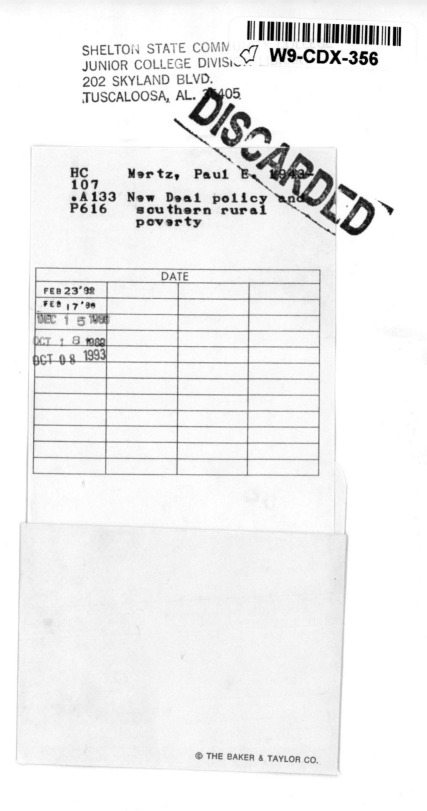

New Deal Policy
and
Southern Rural Poverty

NEW DEAL POLICY
and
SOUTHERN RURAL POVERTY

Paul E. Mertz

Louisiana State University Press

Baton Rouge and London

Design: Dwight Agner
Type face: VIP Caledonia
Composition: The Composing Room of Michigan, Inc.
Printing and binding: Kingsport Press, Inc.

Photographs are by courtesy of the
Library of Congress.

LIBRARY OF CONGRESS CATALOGING IN PUBLICATION DATA

Mertz, Paul E , 1943–
    New Deal policy and southern rural poverty.

    Bibliography: p.
    Includes index.
    1. Rural poor—Southern states. 2. Southern
states—Economic policy. 3. Southern states—Rural
conditions. I Title.
HC107.A133P616   338.975   75–18042
ISBN 0–8071–0289–X

To Lyndall

Contents

Illustrations

Preface

WIDESPREAD poverty has been one of the distinguishing features of the South's historical experience, setting the region apart in a nation which has usually enjoyed material adequacy. At no time was this impoverishment more acute than during the Great Depression. The 1930s, however, were not only years of economic distress in the South, but also the beginning of one of those great periods of readjustment and development that likewise have characterized its past. The Roosevelt administration's attempts to relieve hard times did much to alter the section's industry, labor conditions, and notably, its agriculture. The New Deal and subsequent economic growth elevated the living standards of millions of southerners, and the region has achieved an overall prosperity which contrasts with most of its history. Yet, despite this progress, poverty persists. No longer so pervasive as in the 1930s, it remains in rural pockets, and in the cities, North and South, to which the poor have migrated. Deprivation exists today in a residuum of the population that was obviously not uplifted by the New Deal or anything that has happened since. This study, concentrating on the rural South, will attempt to examine the reasons why an administration noted for reform in behalf of the "forgotten man" at the bottom, and recognizing better than its predecessors that poverty was a special problem, could not alleviate the plight of some of the country's most destitute citizens.

This study was originally written as a Ph.D. dissertation at the University of Oklahoma. It began with a suggestion by Gilbert C. Fite that I undertake a new synthesis of primary materials on the subject of the New Deal's failure to cope with rural poverty. My interest in the 1930s, sharpened by work in Dr. Fite's seminar, and my inclinations toward southern history, guided by John S. Ezell, combined to produce this topic. I have attempted to concentrate my research on manuscript sources wherever possible. I have also tried to survey as thoroughly as I could the inexhaustible quantity of published material on rural and southern conditions of the 1930s, regretting that some things would inevitably be overlooked or not fully exploited, but recognizing that in all research there comes a time when one must write. The works of many other historians have been of great value to me. C. Vann Woodward's interpretation of the southern heritage has been one general influence. More directly, I have benefited from several excellent secondary works on the twentieth-century South and the New Deal. Sometimes my conclusions have concurred with those of the authors, and at other times differed. But in all cases the synthesis has been the result of the best criticism and judgment I could apply to my sources.

Many persons have given essential aid to my research and writing. While preparing the original version of this work I was fortunate to have as a dissertation advisor Gilbert C. Fite, who was generous with his time, advice, encouragement and constructive comments. John S. Ezell also counseled me at various stages of my work, offering valuable insights and suggestions. As a student of these historians, I hope this study can at least approach their high standards of scholarship.

I must also acknowledge a second group of persons who have aided my research. Among these are the staff members of all the research institutions I visited, particularly Joseph Marshall of the Roosevelt Library, Helen T. Finneran and Robert Kvasnika of the National Archives, and Wayne Rasmussen of the Department of Agriculture's history office. Gladys Baker, also of the USDA history office, called my attention to several important documents and made copies available, and gave me the benefit of her insights in agricultural history. Olaf F. Larson of Cornell University also helped locate documents. I am grateful to all those listed in the bibliography who granted interviews, as well as to those who gave permission to use manuscript collections in various libraries. Special thanks is extended to John T. Nixon for allowing me to use the papers of Herman Clarence Nixon. David E. Conrad of Southern Illinois University read portions of the manuscript and offered valuable comments.

In the summer of 1969 I received significant financial aid for research travel through the history department of the University of Oklahoma. Final preparation of the manuscript was assisted by two grants from the Faculty Research Committee of the University of Wisconsin, Stevens Point.

At the University of Wisconsin, Stevens Point, Documents Librarian Arthur Fish patiently helped track down government publications for my research. Graduate students Sally Troyanosky and John Zawadski helped with the endless double-checking in the revision. Virginia Nicholson, Sandy Knapp, Esther Severa and Lyndall Mertz typed the manuscript.

Finally, throughout these years of research and writing, my wife, Lyndall, has given me indispensable help and encouragement. For her patience and understanding I am deeply grateful.

New Deal Policy
and
Southern Rural Poverty

CHAPTER I

Southern Poverty—
A Chronic Problem

ON JUNE 19, 1933, K. D. Wells, a Vicksburg, Mississippi, cotton broker, wrote to the new secretary of agriculture, Henry Wallace. He enclosed a letter from Willie White, a Negro manager of a plantation at Frogmore, Louisiana, to its absentee owner, D. S. Compton of Vicksburg. Wells regarded the letter as "both amusing and tragic" and told the secretary it "pictures truly the situation on cotton plantations in this section." White wrote in answer to Compton's inquiry about the use of ten sacks of oats, intended for mule feed. He reported that "some of the tenants was worr[y]ing me that the[y] had no feed" for their workstock, and not wanting them to neglect their crops he had furnished it. But when the sharecroppers returned to the plantation commissary within a few days and requested more oats, White demanded to know "why the[y] run out so soon." He discovered the reason: "The[y] had to eat all the time out of [the feed] them selves." The Frogmore plantation was probably, like most others in the spring of 1933, in poor financial condition and White evidently had orders to cut expenses by advancing only minimum food and supplies to the croppers. "I am trying to keep them down all I can," he told Compton, but "some are allways coming for some thing and are hungry and cant work without eating and then I give them some thing so the[y] wont have no excuse." Other croppers pressed White to furnish more clothing, and still others were "talking about the[y] no the[y] are going to be sick [with malaria] because the m sceaters are eating them up and [they] ant able to get A bar [mosquito net]." He noted that the tenants were "allways grumbling" about high prices for necessities at the commissary, "but I dont no why the[y think conditions] are much better elce Where." Wells told Wallace he hoped the letter would help "enthuse your co-workers to relieve this situation under the cotton plan which you have announced to-day." Then, recalling another cabinet member's recent remarks on the impoverishment of the South, Wells added, "You might show it to your friend Miss Perkins, and tell her that we need more than shoes in this southern country."[1]

As Wells suggested, distress was widespread in the rural South in 1932 and 1933, at the nadir of the Great Depression. But hunger and deprivation were not new to the region, which had known a persistent and pervasive rural poverty that hard times only worsened. This was widely recognized by scholars during the 1930s. Charles S. Johnson of Fisk University, a leading black sociologist, wrote that "the general depression reached the South when it was already prostrate and sadly crippled by an outworn tenant system." Mordecai Ezekiel, an economist with the Bureau of Agricultural Economics, saw the cotton belt as "the greatest farm problem" because of the low productivity and incomes of masses of its landless farmers. Historian Frank Tannenbaum, writing in 1924, concluded that cotton tenancy had "pauperized the rural South."[2]

---

1   K. D. Wells to Henry Wallace, June 19, 1933, enclosing Willie White to D. S. Compton, June 6, 1933, in "Records of the Office of the Secretary of Agriculture," Record Group 16, National Archives. Wells referred to Labor Secretary Frances Perkins' currently controversial remark that the depressed American shoe industry could develop an "untapped market" if it could "put shoes on the people of the South." Quoted in George B. Tindall, *The Emergence of the New South, 1913–1945* (Baton Rouge: Louisiana State University Press, 1967), Vol. X of 10 vols., in Wendell Holmes Stephenson and E. Merton Coulter (eds.), *A History of the South*, 575.

2   Charles S. Johnson, "The Effects of the Depression and Recovery on the Negro" (Typescript in Charles S. Johnson Papers, Fisk University); Mordecai Ezekiel, "Two Hundred Dollars a Month, the Townsend Aim Is Not Impossible" (Typescript in Agricultural History Office, Economic Research Service, U.S. Department of Agriculture); Frank Tannenbaum, *Darker Phases of the South* (New York: G. P. Putnam's Sons, 1924), 133.

Poverty in the South was no mere circumstance of the Great Depression. In 1929, at the end of a supposedly booming decade, per capita personal income in the former Confederacy ranged from $270 in South Carolina to $521 in Florida. The average for twelve southeastern states was only $368 and that of Texas $478, compared to $703 for the nation. In only five nonsouthern states did 1929 per capita personal income fall below Florida's, the South's highest. As the depression deepened, these incomes dropped still lower; comparable figures for 1932 were $314 in Florida and $126 in Mississippi, averaging $204 in the Southeast, $262 in Texas, and $401 in the nation.[3] Of course, rural incomes were consistently under the general levels. In 1929 the per capita income of the southern farm population varied from South Carolina's $129 to Florida's $419, averaging $183 in the Southeast and $298 in Texas. The measure of southerners' possessions was as disheartening as their low incomes. Per capita wealth in 1930 fell between $1,110 in Mississippi and $2,081 in Virginia, while the national figure was $2,620.[4]

In the early New Deal period relief agencies were probably more aware of the extent and intensity of rural destitution than anyone else in government. Throughout 1933 and 1934 the field reports that poured into the Washington offices of the Federal Emergency Relief Administration (FERA) reflected a realization of the chronic poverty of millions of southerners.

Some of the most impoverished lived in resource-deficient areas of the Appalachian and Ozark mountains. In November, 1934, for example, a state relief director reported that "the average of rural classes on relief in Kentucky have never had an adequate standard of

3   U.S. Office of Business Economics, *Personal Income by States Since 1929: A Supplement to the Survey of Current Business*, ed. Charles F. Schwartz and Robert E. Graham, Jr. (Washington: Government Printing Office, 1956), 142–43. Howard Odum, *Southern Regions of the United States* (Chapel Hill: University of North Carolina Press, 1936), 48, considers still another indicator of income: in 1928 the national average federal income tax payment of $176.97 was exceeded only by North Carolina ($195.23) and Florida ($239.91) among southern states. The region's lowest average payment, that of Mississippi, was only $47.32.

4   Odum, *Southern Regions*, 46, 48, 75, 77. Per capita personal farm income in other regions averaged $366 (twelve northeastern states), $262 (eight midwestern states), $426 (nine plains and mountain states) and $818 (three Pacific states and Nevada). Outside the former Confederacy only Oklahoma and New Mexico had a per capita wealth lower than Virginia's.

living. In the mountain counties... where from 30 to 60 percent of the population is on relief, average standards of living are perhaps higher now than they have ever been—certainly no lower." A Virginia administrator concurred that "among... those 'poor whites' in the remote mountain areas... the relief program is probably bringing them a subsistence standard somewhat higher than that to which they have been traditionally accustomed." Another official observed that hill families in northwestern Arkansas rarely had more than $25 per year in cash and existed on a diet limited to four or five items.[5]

Other poverty resulted from the farming of land that was worn out or never really suitable for agriculture in the first place. In June, 1934, an FERA field investigator described one such area:

Fairly typical, for Western Tennessee, I gather, was a district I visited yesterday. Table land. Thin soil. Terrible housing. Illiteracy. Evidences of prolonged under-nourishment. No knowledge of how to live decently or farm profitably even if they had decent land. "Five years is about as long as you can get any crop on this land," one farmer there told me. "Then it's gone and you have to clear some more and start over again." Crops grown on it are stunted.... Eastern Tennessee is worse of course. There you see constantly evidence of what happens when you cut timber off mountain sides and plant crops there.... And all over the state, in the rural areas, the story is the same—an illiterate, wretched people, under-nourished, with standards of living so low that, once on relief, they are quite willing to stay there the rest of their lives. It's a mess.[6]

Southern relief administrators also found their urban case loads crowded with chronically poor people, many of them recent arrivals from the country. In New Orleans and Houston officials complained to a representative of FERA headquarters that many blacks were living better on relief than they had in their usual agricultural employment and therefore were difficult to remove from the rolls. Another observer for the Washington office reported Carolina textile workers, both employed and on relief, packed into squalid mill

5 George Goodman to Harry Hopkins, November 30, 1934, William A. Smith to Hopkins, November 26, 1934, Edith Foster to Hopkins, February 15, 1934, all in Harry Hopkins Papers, Franklin D. Roosevelt Library, Hyde Park, N.Y.
6 Lorena Hickok to Hopkins, June 6, 1934, *ibid*.

slums, short of food and clothing and afflicted with pellagra, rickets, and other dietary diseases. One doctor told her that every mill worker he examined showed signs of undernourishment. She concluded that "Gaston County is my idea of a place to go to acquire melancholia."[7]

Although poverty was not confined to any particular area in the South, privation was most widespread, and probably most intense, among several million tenant farmers, sharecroppers, and agricultural wage workers. Tenants and croppers were the largest single block of the nation's rural poor. The majority of them grew cotton and were, as the authors of the decade's most authoritative short work on tenancy put it, "the most impoverished and backward of any large group of producers in America."[8] In 1930 they comprised 1,091,944 white and 698,839 black families and accounted for about one quarter of the South's population and half its farmers. They included about 8.5 million individuals (5.5 million whites and over 3 million Negroes) in a southern nonurban population of about 18 million. Their birthrate was the country's highest, helping to make the South the most densely settled farm area in the United States.[9]

As all serious writers on the subject in the 1930s stressed, landlessness was not only widespread, but increasing. In 1880, the first year the census investigated the problem, tenants operated 36.2 percent of all southern farms. By 1920 the percentage had risen to 49.6, and by 1930 to 55.5. These figures were for the whole region;

7   Hickok to Hopkins, April 13 and 17, 1934, and Martha Gellhorn to Hopkins, November 5, 11, and 19, 1934, *ibid.*
8   Charles S. Johnson, Edwin R. Embree, and Will W. Alexander, *The Collapse of Cotton Tenancy: Summary of Field Studies and Statistical Surveys, 1933–1935* (Chapel Hill: University of North Carolina Press, 1935), 1.
9   *Ibid.*, 3–4; Odum, *Southern Regions*, 463. According to U.S. National Emergency Council, *Report on Economic Conditions of the South* (Washington: Government Printing Office, 1938), 17, the region's excess of births over deaths was about ten per thousand, compared to a national average of seven. The high southern rate, compared to a nearly static nonsosthern rate, caused considerable concern in the administration. Some projections showed that, barring changes in the trends, poorly educated, unskilled people of southern rural background would constitute a majority of the American population within 50 years. See Rexford G. Tugwell Diary (Typescript in Rexford G. Tugwell Papers, Franklin D. Roosevelt Library), November 25, 1934; remarks by Tugwell and Roosevelt in Roosevelt Press Conferences, IV, 212, Franklin D. Roosevelt Library.

by 1930 the rate for cotton farms was about 60 percent. Another well-publicized trend was the growing proportion of tenants who were white. In the decade before 1930 white landless farm families increased by 200,000 (or about 1 million persons) compared to only 2,000 additional black families.[10]

Such figures are unrevealing, however, until one considers the gradations of southern tenancy, in which the farmer's status depended upon how much of his own equipment, living necessities, and self-direction he could provide, compared to what his landlord furnished. Relatively rare in the cotton belt were cash tenants, numbering about 205,000 in ten states. These tenants leased land, usually whole farms for several years at a time, and paid as rent a specific sum in money or a stated amount of the crop. They also supplied their own implements, workstock, domestic livestock, seed, feed, and fertilizer, and farmed without supervision. In southeastern cotton areas, ravaged by boll weevils and soil exhaustion, such tenancy increased in the 1920s. This actually reflected the disintegration of plantation farming as absentee owners and corporate holders of foreclosed farms leased land to cash renters.[11]

A second arrangement, involving over a half million farmers, was share tenancy, in which the renter provided at least some of his equipment, draft animals, seed, feed, and fertilizer, as well as most of his food and subsistence goods. Landlords furnished an average of twenty-five acres, a house, and whatever equipment the farmer lacked. If necessary, they also advanced cash, food, or subsistence goods during the year. Share tenants worked on a yearly verbal contract under varying degrees of supervision. The farm owner marketed the crop, and usually gave the tenant three-fourths or two-thirds of the proceeds, less any advances.[12]

10 Johnson, Embree, and Alexander, *Collapse of Cotton Tenancy*, 4–5.
11 U.S. Bureau of the Census, *Fifteenth Census of the United States, 1930: Agriculture*, Vol. II, Pt. 2, p. 31; Arthur F. Raper, *Preface to Peasantry: A Tale of Two Black Belt Counties* (Chapel Hill: University of North Carolina Press, 1936), 4, 146–48.
12 Raper, *Preface to Peasantry*, 146–48; Thomas Jackson Woofter, Jr., *Landlord and Tenant on the Cotton Plantation*, Works Progress Administration Research Monographs, V (Washington: Works Progress Administration, 1936), 36. The twenty-five-acre average was for seven cotton states east of Texas and Oklahoma. Because of variations in crop-

Nearly half of all southern tenants were sharecroppers, "the lowest category of poverty and dependence" among renters. Included were 383,000 whites (16.4 percent of all white farmers) and 392,000 blacks (44.6 percent of all Negro farmers). Concentrated in areas of intensive cotton cultivation, they operated 716,000 small plots of their landlords' holdings, averaging twenty acres each. Sharecroppers were actually propertyless workers paid with a portion of the crops they raised. Landowners not only supplied acreage, houses, workstock, and everything else needed for farming (often including such common implements as hoes), but also advanced food and living necessities, which they deducted from the tenant's share of the crop when they sold it. The cropper contributed only his and his family's labor, worked under much direct supervision, and received half the proceeds of his production.[13]

Planters provided food or subsistence goods to tenants either by arranging limited credit for them with a local merchant, or directly, through a plantation commissary. Since this "furnish" was considered income drawn in advance of the settlement of accounts, landowners tried to restrict it to an amount they estimated the cropper's cotton could cover. The landlord (or merchant creditor) held a statutory lien on the tenant's part of the crop, which entitled him to market it and deduct the cost of all advances, plus interest. Creditors, of course, kept all accounts, with the result that most of the poorly educated croppers were ignorant of the exact extent of their indebtedness.

In his research of southeastern plantations for the Works Pro-

---

sharing arrangements and degrees of landlord supervision, share tenants were a relatively indefinite category. The census table cited in note 11 lists for the old Confederacy and Oklahoma 710,244 "other" tenants, exclusive of sharecroppers and cash tenants. Presumably most of these were share tenants.

13 Raper, *Preface to Peasantry*, 146–48; Johnson, Embree, and Alexander, *Collapse of Cotton Tenancy*, 7. Figures on the number of sharecroppers adapted from U.S. National Resources Committee, *Farm Tenancy: Report of the President's Committee* (Washington: Government Printing Office, 1937), 98–99. In Georgia, South Carolina, and Arkansas the cropper was legally not a tenant, but an employee with only a laborer's lien on the crop. Generally, other states recognized croppers as tenants with an equity in the crops they raised. A landlord, however, had a superior statutory lien on the cropper's production for rent, all advances, and interest. Charles S. Johnson, "Legal Status of Southern Share-Tenants and Share Croppers" (Typescript in Johnson Papers).

gress Administration (WPA), T. J. Woofter discovered that "usury laws are inoperative" in the furnishing system. He found that of 588 North Carolina croppers, 82 percent received cash from their landlords, averaging $109 at 21 percent yearly interest. Such advances were usually extended at a "flat rate" of 10 percent, but since they were made in the spring and repayable as cotton was marketed in the fall, the money was used for less than a year and the real annual rate was much higher. Sixty percent of the croppers obtained food and household goods (worth an average of $113) from landlords at an average 53 percent interest (a "flat" 20 or 25 percent). Forty-one percent received supplies (averaging $54) from a merchant on their landlord's guarantee at an average 71 percent interest. [14]

This pernicious credit system was an inherent part of cotton tenancy. In fact, landlords often found that they could not profit without exploiting and impoverishing their dependents through "furnishing." [15] So long as all phases of cotton growing were unmechanized, making necessary a large force of ignorant and unskilled workers with whom crops were shared, the very terms of the division put strong pressure on planters to maximize profits at their tenants' expense. A perceptive WPA field investigator explained it best. "Every business enterpriser," he wrote, "seeks to reduce his cost of production by all rational means to a minimum [percentage of the product's selling price]. This the share-cropping system prevents, for the cost of production is always one-half the selling price of cotton... *less, of course, what he can recoup in the way of a profit on*

---

14   Woofter, *Landlord and Tenant,* 29–31, 53, 61–63. Landlords usually borrowed from banks in order to make advances. Before the New Deal their bank rates were often high, but by 1934 southeastern landlords obtained credit from banks or federally chartered production credit associations at an average rate of 6.5 percent. Charging exorbitant rates to tenants was often excused because they were poor risks. But Woofter found that for all advances the "flat" rate averaged 19 percent, with an average loss to landlords of 5 percent, leaving a net gain of 14 percent. But since the average duration of credit was only six months, the real annual return was about 28 percent. He concluded (p. 63) that landlords and merchants were "taking care to keep the interest rate well above any possibility of loss from defaulting tenants."

15   Johnson, Embree, and Alexander, *Collapse of Cotton Tenancy,* 9–10; David E. Conrad, *The Forgotten Farmers: The Story of Sharecroppers in the New Deal* (Urbana: University of Illinois Press, 1965), 9.

his 'furnish' to his tenants." In times of declining prices, a 50 percent
cost of production (or even more in the case of share tenancy), combined with interest on a mortgage, taxes, and other overhead expenses, could consume the planter's profit. Therefore, he often had
compelling reasons to appropriate as much of the tenant's share as
possible.[16] The practice of furnishing and his lien on the cropper's
cotton gave him the means to do so.

The workings of the furnishing system deprived many tenants,
whose shares of crops could not cover advances and interest, of all
net income. Charles S. Johnson discovered that in 1932 only 9.4
percent of the landless blacks in Macon County, Alabama, received
any cash profit; all others "broke even" in their accounts or sank further into debt. Such conditions were common throughout the South.
In 1934 Johnson supervised field surveys of croppers in South Carolina, Alabama, Mississippi, and Texas, and found that "few of the
tenants... had cleared cash incomes since 1921, and many had
made nothing since the World War." In 1933 the fortunate few had
averaged $105.43 per family.[17]

During the 1930s numerous studies emphasized the cotton tenants' persistently low incomes. In 1934 T. J. Woofter made an
exhaustive survey for the WPA of 646 plantations in the Carolinas,
Georgia, Alabama, Mississippi, Arkansas, and Louisiana. He found
that the average per capita net income for all residents, including
owners, was only $110 per year, ranging from $89 in the Alabama
black belt to $127 in the Atlantic coastal plain. Sharecropper families
averaged a net annual income (cash and subsistence advances) of
only $312 (or $71 per capita), while share tenant families received
$417 (or $92 per capita). Actual cash incomes were, of course, lower:
$122 and $202 per year for cropper and share tenant families, respectively. Woofter concluded that such figures reflected the low
productivity of hand labor on small cropper acreages and "indi-

16　Pierce Williams, "The Problems Created by the Diminishing Demand for Casual Ag-
　　ricultural Labor in Texas" (Typescript report to Harry Hopkins, March 27, 1936, in
　　Hopkins Papers). Italics added.
17　Johnson, Embree, and Alexander, *Collapse of Cotton Tenancy*, 12–13.

cate[d] the seriousness of the problem of raising the standard of living among the tenant and farm labor classes."[18] Mordecai Ezekiel of the Bureau of Agricultural Economics also saw low productivity as "the real reason for Southern poverty." He wrote that "usually the labor of an entire family goes to handle about 20 acres of cotton and to produce at best 5 to 12 bales. At 12¢ a pound . . . the gross value of this family's output is only $360–$720. Even at pre-depression prices in 1929," he added, "cotton farms . . . averaged only $684 cash income. . . . With the sharecropper, half of this goes to the landlord . . . leaving at most but $250 to $500 for the . . . family's cash income for the year."[19]

These chronically low incomes, of course, declined during hard times. Arthur Raper, a young sociologist working for the Atlanta-based Commission on Interracial Cooperation, began his intensive studies of the Georgia black belt in the 1920s. He found that landless Negro farm families in one county averaged $302.06 per year in 1927, but only $150.74 in 1934, and in another county black tenants' incomes declined from $380.79 to $299.56 in the same period. In the spring of 1933, Will Alexander, Raper's mentor and executive secretary of the interracial commission, reviewed these trends for the organization's board of directors and stated what knowledgeable people already suspected. "The present depression," he wrote, "is merely aggravating the low earnings of the South's rural dwellers, which in normal times are very low."[20]

As pathetically small as were croppers' incomes, those of farm wage workers were even lower. One planter, sympathetic to the poor, told Henry Wallace that although he would not defend the sharecropping system, he could "safely and confidently assert that it is a blessed haven of affluence and security for cotton workers in the high yield districts as compared to a day labor economy."[21]

---

18 Woofter, *Landlord and Tenant*, 72–73, 83–86.
19 Ezekiel, "Two Hundred Dollars a Month."
20 Raper, *Preface to Peasantry*, 36; Will Alexander, "National Services in the Alabama and Georgia Rural Black Belt" (Typescript memorandum, spring, 1933, in Commission on Interracial Cooperation Papers, Atlanta University).
21 Undated article by Thad Snow, enclosed in Irving Brant to Mordecai Ezekiel, December 22, 1936, in RG 16, NA.

Throughout the 1930s the ranks of these laborers swelled as the decline of the furnishing system, the effects of New Deal crop control measures, or, by the middle of the decade, increasing mechanization displaced tenants. By October, 1933, an estimated 200,000 dispossessed rural families received federal relief in cotton counties from Arkansas and Louisiana eastward. In 1940 casual laborers numbered over 842,000 in the same general area. Although they might occupy shacks on farms, they received no food or supplies and found work only at irregular intervals during the crop season. In 1934 Raper noted Georgia pay scales of forty to sixty cents per day for men and thirty to fifty cents for women. He estimated that the efforts of whole families might yield between $128 and $160 in 1933 or 1934. Similar conditions prevailed in western cotton areas. A 1936 WPA survey in eastern Arkansas found that wage hands netted an average of $203 per year, and more than half subsisted on less than $200.[22]

Income figures, of course, only begin to suggest the intolerable living conditions of millions in the South, the squalor of their housing, the paucity of their possessions, their malnourishing diets, debilitating diseases, ignorance, and economic dependence. By the early 1930s, their normally low standards had declined to the point that they shocked almost to despair observers who thought they knew the South well. For example, Frank Tannenbaum, returning to the cotton belt in 1934 after an absence of ten years, exclaimed to Will Alexander that living conditions had "collapsed" and "there's nothing you can do to the system that's running now to make it support people."[23]

The typical cotton tenant was housed in a two- or three-room unpainted frame cabin, supported on stone or concrete blocks, constructed of inferior lumber and rarely weatherproof. Roofs were of "tin" (galvanized sheet iron) or pine shingles, doors and windows

22 Woofter, *Landlord and Tenant*, 145–46; Tindall, *Emergence of the New South*, 412; Raper, *Preface to Peasantry*, 39; Stanley V. White, "Report of Survey of Factors Contributing to the Economic Insecurity of Workers in the Mississippi Delta Cotton Region" (Typescript report, October, 1936, in Hopkins Papers), 14.

23 "Reminiscences of Will W. Alexander" (Typescript, 1952, in Oral History Collection, Columbia University), 377.

were without glass and unscreened, and interiors were unceilinged. Plumbing, running water, electricity, sanitary wells, and frequently even privies were lacking. In 1930 the average renter's house in the cotton belt was valued at $350; those inhabited by sharecroppers were undoubtedly worth much less.[24]

Family possessions were meager. Sharecroppers of course lacked mules, domestic livestock, wagons, and farm implements. They frequently had few household furnishings and no cookstoves—cooking over open hearths was common in cotton country. Relief officials in the Deep South discovered that about 20 percent of their cotton-growing clients had never owned a mattress until they received one from the FERA. According to one study, the personal belongings of landless whites in Tennessee were worth less than $100 on the average. And Robert W. Hudgens, director of the Resettlement Administration and later the Farm Security Administration (FSA) for South Carolina, Georgia, Alabama, and Florida, reported that large numbers of black belt cotton families owned goods valued at $20 or less.[25]

Probably the most enervating aspect of the tenant's life was his diet, inadequate even in quantity and a positive menace nutritionally. "Furnish" rarely consisted of more than a dozen items; "meat" (fat salt pork), flour, cornmeal, molasses, and dried peas and beans were usually provided. Since vegetable gardens used land which the crop lien system demanded for cotton and reduced furnishing profits, landlords often discouraged tenants from planting them. Likewise, few croppers had cows, pigs, or even poultry; Raper reported that in two Georgia counties one-seventh of the families ate neither chicken nor eggs during an entire year. Nevertheless, such food as the poor obtained consumed most of their earnings. In eastern Arkansas, for example, the WPA found that croppers spent 69 percent of their income for food, including 12 percent for meat, 17

24　Good accounts of tenant housing include Johnson, Embree, and Alexander, *Collapse of Cotton Tenancy*, 15–16; Raper, *Preface to Peasantry*, Chap. 4; National Emergency Council, *Economic Conditions of the South*, 33–36.
25　Johnson, Embree, and Alexander, *Collapse of Cotton Tenancy*, 16; Raper, *Preface to Peasantry*, 65–68; "Reminiscences of Will W. Alexander," 522; interview with Robert W. Hudgens, July 8 and 9, 1970.

percent for lard, and 33 percent for flour and meal. In addition these destitute people spent another 12 percent for clothing.[26]

Not surprisingly, these wretched living conditions undermined the health, and therefore the economic productivity, of the poor. Malaria flourished; about 2 million cases were estimated for the South in 1938. Malnourishing food caused rickets and pellagra, and lack of sanitation resulted in hookworm infection among rural people who could not afford shoes. In February, 1934, a Florida public health official told a representative of the FERA that the state had 250,000 cases of hookworm and 80,000 or 90,000 of malaria. In 1938 the National Emergency Council's well-known *Report on Economic Conditions of the South* succinctly described the cotton states as a "belt of sickness, misery and unnecessary death."[27]

Tenancy had still other culturally and economically blighting effects, frequently described in the 1930s and since. Because land tenure was based on one-year verbal contracts, tenants moved as often as every year or two, crowding southern highways in midwinter in search of a better "situation." This transience, and the fact that there were no provisions in law for compensation of tenants for farm improvements they made, destroyed incentives for conservation of the soil and maintenance of farm buildings, houses, and other property. Employment of whole families in the fields and constant moving led to sporadic school attendance and low levels of literacy. Moreover, as Raper observed, the cropper's long years of looking to landlords for credit and supervision of his farming left him "schooled in dependency" and "unaccustomed to responsibility."[28] Similarly, Charles S. Johnson described black tenants in Macon County, Alabama, as "individuals of uniformly low education, low earning

---

26 Johnson, Embree, and Alexander, *Collapse of Cotton Tenancy*, 16–19; Raper, *Preface to Peasantry*, 42–43, 52–53; Rupert B. Vance, *Human Factors in Cotton Culture: A Study in the Social Geography of the American South* (Chapel Hill: University of North Carolina Press, 1929), 247–48, 298–99; White, "Economic Insecurity of Workers in the Delta Cotton Region," 22.

27 Hickok to Hopkins, February 5, 1934, in Hopkins Papers; National Emergency Council, *Economic Conditions of the South*, 29–32.

28 Conrad, *Forgotten Farmers*, 13–14; Johnson, Embree, and Alexander, *Collapse of Cotton Tenancy*, 20–23; Raper, *Preface to Peasantry*, 4.

power, limited skill, primitive domestic life, high mobility and almost complete mental and economic dependence upon the landlord. The average years of schooling is less than four, and illiteracy is high. In the plantation areas this tenant population has been effectively isolated from the dominant currents of American life. . . . The level of this circumscribed life has, of necessity, been low."[29] His observations could have applied with equal force to croppers of both races throughout the region.

Beginning about 1925, the fundamental poverty of the South was compounded by prolonged agricultural depression. Both the output and price of the region's great staple, cotton, had always been subject to sharp fluctuations. A period of high returns usually stimulated increased planting to the point of overproduction, which resulted in a price decline. This occurred in the 1920s and early 1930s.[30]

Cotton returns were high during and just after World War I (reaching an average thirty-five cents per pound in 1919), but dropped precipitously (to less than sixteen cents) along with most American farm commodities in the "price break" of 1920–1921. Then, from 1921 to 1924 short crops drove prices up, to a peak of twenty-eight cents per pound in 1923. After 1923, acreage increased steadily, partly because of new cultivation in the lower Mississippi Valley and southwestern plains, and also because of the recovery of some southeastern regions from serious boll weevil infestation. Prices held above nineteen cents through 1925, but sagged the next year to twelve cents. In 1927 cotton brought twenty cents per pound, but then decline set in until 1933. The 1929–1930 crop sold for $1,470,000,000 but that of 1932–1933 was worth only $431 million, or a disastrous six cents per pound.[31]

Because of this general depression, the tenancy system, especially in the Southeast, showed unmistakable signs of deterioration

---

29 Charles S. Johnson, "Is Share Tenancy Inevitable in the Cotton Economy of the South? A Discussion with Particular Reference to the Negro" (Typescript in Johnson Papers), For full treatment of the dependence of sharecroppers see Johnson's *Shadow of the Plantation* (Chicago: University of Chicago Press, 1934).

30 Woofter, *Landlord and Tenant*, 3.

31 *Ibid.*, 39–40; Theodore Saloutos, *Farmer Movements in the South, 1865–1933* (Berkeley: University of California Press, 1960), 254–56.

before the New Deal. Even before the crash in 1929 there was widespread depression in the old cotton belt, as well as decline of landownership, and loss of workstock by share tenants. The Southeast suffered from soil exhaustion, overproduction, and subsequent low prices. In certain areas, Georgia and South Carolina particularly, falling prices in the 1920s coincided disastrously with eastward advancing boll weevil infestation. After 1929 still more disorganization of prices and finances occurred. In their straightened circumstances many landlords attempted to lighten their financial obligations by discontinuing furnishing. But this drove their sharecroppers out of agriculture, except as irregular wage hands. In 1934 a study of 825 dispossessed tenants in North Carolina revealed that about three-fifths of them had been displaced between 1929 and 1932. Fewer were dislocated in 1933, but the number increased again in 1934 due to New Deal acreage restriction.[32] By October, 1933, depression conditions had forced on relief more than one-eighth of the families in seven southeastern cotton states. This relief load included 500,000 cases, of whom 300,000 were in cotton counties, mostly rural people or town residents dependent on cotton for employment.[33]

As the depression deepened, the federal government tried to bolster agriculture and relieve the unemployed. One of its first efforts, instituted by the Hoover administration, was an extension of low-interest credit to farmers for seed, feed, and fertilizer. Intended to aid financially pinched farmers to make their crops, these federal seed and feed loans became, in parts of the South, almost a necessity for farming.[34] In the cotton belt they readily fit into the landlord-

32 Woofter, *Landlord and Tenant*, 39–40; Johnson, Embree, and Alexander, *Collapse of Cotton Tenancy*, 61–62.

33 Woofter, *Landlord and Tenant*, 145–46. According to Woofter (pp. 49, 148), southeastern landlords required an average of $3,500 to meet crop expenses for a season, $1,200 to furnish tenants, and $150 for miscellaneous wages. They usually depended on bank loans for these sums. As cotton prices declined, abandonment of furnishing was often a first step in cutting expenses. See also Calvin B. Hoover, "Human Problems in Acreage Reduction in the South" (Typescript, spring, 1934, in "Records of the Agricultural Stabilization and Conservation Service," Record Group 145, National Archives). For a WPA assessment of the deterioration of tenancy in the Southwest see Williams, "The Problems Created by the Diminishing Demand for Casual Agricultural Labor in Texas."

34 Alexander, "National Services in the Black Belt."

tenant system. The operation of the loans revealed generally how planters tried to manipulate federal programs for their own maximum benefit, and also indicated the extent of financial distress of their plantations.

Feed and seed credit was administered by local committees, which approved the loans. In the black belt these were usually made up of planters and merchants. Farm owners received loans, but tenants did not unless landlords cooperated. Government money could not be extended to the landless for the same reason that banks never lent to them. Lenders needed collateral. A landowner could offer real or chattel mortgages for long or short terms, but the property-less farmer could offer only a lien on his share of a prospective crop. Landlords, however, already held this security and unless they agreed to waive their liens, no one else could finance their share-croppers. The government required waivers before making seed and feed loans to tenants. Thus the traditional credit system limited the effectiveness of a federal program in reaching the neediest farmers. [35]

There were, however, some planters and bankers with foreclosed land to operate who waived liens and allowed their tenants to obtain government credit, in order to relieve themselves of furnishing expenses. Thus some of the poor were able to get money and buy necessities at cash prices. But more frequently landlords took over the loans by refusing to waive liens in the first place unless the croppers surrendered their checks. Planters had traditionally borrowed directly from banks and then reallocated part of the funds to tenants at higher interest rates. By taking charge of the feed and seed checks they proceeded to do the same with government credit. [36]

---

35 *Ibid.;* Woofter, *Landlord and Tenant,* 55–56. Similar New Deal credit agencies, the production credit associations (authorized by the 1933 Farm Credit Act) were also limited by the plantation system for the same reason—tenants, having given one lien, could offer no other security. Production credit associations lent to farmers for general agricultural purposes, and in the seven southeastern states in Woofter's study, 147 associations (one fourth of those in the country) were organized by the end of 1934. They provided $17 million (18 percent of all such credit in 1934) in loans averaging $355 at 5 percent interest. This low rate necessitated good security; hence loans were made almost exclusively to farm owners.

36 Alexander, "National Services in the Black Belt."

In some cases landlords deposited the checks in their accounts and issued cash back to tenants, as they thought they needed it, at 8 or 10 percent interest. Thus tenants paid interest twice: 6 percent to the government and again to the landlord, who held the money and "advanced" it to them. Will Alexander reported to the interracial commission that "this practice is common in . . . the Georgia Black Belt." Other planters who had commissaries reissued tenants' loans to them in supplies at time-credit prices. This not only deprived the croppers of the benefit of cash buying, but also gave the planter the means to obtain goods for resale—in effect the government subsidized an exploitive furnishing business which had become burdensome in hard times. According to Alexander this procedure was followed "quite freely" in the Alabama black belt. Still other landlords secured the checks and applied them to croppers' back debts, an action that was illegal.[37]

There were other instances of sheer fraud, in which planters, aided by local postal authorities, secured loans upon the names of their Negro tenants, who never knew of the money. Another inequity was that some black farm owners were prevented from obtaining loans. In some cases, planter-merchants, having qualified their own tenants to avoid the expense of furnishing them, desired to profit by financing the most industrious and propertied Negro farmers. Sitting on loan committees, they offered to finance those blacks at high interest rates, thus giving them the "available credit" which disqualified them for federal loans.[38]

In the feed and seed loan program some landlords appropriated for their own use benefits which should have gone to tenants and croppers. These injustices, although on a smaller scale, were essentially like those which later plagued the Agricultural Adjustment Administration (AAA) in distributing its payments.[39] This suggests that although both the AAA cotton contract and the feed and seed loan procedures provided opportunities for abuse of tenants' rights,

37   *Ibid.*
38   *Ibid.*
39   Robert C. Weaver, "The New Deal and the Negro, A Look at the Facts," in Howard Zinn (ed.), *New Deal Thought* (Indianapolis: Bobbs-Merrill, 1966), 327.

the fundamental problem of the poor was less the workings of specific government policies than their complete dependence on landlords in an exploitive system.

Planters also influenced the operation of early relief agencies in the cotton belt in a way which presaged their attitude toward later New Deal efforts. The Red Cross provided rations for the destitute during the first years of the depression and was credited with keeping many rural southerners alive in the winter of 1932–1933. Its program was administered by local committees of planters and businessmen. In many cases farmers used the Red Cross to furnish their tenants, for whom they secured places on its rolls. But in many other instances landlords charged their tenants or required labor of them for Red Cross rations which they claimed to have secured for them.[40]

Similarly, in the Alabama black belt in 1932 several counties conducted work relief projects with funds borrowed from the Reconstruction Finance Corporation (RFC). As with the Red Cross, planters welcomed the opportunity to shift furnishing responsibilities, but apprehended that work relief wages higher than those they customarily paid would "disorganize labor." For example, in county seat towns RFC paid seventy-five cents per day for as many as three days per week, but due to planter influence, offered only one day's work per week at fifty cents in rural areas. During the spring plowing season planter-dominated RFC administrators cut town wages to the rural level and dropped from employment those wanted for field labor, thus forcing them to accept "available work" offered by farmers, often at no more than thirty-five cents per day.[41] Later many planters would expect the New Deal's FERA and WPA to operate in the same manner.

The limited farm credit and relief measures of the Hoover years were, of course, far from adequate to cope with the distress of the rural South. Indeed, by the time the New Deal commenced, many of the region's longstanding problems had reached a crisis point. The

---

40   Alexander, "National Services in the Black Belt."
41   *Ibid.*

tenancy system, although deteriorating, still exploited and impoverished millions. Some scholars and journalists recognized that the section's destitution was chronic and pervasive. But public awareness of the South's condition centered on the general depression which intensified its poverty. Of particular concern was the disastrous level of cotton prices. It was to that matter that the New Deal turned first.

CHAPTER II
Parity and Poverty

THE NEW DEAL'S involvement in the South's problems began in May, 1933, with the passage of its major farm policy, the Agricultural Adjustment Act. This measure was hastily drafted and enacted during the emergency-packed "Hundred Days." But the law's fundamental principle, price parity, was not new; it had been current in various forms throughout the 1920s. First developed by George N. Peek in 1921, parity was a plan for "equality for agriculture" in a time of depressed crop prices. It was the basis for the unsuccessful McNary-Haugen bills of the Coolidge era and "finally became an accepted part of American farm policy" with the passage of the Agricultural Adjustment Act.[1]

The idea of parity was to create, or actually restore, a "fair exchange value" between agricultural commodities and industrial and consumer goods. This would require an increase in the prices farmers received for their principal crops until they were the same, in relation to general prices, as in the last five years before World War I, a time of comparative prosperity for agriculture.[2]

Peek and others saw overproduction as the main factor depress-

---

1 Gilbert C. Fite, *George N. Peek and the Fight for Farm Parity* (Norman: University of Oklahoma Press, 1954), 38.
2 *Ibid.*, 39–40.

ing staple crop prices and reasoned that the key to raising them was elimination of surpluses. During the 1920s there were two main ideas on how to accomplish this goal. Peek proposed that the government subsidize the sale of the surplus abroad, even at a loss. With the excess disposed of in this manner, he expected domestic prices to rise to an acceptable level. The second method, never favored by Peek but embraced in the late 1920s by Chester Davis and some of his other associates, was to curtail production of staples, probably by limiting the acreage planted. This was a recurrent idea in the South whenever large cotton crops lowered prices and cut profits. The period from 1929 to 1932, for example, saw several futile campaigns to institute voluntary or state-imposed controls.[3]

By 1924 Peek's idea of parity and how to achieve it (expressed in the McNary-Haugen bills) had become a powerful movement in the Midwest. Serious southern interest began in 1926 as cotton prices dropped from previously satisfactory levels and prewar incomes suddenly looked increasingly attractive. With both southern and midwestern backing, McNary-Haugen legislation was enacted by Congress in 1927 and 1928, but vetoed by Coolidge. During the Hoover years parity measures were further frustrated by the president's known hostility to them and by the administration's unsuccessful efforts to control surpluses through its Federal Farm Board.[4]

With the passage of the Agricultural Adjustment Act on May 2, 1933, price parity became national policy. The act's declaration of purpose made clear that it was commodity legislation. It proposed: "to establish and maintain such balance between the production and consumption of agricultural *commodities*...as will reestablish prices to farmers at a level that will give agricultural *commodities* a purchasing power with respect to articles that farmers buy, equivalent to the purchasing power of agricultural commodities in the base period.... August 1909–July 1914." The act permitted the secretary of agriculture, as one means of inducing farmers to withdraw land

3 *Ibid.*, 39, 84–85, 162, 170, 180–81; T. Harry Williams, *Huey Long* (New York: Alfred A. Knopf, 1969), 520–33.
4 Fite, *George N. Peek*, 71, 162, 170, 177–81; Theodore Saloutos, *Farmer Movements in the South, 1865–1933* (Berkeley: University of California Press, 1960), 268–75.

from production of staples, to offer them contracts providing for "rental or benefit payments" in amounts that the secretary deemed "fair
and reasonable."[5]

Many backers of the bill argued that improved prices and government payments would generally boost farmers' incomes and
promote depression recovery.[6] But the law did not assure increased
personal incomes to all persons dependent on agriculture for a living, desirable as that aim was. Its specific language linked increased
purchasing power to the prices of major crops—indeed that relationship was the whole import of the decade-long drive for parity
legislation which found final expression in the AAA.[7] Moreover, the
law said nothing about how any benefit payments should be distributed among farmers; those matters could only be covered in the
acreage reduction contracts between the secretary and the producers. Thus the specific language of the act could allow its administrators to concentrate narrowly on the parity aim and conduct the
AAA as a commodity-price agency. One result was the gross unfair-
ness of the practical distribution of benefits under AAA contracts.

The AAA was forced to operate its cotton program on an emergency basis during the 1933 crop season. When the act was passed
farmers had already planted a crop of record proportions and a huge
surplus was expected. Since it was too late to curtail planting, the
only alternative was the famous "plow up." According to hastily devised agreements, farmers plowed under one-third of their acreage.
In return they received cash benefits of seven to twenty dollars per
acre (depending on their average yield) or six to twelve dollars per

---

5 U.S., *Statutes at Large*, Vol. XLVIII, Pt. 1, pp. 32, 34. Italics added.
6 Van L. Perkins, *Crisis in Agriculture: The Agricultural Adjustment Administration and
   the New Deal, 1933*, University of California Publications in History, LXXXI (Berkeley:
   University of California Press, 1969), 41–42; Edwin G. Nourse, Joseph S. Davis, and
   John D. Black, *Three Years of the Agricultural Adjustment Administration*
   (Washington: Brookings Institution, 1937), 23.
7 Donald H. Grubbs, *Cry from the Cotton: The Southern Tenant Farmers' Union and the
   New Deal* (Chapel Hill: University of North Carolina Press, 1971), 35–36, takes AAA
   chief Chester Davis to task for denying the "avowed purpose of the act" when Davis
   wrote in 1934 that "it is not intended that the act should . . . deal with deep-seated social
   problems." The difficulty with an interpretation which implies that the AAA's avowed
   purpose was to deal with social problems is its failure to place the Agricultural Adjustment Act in the context of a dozen years of agitation for commodity price parity.

acre plus options to purchase (before January 1, 1934) surplus government cotton, equivalent to that destroyed, at only 6 cents per pound, with the intention of reselling it at a profit as prices rose. During the summer 10.4 million acres were taken out of production, reducing the crop from an estimated 17 million bales to 13 million. Farmers received $161 million in cash and options. The price of cotton climbed to 11 cents per pound in July, then settled between 8 and 10 cents in the fall. Parity was considered to be 12.7 cents.[8]

The distribution of plow-up benefits was shot through with abuses. Landlords, as contract signers, received the checks, but AAA required them to divide payments with tenants according to their interests in the destroyed cotton—for example, half for a sharecropper and two-thirds or three-fourths for a share tenant. This conformed to traditional procedures in which planters allocated credit or profits to their dependents, and it was also reminiscent of their manipulation of federal feed and seed loans in 1932. As Department of Agriculture economist Calvin B. Hoover later pointed out, a landlord holding the check was in a position to make any settlement he wished. The resulting inequities were common knowledge by 1934. Some tenants received no plow-up money and others received a portion less than their equity in the crop. A considerable number of landlords simply applied tenants' benefits to their debts for advances. At first glance this reduction of indebtedness would seem to be to the tenants' advantage, except that many illiterate croppers were ignorant of how much they owed, and in any case their accounts usually included exorbitant interest charges.[9] Nevertheless, the AAA legal division later ruled that such "set-offs" were legal unless prohibited by state law.[10]

---

8   David E. Conrad, *The Forgotten Farmers: The Story of Sharecroppers in the New Deal* (Urbana: University of Illinois Press, 1965), 44, 47; George B. Tindall, *The Emergence of the New South, 1913–1945* (Baton Rouge: Louisiana State University Press, 1967), Vol. X of 10 vols., in Wendell Holmes Stephenson and E. Merton Coulter (eds.), *A History of the South*, 394.

9   Conrad, *Forgotten Farmers*, 43–50, 64–67; Calvin B. Hoover, "Human Problems in Acreage Reduction in the South" in "Records of the Agricultural Stabilization and Conservation Service," Record Group 145, National Archives.

10 Francis Shea to Margaret Bennett, November 14, 1934, in RG 145, NA.

In October, 1933, less than six months after AAA operations began, a contract covering both the 1934 and 1935 crop seasons was drawn up. Under this plan the government proposed to "rent," through voluntary agreements, 15 million acres, or about three-eighths of the nation's cotton land, to keep it out of production. In return it offered growers a payment of 4.5 cents per pound of the average yield (1928–1932) of the "rented acres." [11]

This payment was divided into two parts. The major portion, 3.5 cents per pound, was a "rental" paid to the landowner. There were two exceptions to this rule. A cash tenant, due to his independent status, was entitled to the full rental. Likewise, a "managing share tenant" was supposed to receive half of it. The contract defined a managing share tenant as a share tenant who had actual control of leased land, paid a percentage of the crop as rent, and farmed without landlord supervision. Just which of the more independent share tenants qualified became a matter of extreme controversy. The second part of the AAA benefit, 1 cent per pound, was called the "parity payment" and was to be divided between landlord and tenant according to the interest each had in the crop. Cash tenants would receive all of it, share tenants three-fourths or two-thirds, and sharecroppers half. As in the plow-up, landlords received the checks and distributed the tenants' portions. This apportionment of benefits gave the average landlord with sharecroppers the full rental of 3.5 cents per pound of the average yield of his rented acres and half the parity payment (0.5 cent per pound) and left the cropper with 0.5 cent per pound. In addition they both could hope to receive an improved price on the reduced amount of cotton they grew. Thus the landlord received eight-ninths of the government benefit. [12]

This disproportionate division was a unique feature of the 1934–

11　U.S. Department of Agriculture, Agricultural Adjustment Administration, Production Division, "1934 and 1935 Cotton Acreage Reduction Contract, Form No. Cotton 1," and "Essentials of the Cotton Plan for 1934–35," AAA press release, both in RG 145, NA.

12　Department of Agriculture, "1934 and 1935 Cotton Acreage Reduction Contract," Hoover, "Human Problems in Acreage Reduction in the South," and "Essentials of the Cotton Plan for 1934–35," all in RG 145, NA. For a secondary account see Conrad, *Forgotten Farmers*, 52, 54–61.

1935 cotton contract. The rationale for it revealed much about the prolandlord outlook of the AAA cotton section. According to Calvin Hoover, who in 1934 critically assessed the operation of the program for the AAA, cotton landlords would receive a smaller cash amount per acre from the government than the signers of corn-hog and tobacco agreements if the benefits were divided proportionately to crop interests as in the case of those commodities. Accordingly, Hoover wrote, the cotton section feared that landlords would not cooperate with the AAA unless they received significantly more favorable terms. Thus they were given nearly 89 percent of the payment compared to the croppers' 11 percent and "induced to sign the cotton contract by [benefits] obtained at the expense of the share tenant and the share cropper."[13]

Section 7 of the contract, an imprecise paragraph, attempted to protect tenants by placing three general obligations on landlords. To compensate tenants for the paucity of their government payments, landlords were to permit them to cut plantation wood for fuel without charge, and to use an "adequate portion" of the "rented acres" to grow food. The contract writers calculated that if croppers had actually received half, rather than one-ninth, of the government benefit for the average of six acres they no longer cultivated, they would get about $3 more per acre, or a total of $18.21. Compensatory use of "rented" land was thought to be worth at least that much. But as Hoover remarked, that assumed that croppers would really have full use of the land. Secondly, "as nearly . . . as practicable" contract signers were to prorate the acreage reduction among tenants to avoid leaving some with little or no land to make a crop in which they could share. Finally, to prevent the displacement of their workers, farm owners were "insofar as possible" to "maintain on this farm the normal number of tenants and other employees" and "permit all tenants to continue in the occupancy of their houses . . . rent free, for . . . 1934 and 1935." A loophole, however, allowed the evic-

---

13 Hoover, "Human Problems in Acreage Reduction in the South," in RG 145, NA. Cotton planters had, however, signed (though perhaps they did not fulfill) the plow-up contract that divided benefits proportionately to crop interests.

tion of those who became a "nuisance or a menace to the welfare of the producer."[14]

The authors of these provisions were Cully Cobb, a former Georgia farm editor and chief of the AAA cotton section, and Oscar Johnston, head of the finance division and manager of the Delta and Pine Land Company of Scott, Mississippi, the nation's largest plantation. They intended paragraph 7 to constitute only a "moral obligation" for landlords.[15] When Socialist leader Norman Thomas later excoriated AAA administrator Chester Davis for writing "pious hopes into a contract as if they were legal provisions,"[16] he was not far wrong.

Actually, however, when the section was written there were objections to it from within the AAA. Alger Hiss, a staff member of the legal division, participated in the drafting and expressed grave doubts about the enforceability of paragraph 7 because of its vagueness. He was supported in this view by Jerome Frank, head of the legal division. But Hiss, unable to change the substance of Johnston's and Cobb's policy, acquiesced in the final wording. Another critic, D. P. Trent, assistant director of the commodities division and an authority on tenancy, told Chester Davis he thought the division of benefits was unfair and predicted it would cause dissatisfaction and play into the hands of radicals. He suggested revising the contract to distinguish between cotton tenants in nonplantation districts (mostly white, often former farm owners of some ability, and not wards of their landlords) and those on large plantations (by implication the more dependent blacks). Trent thought the proposed one-ninth benefit might be adequate for the latter, but the abler croppers should receive 25 percent of the rental as well as half the parity payment. While Davis agreed with Johnston and Cobb on basic policy, he was sufficiently impressed by Trent's arguments to press them upon Johnston, although unsuccessfully. In November, after the contract was written, Davis evaluated it for George Peek,

---

14 *Ibid.*; Department of Agriculture, "1934 and 1935 Cotton Acreage Reduction Contract," in RG 145, NA.
15 Conrad, *Forgotten Farmers*, 58–59.
16 Norman Thomas to Chester Davis, March 22, 1935, in RG 145, NA.

then AAA's administrator. "I want to call your attention to the fact that... there is no legally enforceable provision that will hold on the farms the normal number of tenants," he wrote. Then he predicted that the paragraph would become a source of trouble, but like Trent, he expected the objections to come from white nonplantation croppers dissatisfied with payment divisions.[17]

The tenancy provisions of the 1934–1935 contract were unenforced, if not unenforceable, and, beginning about the middle of 1934, aroused a storm of public criticism against the AAA. Reliable observers agreed that violations were widespread. By the end of the year four competent assessments of the situation had appeared, which, taken together, can be considered conclusive evidence of the general charges. The first of these evaluations was AAA's own. The agency, responding to attacks from the press and elsewhere, appointed Calvin B. Hoover, a Duke University economist attached to the AAA, to review the cotton program.[18] Drawing upon his expertise in southern agricultural matters, he wrote a report, "Human Problems in Acreage Reduction in the South," which was made public in the spring of 1934. The fact that Hoover was an official of the AAA, and had no particular intention of discrediting it or the New Deal lent special significance to his penetrating criticism.

Slightly later in 1934, Socialists censured the AAA. Norman Thomas, the party's 1932 presidential candidate, wrote *The Plight of the Sharecropper*, which succinctly described the tenants' living conditions and included a suggestion for government landownership and cooperative farming.[19] Appended to it was a report of a thorough survey of croppers in the region surrounding Memphis. It was prepared by William Amberson, a physiologist at the University

17 Memorandum by Alger Hiss, November 9, 1933, in AAA legal office files in "Records of the Office of the Secretary of Agriculture," Record Group 16, National Archives; D. P. Trent to Davis, October 30, 1933, and Davis to George Peek, November 11, 1933, both in RG 145, NA. According to Conrad, *Forgotten Farmers*, 57–58, Hiss did obtain a contract provision giving the secretary of agriculture "final and conclusive" determination of producers' fulfillment of all contract terms, which could have enabled the secretary, through policy decisions, to clarify paragraph 7.
18 Conrad, *Forgotten Farmers*, 123–24.
19 Norman Thomas, *The Plight of the Sharecropper* (New York: League for Industrial Democracy, 1934).

of Tennessee medical college in Memphis and active Socialist.[20]
Both these works were anti-New Dealish in tone, but factual and
based on reliable observation.

A fourth critical report was that of the Committee on Minority
Groups in the Economic Recovery, which represented a southern
liberal point of view not adverse to the New Deal as a whole. The
committee consisted of Will Alexander of the Commission on Interracial Cooperation, Charles S. Johnson, Edwin Embree of the Julius
Rosenwald Fund, and Frank Tannenbaum. During the summer of
1934 Johnson directed extensive investigations throughout the cotton belt, and in December Tannenbaum delivered a summary of the
results to the Agriculture Department. The committee later published its findings as *The Collapse of Cotton Tenancy*, the decade's
most scholarly short work on the subject.[21]

The injustices which these critics noted fell into several
categories. The first was that some landlords simply did not distribute parity payments. In other instances tenants received only part of
their due, were coerced by landlords to sign away their shares of the
payments, or had benefits applied to their indebtedness as in the
1933 plow-up. The threat of eviction, of course, could forestall their
complaints to the AAA. The fundamental problem in these cases was
that the agency made checks only to farm owners and relied on them
to allocate the money properly. This was partly a matter of administrative convenience, but it also conformed to the old plantation pattern in which the landlord dispensed credit or profits to his dependents, often according merely to his estimation of their needs and his
own.[22]

20   William R. Amberson, "The Social and Economic Consequences of the Cotton Acreage
      Reduction Program: Report of Survey Made by Memphis Chapter L.I.D. and the
      Tyronza Socialist Party Under Direction of William R. Amberson," appendix in
      Thomas, *Plight of the Sharecropper*, 19–24.
21   Frank Tannenbaum to Paul Appleby, December 29, 1934, in Frank Tannenbaum Pa-
      pers, Columbia University; Charles S. Johnson, Edwin R. Embree, and Will W. Alex-
      ander, *The Collapse of Cotton Tenancy: Summary of Field Studies and Statistical Sur-
      veys, 1933–35* (Chapel Hill: University of North Carolina Press, 1935).
22   Thomas, *Plight of the Sharecropper*, 14; Amberson, "Social and Economic Conse-
      quences of the Cotton Acreage Reduction Program," 28–30; Hoover, "Human Prob-
      lems in Acreage Reduction in the South," in RG 145, NA.

Secondly, the division of payments, in which the higher strata of landless farmers received more than those of lower status, encouraged landlords to downgrade tenants whenever possible. This was especially true in the case of the ill-defined "managing share tenant," who was entitled to half the rental payment (which amounted to nearly 39 percent of the total benefit). Farm owners who rented to self-directing share tenants often claimed to exercise a supervision that disqualified them as managers with a stake in the rental. Similarly, because ordinary share tenants received more of the parity payment than sharecroppers, they were often demoted to that level. And a planter who could redefine his croppers as wage hands could reap maximum profits from the government because the contract gave day laborers nothing whatever. Moreover, as Calvin Hoover summarized the situation, "the more favorable the division of... payments is to the tenant, the stronger will be the motive for the landlord to reduce the number of his tenants" and substitute wage labor.[23]

The most serious abuse of the contract was the outright eviction of croppers, despite the planters' obligation "insofar as possible" to keep the normal number. "The simplest and surest way... to avoid the division of the payment with sharecroppers is to have no sharecroppers," one planter later admitted.[24] The displacement was of massive proportions. The total number of sharecroppers in the South declined between 1930 and 1935 for the first time in more than five decades.[25] In January, 1935, the federal farm census counted 76,000 sharecroppers in Texas, as compared to 105,000 in April, 1930.[26] The Federal Emergency Relief Administration, which recognized this problem well before the Agriculture Department

23 Hoover, "Human Problems in Acreage Reduction in the South," in RG 145, NA.
24 Undated article by Thad Snow, enclosed in Irving Brant to Mordecai Ezekiel, December 22, 1936, in RG 16, NA.
25 U.S. National Resources Committee, *Farm Tenancy: Report of the President's Committee* (Washington: Government Printing Office, 1937), 39, 99. Between 1930 and 1935 the percentage of southern farmers who were tenants declined from 55.5 to 53.5. The number of sharecroppers dropped from 775,000 to 715,000.
26 Pierce Williams, "The Problems Created by the Diminishing Demand for Casual Agricultural Labor in Texas," (Typescript report to Harry Hopkins, March 27, 1936, in Harry Hopkins Papers, Franklin D. Roosevelt Library, Hyde Park, N.Y.).

did, felt compelled as early as February, 1934, to create a special division to reestablish dispossessed farmers.[27]

Certainly not all displacement was directly attributable to the AAA. Already in parts of the Southwest fewer croppers were needed due to the increased use of tractors. In the Southeast, planters sought to escape furnishing responsibilities, deemed "one of the chief trouble spots for the landlord."[28] But the AAA contract was a compelling reason for discontinuing sharecropping. In 1936, one Missouri planter, who was sympathetic to tenants, considered the trends of the past few years toward wage labor and remarked on the planter outlook:

The [planter-businessman] has absorbed plenty of punishment in years gone by, but he remained optimistic and is always willing to risk all his own money and all he can borrow on a cotton crop. Now businessmen[,] when they have obtained an advantage by special legislation . . . do not . . . rush forward cheerfully to share the advantage with their work people. This reluctance is said to be inherent in business. We cotton planters are sufficiently businesslike to be that way too. We have secured an advantage by special legislation which . . . more or less assures us a remunerative price for high yield cotton and also gives us real money for reducing our acreage. And does it seem reasonable to us that we should share this advantage with our work people, and do we do it gladly? It does not, and we do not. . . . We merely take the industrialist view.

He concluded that planters converted to wage labor because it paid to do so. Furthermore, any contract provisions to the contrary amounted to little more than "moral suasion," bound to be ineffective, because of a "long established habit of thought, part of the Southern culture, in fact, that rejects the idea that the cotton cropper is entitled to or benefited by a money income more than sufficient to supply his most pressing bodily needs." And in 1934 an investigator posing as a sharecropper seeking a place to farm had heard this planter attitude expressed in its bluntest terms by a "riding boss" for

27 See Chapter IV, herein.
28 Williams, "The Problems Created by the Diminishing Demand for Casual Agricultural Labor in Texas"; Paul S. Taylor to Henry Wallace, June 3, 1937, confidential report in RG 16, NA; Thomas Jackson Woofter, Jr., *Landlord and Tenant on the Cotton Plantation*, Works Progress Administration Research Monographs, V (Washington: Works Progress Administration, 1936), 29, 39.

the R. T. Kuhn plantation in Crittenden County, Arkansas. "We don't intend to give these niggers a share-crop," said the overseer. "We're going to wait until it is too late to get a crop anywhere else, and then work them at day labor at 6 bits a day."[29]

The formation of the Southern Tenant Farmers' Union (STFU) in July, 1934, was the most significant reaction of poor farmers themselves to the inequitable workings of the AAA. The union originated with a biracial group of sharecroppers on the Hiram Norcross plantation near Tyronza, in Poinsett County, Arkansas. Significantly, this strongest of tenant organizations began in a fertile delta area which had been brought into cultivation mostly since 1910 and where, in contrast to the older plantation regions of the Southeast, both cotton planting and sharecropping were expanding until the early 1930s. The Norcross tenants turned for leadership to H. L. Mitchell and Clay East of Tyronza, local Socialists who had recently discussed the possibilities of tenant labor union activity with Norman Thomas. Their organizational efforts spread STFU locals throughout northeastern Arkansas and enrolled a membership of perhaps 1,500 by the end of 1934.[30]

Although the STFU later became outspokenly critical of most New Deal tenancy policy and antipoverty efforts, its original objectives were much narrower. Chiefly concerned with establishing union bargaining power with landlords and assuring tenants equitable treatment under existing AAA regulations, it began bombarding the agency with reports of evictions and contract violations. Meanwhile, local reaction to the union was, at first, limited to suspicion of its aims and its racially mixed membership. But by January, 1935, a violent union-breaking compaign by planters and local law enforce-

---

29   Undated article by Thad Snow, enclosed in Brant to Ezekiel, December 22, 1936, in RG 16, NA; typescript notes for Amberson, "Social and Economic Consequences of the Cotton Acreage Reduction Program," in William R. Amberson Papers, Southern Historical Collection, University of North Carolina, Chapel Hill.

30   Grubbs, *Cry from the Cotton,* 7, 29, 62–64, 67; Conrad, *Forgotten Farmers,* 85–87, 93; "Reminiscences of Harry Leland Mitchell" (Typescript, 1957, in Oral History Collection, Columbia University), 20–25. Early estimates of Southern Tenant Farmers' Union membership ranged from 1,200 to 1,500. See William Amberson to Appleby, November 21, 1934, and memorandum accompanying STFU list of contract violations, December, 1934, both in AAA legal office files in RG 16, NA.

ment officials broke out in Arkansas and dragged the AAA's tenant problems into full public view.[31]

Early in 1935 the growing tenancy controversy split the AAA and resulted in both the dismissal of most of its legal staff and an implicit reaffirmation of the agency's price parity aims. The general outlines of this episode, known as the "AAA purge," are well known and need be sketched only briefly.[32]

There had always been friction within the AAA between the traditional agriculturalists who dominated it (men like Chester Davis who became administrator in December, 1933) and viewed its sole objective as price parity, and certain staff members of the legal division who leaned toward making the agency more responsive to consumers' needs and toward social reform in general. Included in this latter "liberal" group were AAA General Counsel Jerome Frank, Alger Hiss, Francis Shea, Lee Pressman, Margaret Bennett, Robert McConnaughey, and Gardner Jackson, who was an assistant in the office of the AAA consumers' counsel.[33] By the fall of 1934 the legal division began to investigate the complaints emanating from STFU territory in eastern Arkansas. This interest led directly to a clash with the cotton section over interpretation of the AAA contract.

The immediate issue concerned the eviction of sharecroppers from the Norcross plantation for membership in the STFU. The tenants had sued their landlord in the state courts of Arkansas to enjoin him from dismissing them, contending that their union membership was not a legal reason, under the contract, for such action. They also requested the secretary of agriculture to halt the evictions pending investigation. Finally, the STFU's attorney asked the AAA to intervene in the case for the tenants.[34]

---

31 Conrad, *Forgotten Farmers*, 87, 95, 97, and Chap. 9; Grubbs, *Cry from the Cotton*, 70–74; "Reminiscences of Harry Leland Mitchell," 25; Southern Tenant Farmers' Union list of 266 contract violations, December, 1934, in AAA legal office files in RG 16, NA.

32 The best secondary accounts of the purge are Conrad, *Forgotten Farmers*, Chap. 8, and Grubbs, *Cry from the Cotton*, Chap. 3.

33 Conrad, *Forgotten Farmers*, 105–107, 110–116.

34 *Ibid.*, 136; Paul Porter to Jerome Frank, January 3, 1935, eleven Norcross sharecroppers to Wallace, December 12, 1934, C. T. Carpenter to Frank, January 11 and 15,

This matter and others were referred to a special three-member AAA committee on contract violations. Its chairman and the cotton section's representative held that Norcross had not contravened the letter of the agreement because, although he had dismissed share-croppers, he had not reduced the number of his tenants. This conformed to the cotton section's standard view concerning evictions. Therefore the majority counseled the secretary that it was "inadvisable administratively and not in accordance with public policy" to use the threat of contract revocation to force landlords to keep the same persons as tenants, rather than merely the same number. Of course they also objected to intervention in the suit.[35]

In a minority report endorsed by Assistant General Counsel Alger Hiss, Margaret Bennett, the legal division's member of the committee, argued that union membership was neither a "nuisance" nor a "menace" under the contract and therefore not cause for eviction. Furthermore, as the legal division now read the regulations, landlords were bound to keep the identical 1934 tenants during 1935. Therefore, the secretary should "enforce the contract," as interpreted by the legal division and forbid Norcross to discharge his croppers.[36]

Another development, in January, 1935, intensified the AAA dissension. Frank sent an agency lawyer, Mary Conner Myers, to Arkansas with a mandate for thorough investigation of all contract irregularities. On January 18 she wired Frank from Memphis that she found the contract "openly and generally violated." After several days in the Delta she filed a report which reputedly was trenchantly critical of the AAA. But it was withheld from publication, probably on Chester Davis' direct order, and later removed from AAA files.[37]

The suppression of the Myers report became, in itself, a cause

1935, Carpenter to Appleby, January 15, 1935, and Bennett to Frank, January 10, 1935, all in AAA legal office files in RG 16, NA.

35 Majority of Committee on Violations of Rental and Benefit Contracts to Wallace, memorandum, January 10, 1935, in AAA legal office files in RG 16, NA.

36 Bennett to Wallace, and Frank to Wallace, memoranda, both January 12, 1935, in AAA legal office files in RG 16, NA.

37 Frank to Wallace, January 12, 1935, Mary Conner Myers to Frank, January 18, 1935, in AAA legal office files in RG 16, NA; Conrad, *Forgotten Farmers*, 139–41, 185.

for even more public censure of the AAA. The agency's standard reply to those who demanded publication was that it could not be released since it named specific violators (which seems likely) who might be subject to future prosecution (much less likely) and besides it contained nothing new. The latter part of this explanation was probably true. Writing in the spring of 1935, STFU executive secretary H. L. Mitchell reconstructed the report on the basis of his conversations with Myers. His outline differed little from the criticisms of AAA published by Thomas, Amberson, or Hoover, or those submitted to the Agriculture Department by Frank Tannenbaum.[38] The evidence suggests, however, that Myers indicted the cotton program in strong language which the agency simply found too embarrassing to make public. She may also have condemned planters in blunt terms. After one day in the Delta she wired Frank that the violations she found revealed "one long story of human greed." While in Memphis she called on William Amberson, who reported that she "turns out to be very sympathetic to our cause." Indeed, she may have been even more outspoken than Amberson, since he found himself trying to convince her that "not all planters are dishonest, as she is prepared to believe on the basis of her first two days' stay."[39] In any case, the publication by AAA of any report attacking its planter constituency would have been politically devastating to the agency.

The AAA's internal struggle climaxed early in February, 1935. Jerome Frank's legal division, during Chester Davis' absence from Washington, prepared a reinterpretation of paragraph 7. The new opinion, written by Francis Shea with assistance from Hiss, required landlords to retain the same tenants throughout 1935 as they had had in 1934, not merely the same number. This would, of course, greatly restrict planters in ridding themselves of unwanted croppers. The move raised a direct jurisdictional dispute concerning power to

---

38   Davis to Roger Baldwin, March 2, 1935, Porter to Walter White, March 26, 1935, H. L. Mitchell to Porter, March 27, 1935, all in RG 145, NA.

39   Myers to Frank, January 18, 1935, in AAA legal office files in RG 16, NA; Amberson to Baldwin, January 19, 1935, to Margaret Marshall, to Carpenter, and to Clay East, all January 21, 1935, and to Thomas, January 25, 1935, all in Amberson Papers.

construe the contract. Although such matters are normally the responsibility of a legal staff, no one outside Frank's division had ever asked for an interpretation of the tenancy paragraph. The cotton section, already suspicious of the general counsel's office, saw the action as a challenge to its control of its program.[40]

Davis was thoroughly angered when, returning to Washington, he discovered that the new interpretation had been announced and sent to the field. For two hours on the afternoon of February 2 he conferred with Wallace. He told the secretary of the legal division's action, complained bitterly of an "intrigue" against him by Frank and others, and said that he was considering resigning to return to private life.[41]

Wallace's first reaction was that Davis had exaggerated the problem, and after conferring with Undersecretary M. L. Wilson, he wanted to avoid hasty action. But he received other advice that the situation was critical. Economic advisor John D. Black wrote that Davis had "reached the end of his endurance" and might demand changes in the agency which Wallace would find difficult to make. Moreover, Black advised, Davis was essential to the AAA, not only as the only administrator "who can carry the ball in the next year or two," but also because "there is no mistaking the general approval of him among agricultural folks." Finally, Black suggested that if Davis resigned other AAA officials might leave with him. Such counsel must have inclined Wallace toward the view that Davis was indispensable.[42]

On February 4 Wallace saw Davis again, along with department solicitor Seth Thomas. The secretary already believed that Frank and others in the "extreme liberal group" had an unfortunate lack of agricultural background and wanted to accomplish reform too

40 Conrad, *Forgotten Farmers*, 141–43, 146. For the opinion see Shea to Robert McConnaughey, February 4, 1935, in RG 145, NA.

41 Henry A. Wallace Diary (Typescript in Henry A. Wallace Papers, University of Iowa), February 2, 1935. Davis also charged that Assistant Secretary Paul Appleby was part of the "intrigue."

42 *Ibid.*, February 2, 3, and 4, 1935; John D. Black to Wallace, February 3, 1935, in Wallace Diary.

rapidly.[43] After agreeing with Davis that the lawyers' "social pre-conceptions" had influenced their judgment, Wallace was then persuaded that their interpretation was "indefensible from a practical agricultural point of view," as well as legally unsound. Finally, speaking alone with Wallace, Davis said that for him the situation had reached the breaking point and asked for authority to fire Frank, Shea, and Lee Pressman.[44]

After this meeting Wallace was convinced of the need for immediate action to prevent the loss of Davis. Furthermore, the secretary had reason to expect a storm of planter and congressional objection if he upheld any changes in the cotton section's application of the contract. In January, for example, he had been warned by the president of the American Cotton Cooperative Association that requiring landlords to keep the same tenants would "reverse completely the sentiment of thousands of the friends of crop control" and "break... faith with the cotton growers." And just three days previously Wallace had met with a delegation of Arkansas planters who came with their congressman to protest the announcement of the change.[45]

Influenced by these considerations, Wallace told Davis, who telephoned for a decision on the evening of the fourth, that he "had the green light." On the fifth Davis dismissed Frank, Shea, and Pressman, as well as Gardner Jackson from the consumers' counsel's office. Alger Hiss resigned slightly later. Wallace then promulgated a final interpretation of the contract which reaffirmed the cotton section's position. Although the purge embarrassed the secretary and angered prominent New Dealers outside the AAA (Undersecretary Rexford Tugwell almost resigned when he heard of it), Wallace consistently justified it as necessary to maintain AAA's effectiveness and its support among commercial farmers.[46]

---

43 Wallace Diary, February 2, 1935. Wallace included Paul Appleby and Rexford Tugwell in the "extreme liberal group."

44 *Ibid.*, February 4, 1935. Davis found no fault with Hiss, who he thought was merely being loyal to Frank, and did not ask to fire him.

45 *Ibid.*, February 1 and 4, 1935; N. C. Williamson to Wallace, January 16, 1935, in RG 16, NA.

46 Wallace Diary, February 4 and 11, 1935; Davis to Wallace, February 5, 1935, in Wallace Diary; Conrad, *Forgotten Farmers*, 148. Tugwell thought the dismissals were "part

The AAA purge involved at least two policy issues. One question was the extent to which the agency should try to prevent the tenant displacement that resulted from production control, and a narrow view won out. A less immediate issue was an indirect challenge by the AAA liberals to the preeminence of the agency's price parity aims. This was implied in two of the legal division's main policy statements in the dispute—Margaret Bennett's dissent from the majority report of the committee on contract violations and Francis Shea's reinterpretation of paragraph 7, approved by Frank and Hiss. These key documents also stressed several social considerations which, if accepted, could have reinforced the reformist outlook.

Miss Bennett argued that the secretary should require landlords to keep the same tenants in 1935 as in 1934 because, in her opinion, anything less would allow them latitude to discharge their dependents for any reason, regardless of whether the secretary judged the evictions socially desirable. She further maintained that "it is not unreasonable to ask [a landlord] to contribute . . . to the welfare of the community in which he lives" by not evicting croppers who would otherwise become part of a "destitute floating population" and a public burden. [47] This was a good point as social policy which Bennett might have strengthened by relating it to the contract requirement that producers cut acreage "in such a manner as to cause the least possible amount of labor, economic and social disturbance."

Concerning the immediate issue of the Norcross case, Miss Bennett urged the secretary to forbid evictions which were solely for STFU membership. She argued solidly that Norcross had never claimed dissatisfaction with his tenants' work and that merely joining a union did not make his sharecroppers a "nuisance" or a "menace"

---

of Davis' studied plan to rid the Department of all liberals" and give "reactionary farm leaders" control of agricultural policy. Rexford G. Tugwell Diary (Typescript in Rexford G. Tugwell Papers, Franklin D. Roosevelt Library), February 10, 1935. Wallace did not see Frank and Hiss until late in the day, after the dismissals. When they outlined their position it "sounded entirely reasonable and . . . just as good as that presented by Chester Davis," but Wallace still upheld Davis because of his concern for AAA's administration. See Wallace Diary, February 5, 1935.

47 Bennett to Wallace, January 12, 1935, in AAA legal office files in RG 16, NA.

under the contract.[48] In his treatment of the eviction question, Shea considered the cotton section's emphasis on the producer's obligation to "maintain on this farm the *normal number* of tenants and other employees." In response he stressed the requirement, immediately following, that landlords "permit all tenants to continue in the occupancy of their houses on this farm...for...1934 and 1935." He contended that this language, read in the context of the whole paragraph, permitted no dismissals, except of those who were unquestionably a nuisance or menace. Unless landless farmers moved voluntarily, a plantation's 1935 tenants had to be identical to those of 1934.[49] These arguments, which made the most of the contract's vague wording, were by far the legal division's strongest and should have sufficed to support the AAA liberals' case against evictions.

Both Shea and Bennett, however, dealt not only with the language of the contract, but also interpreted the Agricultural Adjustment Act. Summarizing her position, Bennett advised Wallace to stop the growing criticism of the AAA by "attempting to carry out the declared policy of the Act (that is, to increase not only the price of agricultural commodities, but also the purchasing power of *all farmers*)." Likewise, Shea attributed to the act itself, rather than to the contract alone, the purpose of distributing as broadly as possible purchasing power in the form of benefits. He saw the law's "declared policy" as the "reestablishment of the purchasing power and economic welfare of the whole farm community" including not only tenants but even wage laborers as well.[50] Thus, both lawyers tied the

48   *Ibid.* Bennett also argued that dismissals for union membership contravened congressional policy which, as expressed in Section 7-a of the National Industrial Recovery Act, recognized collective bargaining. But here she was unconvincing, since there were no AAA contract obligations analogous to the National Industrial Recovery Act's 7-a.

49   Shea to McConnaughey, February 4, 1935, in RG 145, NA. Italics added. This paragraph has benefited from the discussions of the strength of this particular legal division argument found in Conrad, *Forgotten Farmers*, 142–43, and Grubbs, *Cry from the Cotton*, 55.

50   Bennett to Wallace, January 12, 1935, in AAA legal office files in RG 16, NA; Shea to McConnaughey, February 4, 1935, in RG 145, NA. Italics original. While Bennett and Shea may have been close to the intent of some of the act's framers, their version of its "declared policy" is hard to extract from the language of the statute's statement of policy. To support his opinion Shea cited a House Agriculture Committee report, *Relieve*

objective of increasing farm purchasing power (which the statute linked to commodity prices) to the admittedly desirable aim of increasing the income of all persons engaged in agriculture. Acceptance of this last interpretation would have weakened the agriculturalists' view of price parity as the fundamental concept of the AAA.

Price parity continued as a major New Deal commitment. A few claimed that it was sufficient to uplift the poor. For example, at the height of the AAA controversy the chief of the cotton section, Cully Cobb, told Chester Davis that production control and enhanced prices had pulled landlord and tenant alike out of debt and put them "in a far stronger economic position than they were in the early months of 1933." He saw the cotton program as a "new opportunity to tenants" and a "first step towards economic independence," at least for the "more efficient."[51] But a much more frequently expressed view was that parity was the region's major economic need—an expectation that the overall prosperity of the South was largely a matter of twelve-cent cotton. Even Roosevelt, whose understanding of southern poverty was broader than such commodity views, could occasionally overstate the benefits of parity. For example, in December, 1934, as public criticism mounted against the AAA for helping the few rather than the many, he remarked in a press conference that "the objective is a parity price. . . . If we can maintain something pretty close to parity for three or four years more all through the cotton raising area . . . it is going to do more for the south than has been done at any time before in our lifetime."[52]

One of the best examples of southern landowners' and agriculturalists' faith that parity prices could assure the region's general prosperity was the cotton section's hearings on a 1936 production control contract in Memphis in October, 1935. Equally important,

---

the Existing National Economic Emergency by Increasing Agricultural Purchasing Power, 73rd Cong. 1st Sess. (H. Rept. 6 to accompany H. R. 3835), p. 7, which stated that "additional return [presumably benefit payments] received by farmers by reason of this Act will be money promptly spent . . . in ways that will decrease unemployment and add to the profits of business." But this merely indicated that those who received benefit money would spend it and said nothing specifically about broad distribution of benefits.

51 Cully Cobb to Davis, January 5, 1935, in AAA legal office files in RG 16, NA.
52 Roosevelt Press Conferences, IV, 257–58 in Franklin D. Roosevelt Library.

these hearings were notable for the efforts of a small group of southern liberals to persuade the AAA to make its program more equitable for poor farmers.

At the end of the 1935 crop season the agreement with producers expired and a new one was needed. The law required the secretary of agriculture, before promulgating any crop contract, to call public hearings at which all interested persons could present their views. Accordingly, Wallace announced a conference for October 11–12 in Memphis. In order to confine the discussion to commodity price matters, the official notice called for testimony specifically concerning the effectiveness of the AAA in achieving parity and whether acreage and production control were the most practicable means of attaining that goal.[53]

At this point Will Alexander, the assistant administrator of the newly established Resettlement Administration (RA), perceived that the hearings offered an opportunity, while a contract was still being developed, to bring public pressure on the AAA to improve benefits for poor farmers. As an official of the RA, Alexander was unable directly to attack the procedures of another government agency, but he sought out private citizens who would. On October 4 he contacted Francis P. Miller, a Virginian who had recently organized the Southern Policy Committee (SPC), a network of prominent southerners interested in various regional reforms, especially those to alleviate the plight of landless farmers. Alexander persuaded Miller that the SPC should send a representative to Memphis to press the AAA vigorously to change its tenant policies.[54]

Miller contacted the SPC's president, Herman Clarence Nixon, professor of government at Tulane University, who agreed to undertake the mission. Miller thought the issue to stress was that the AAA

53 U.S. Department of Agriculture, "Official Report of Proceedings Before the Agricultural Adjustment Administration in Re: Hearing on Proposed Adjustment Program for Cotton. Memphis, Tennessee, October 11, 1935," in RG 145, NA. The notice of hearing is on p. 8.
54 Francis P. Miller to Herman Clarence Nixon, October 5, 1935, in National Policy Committee Papers, Library of Congress, hereinafter cited as NPC Papers; Alexander to Johnson, October 7, 1935, in Commission on Interracial Cooperation Papers, Atlanta University.

was "organized and managed in the interest of the upper-class planter." He charged that Cully Cobb privately "makes no bones about this. He says he is doing for the planters what Hamilton did for the industrialists in the latter part of the eighteenth century." This inclination of the AAA, Miller thought, should be held up to public attention. Therefore he saw the hearings as the occasion for the SPC "to *turn on the heat* on the cotton section" to devise a fairer 1936 contract. Moreover, Nixon could present the case persuasively. Not only was he well known as an academic advocate of improved southern rural life (he was one of the twelve "Nashville Agrarians" of 1930), but as the absentee owner of an Alabama plantation with eleven tenants he could appear as a landlord and contract signer. Finally, Miller had arranged for Charles S. Johnson, who had conducted the field surveys for the recently published *Collapse of Cotton Tenancy*, to attend and supply Nixon with technical data on AAA's effects on the poor.[55]

As the hearing approached, Miller foresaw a possible complication. He hoped that a trenchant criticism of the AAA by the SPC would arouse the "rational and liberal elements in the South" to demand reform of the contract. But he feared that the "semicommunist" STFU, or its local advisor William Amberson, might appear and by intemperate condemnation of the New Deal overshadow Nixon's presentation. Therefore he warned Nixon to be alert for Amberson's possible attendance and if necessary try to dissuade him from testifying.[56]

On October 11 the hearings convened at the Chisca Hotel in Memphis with Robert McConnaughey presiding. A long succession of planters, farmers, and Agricultural Extension Service officials testified, filling most of the 452-page transcript with lavish praise for the AAA. Most of them stressed that the agency, while not lifting prices to full parity, had greatly increased the value of the cotton

---

55 Miller to Nixon, October 5 and 9, 1935, Nixon to Miller, October 6 and 10, 1935, in NPC Papers; Johnson to Nixon, October 5, 1935, in Herman Clarence Nixon Papers, in possession of the Nixon family, Nashville. Quotations (italics original) are from Miller's letter of October 5.

56 Miller to Nixon, October 5, 1935, in NPC Papers.

crop. Consequently, farmers had paid debts, added to bank deposits, and bought consumer goods. This increased spending had in turn stimulated industrial production and retail trade. For example, one spokesman presented statistics to show that general merchandise sales in the South had increased nearly 25 percent from 1933 to 1934. Another read a letter from the president of Sears, Roebuck and Company citing greatly improved catalog business in the region. Most of the witnesses made little reference to tenants, except personal assurances that they received adequate government payments. On the whole the hearings seemed to produce remarkable unanimity that AAA had benefited the South. Some even declared that it should be made permanent.[57]

Toward the end of the hearing Nixon took the stand. He agreed that the AAA had increased agricultural purchasing power, but pointed out that it had obviously failed to distribute it democratically. He referred to *The Collapse of Cotton Tenancy* and other studies as evidence that contract abuses had deprived tenants of their already inadequate payments and concluded that the landless were as impoverished as they had been two or three years earlier. Nixon recommended larger payments for them without reducing what landowners received. He argued that such an expansion of benefits would improve the South's general economy even more than had landlord's AAA checks. Poor farmers would, for example, buy cotton clothing, thus stimulating the region's textile industry and providing employment for another large needy group, the mill hands. Finally, Nixon advocated the pending Bankhead tenancy bill as a measure that could help alleviate poverty by assisting some tenants to own small farms.[58]

Charles S. Johnson followed Nixon and eloquently supplemented his colleague's remarks about the AAA's injustices for the landless. Since the STFU, to the surprise of many, made no formal appearance, the two SPC spokesmen sounded the only discordant note amid the

---

57 Department of Agriculture, "Hearing on Program for Cotton," 22–29, 55–57, 152–57, 171–75, 177–80, 215–16, 226.

58 *Ibid.*, 356–84.

praise for the agency.[59] Moreover, except for limited efforts by some AAA officials in the fall of 1933, they were the only ones who ever advocated before the cotton section better benefits for poor farmers while a contract was still being developed.

After the hearings Nixon and Johnson submitted specific recommendations to Secretary Wallace. They suggested that the new contract avoid a major difficulty of the old one by clarifying the definition and rights of managing share tenants. Similarly, they proposed to redefine acreage rental as a general benefit payable to those who contributed labor, workstock, or equipment as well as to those providing land. Thirdly, they advocated limiting the percentage of a sharecropper's payment which the landlord could apply to back debts. Furthermore, the agreement should provide for a diminution of the planter's receipts from the government proportionate to any unwarranted reduction in the number of his tenants. Nixon and Johnson recommended that the AAA make checks to every individual beneficiary, rather than rely on landlords to distribute the money. And finally, when assigning acreage allotments to states and counties, the agency should consider the suitability of different parts of the South for continued cotton growing and encourage a gradual shift away from it in the less productive areas of the Southeast.[60]

On December 3, 1935, the AAA announced a new contract for the crop seasons of 1936–1939, which was patterned after the old one, but "designed to eliminate inequities revealed in the operation of the previous program." The modifications were undoubtedly a response to the attacks of many critics since 1934, but it is significant that some of the changes followed SPC suggestions and the agency cited the Memphis hearings in making them. Crop reduction payments were to be divided somewhat more advantageously for tenants. A share of 37.5 percent would go to the person who furnished land, whereas the one who provided workstock and equipment could claim 12.5 percent. The remaining 50 percent would be split

59 *Ibid.*, 385–410; Nixon to Miller, October 13 and 15, 1935, in NPC Papers.
60 Nixon and Johnson to Wallace, November 4, 1935, in President's Personal File 660, Franklin D. Roosevelt Library.

in the same manner as the crop. This apportionment made the benefits not dependent upon vague classification such as "managing share tenant." It gave the ordinary sharecropper with half interest in his cotton 25 percent of the payment, rather than about 11 percent as before. A self-equipped share tenant could get as much as 50 percent rather than about 22.5 percent. Moreover, the plan required AAA to pay landless farmers by individual checks.[61]

Although the new terms improved tenant benefits, it is not likely that they could have halted the advancing displacement of croppers and the shift to wage labor, even had the Supreme Court not prevented their implementation by declaring the Agricultural Adjustment Act unconstitutional one month after their announcement. The contract still required signers "insofar as economically possible" to retain the same number of tenants and other employees from year to year, but imposed no effective penalties on those who did not. The parity programs that succeeded the AAA—the Soil Conservation and Domestic Allotment Act and the AAA of 1938—had the same general defects.[62]

Despite the great faith of southern farmers and administration officials in the benefits of price parity for the South's economy, the New Deal's production control policies were not an answer to the fundamental problems of the poor. These programs reduced poor people's security on the land and did nothing to lessen the dependence of the destitute, improve their farming skills or general competence, or give the abler tenants a chance for small farm ownership. These problems became the concern of other New Deal agencies.

61 "AAA Announces New Four Year Cotton Adjustment Program," December 3, 1935, AAA press release in RG 145, NA.

62 *Ibid.*; Nixon to Miller, December 8, 1935, in NPC Papers; Donald H. Grubbs, "The Southern Tenant Farmers' Union and the New Deal" (Ph.D. dissertation, University of Florida, 1963), 360–62; Louis Cantor, *A Prologue to the Protest Movement: The Missouri Sharecropper Roadside Demonstrations of 1939* (Durham, N.C.: Duke University Press, 1969), Chap. 12.

CHAPTER III

The FERA Discovers Rural Poverty

T HE ROOSEVELT administration's first real program to improve conditions for the rural poor originated not in the parity-minded Agriculture Department, but in the relief establishment, which was forced by circumstances to consider their plight. To understand why this was true, it is necessary to examine the operation of federal relief in the South during the first year of the New Deal.

The primary relief agency was the Federal Emergency Relief Administration, which operated under annual appropriations beginning in 1933. Headed by Harry Hopkins, FERA granted funds to state Emergency Relief Administrations (ERAs), which administered their own programs, under general federal oversight but with much variation of policy. Usually ERAs furnished direct relief, although they also conducted some work projects. Federal money was supposed to supplement whatever funds states could provide, but throughout the South FERA paid nearly 100 percent of the costs.[1]

Early in the New Deal it was evident that the rural South was heavily dependent on direct federal relief. A survey in July, 1933,

---

1   U.S. Federal Emergency Relief Administration, *Monthly Report, December 1–31, 1933* (Washington: Government Printing Office, 1934), 78–87.

revealed that in seventy selected southern rural counties 37,000 families out of 250,000, or 15 percent, received ERA aid. In the south Atlantic census region 18 percent of the rural families were on relief, in the east south central region 16 percent, and in the west south central 10 percent. Except for the mountain west's 12 percent, no other region exceeded 6 percent. Monthly relief per family was low in the South, varying from $4.57 per family (east south central) to $6.28 (south Atlantic) and $6.76 (west south central). Figures elsewhere ranged from $10.20 (west north central) to $25.70 (New England).[2]

Hopkins directed a second agency, the Civil Works Administration (CWA). This was an emergency organization, created specifically for the winter of 1933–1934 and never intended to be permanent. The federal government funded it completely and determined all its policies, although state ERA directors were usually designated CWA administrators in their states. CWA's program was work relief, generally on public construction. In the rural South this was mostly road work. Standard pay in the region was thirty cents per hour for common labor, which accounted for about 60 percent of all southern CWA employment. At its high point, in January, 1934, the agency enrolled approximately 1,024,000 persons in the former Confederacy.[3]

FERA and CWA were not specifically designed for the rural South, and in fact were anomalous in a tenancy system in which

---

2 E. D. Tetreau to Henry Wallace and Rexford G. Tugwell, October 11, 1933, in "Records of the Work Projects Administration," Record Group 69, National Archives.

3 Federal Emergency Relief Administration, *Monthly Report, December 1–31, 1933*, pp. 16–17, 93; transcript of Harry Hopkins' testimony to the Bureau of the Budget, January 22, 1934, in Harry Hopkins Papers, Franklin D. Roosevelt Library, Hyde Park, N.Y. Like all New Deal work relief, Civil Works Administration pay scales had regional differentials, with the lowest rates in the South. In each state half the CWA employees were supposed to be drawn from relief rolls and the rest from the unemployed registered with the National Reemployment Service job offices. But in several states, e.g. Georgia and Florida, enough relief cases were transferred *en masse* to fill the quota. This still left many on relief and led to a public belief that to become eligible for CWA one first had to get on relief. As a result many middle-class unemployed, having avoided the stigma of the FERA "dole" while awaiting work relief, crowded onto the rolls and resented those earlier (and fundamentally poorer) reliefers who received CWA jobs. See Lorena Hickok to Harry Hopkins, January 11 and 28, 1934, in Hopkins Papers.

landlords were supposed to employ agricultural workers and provide them subsistence during slack seasons. But with the system breaking down, relief was the only immediate way to meet the needs of the destitute. The original purpose of FERA was to relieve depression unemployment, but because agricultural work was so seasonal and normal living standards so low, it was often hard to define unemployment in rural areas. As a federal relief official in Georgia told one of Hopkins' representatives, "a farmer considers every nigger\ living in a house—or the worst kind of shack you ever saw—on his place employed, whether he is paying him anything or not. For a few weeks each year, perhaps, he actually will pay the head of the family 30 or 40 cents a day."[4]

Federal unemployment relief was not necessarily intended to raise living standards or correct poverty conditions. Whether FERA should accept these additional responsibilities became a major policy question. In April, 1934, the director of the Texas state office wrote to Hopkins' assistant, Aubrey Williams, about growing rural case loads. Many county offices, she told him, had assumed, without much analysis of "what they are getting into from a viewpoint of long time relief and rehabilitation," their communities' burdens of general dependence and poverty, including many Negroes and Mexican-Americans she thought could be self-sustaining, at least during the summer. She recommended removing from relief all persons "who have not really been affected seriously by the depression and [who] present a perennial picture of low standards of living." Instead of attempting to improve their condition, the ERA should concentrate on its "real function" of aiding those jobless on account of the depression. Williams agreed that those on relief for reasons other than depression unemployment should be forced back upon local resources, but he urged the Texas administrator to "keep the back door open" in case some chronic dependents faced starvation.[5]

On the other hand, some believed FERA could not ignore the question of living standards. Considering the adequacy of work relief

4   Hickok to Hopkins, January 23, 1934, in Hopkins Papers.
5   Marie Dresden to Aubrey Williams, April 24, 1934, and Williams to Dresden, May 1, 1934, in RG 69, NA.

wages, a Tulane University professor of social work told Williams, "I do not know whether it's sound to attempt to raise standards of living thru relief." But failure to set minimums for clients would squander money by "perpetuating a standard of living that makes for continued illness and human waste. . . . To set a relief standard lower than some tenant farmers and rural laborers get is to . . . set [it] below the pittance paid by sweated industries. We do not do this in cities, why should we do it in rural areas?" [6]

Landlords' attitudes toward relief in 1933 and 1934 were ambivalent. Paternalistic tradition made them responsible for their tenants' subsistence. In December, 1933, an FERA researcher found belief in that tradition still strong among Alabama landlords. With some consistency they also regarded relief as "demoralizing" for labor, because it tended to remove tenants and wage hands from their direct control. Despite this concern, there was a growing desire to shift the responsibility for "carrying" tenants to the FERA. Relief, in fact, was an important factor contributing to the breakdown of traditional tenancy. Lorena Hickok, an investigator for Hopkins, found instances of tobacco farmers moving their surplus sharecroppers into Wilson, North Carolina, and even paying their first week's rent to qualify them for relief. Another field report, from Arkansas in April, 1934, told of a planter attitude that relief was a method of keeping cheap labor available, until needed, without local expense. [7] But as the 1934 planting season approached there were frequent complaints that CWA preempted labor needed by farmers. The source of this objection was that, although there was no labor shortage, relief pay was actually higher than customary agricultural wages or sharecroppers' incomes.

Throughout the New Deal relief agencies found themselves beset by landlords desiring cheap seasonal labor. For example, in the fall of 1933 Malcolm Miller, South Carolina ERA administrator,

6 Florence Sytz to Williams, November 27, 1934, in Aubrey Williams Papers, Franklin D. Roosevelt Library.

7 Harold Hoffsomer, *Landlord-Tenant Relations and Relief in Alabama* (Washington: Federal Emergency Relief Administration, Research Bulletin Series II, no. 9, November 14, 1935), 7, copy in RG 69, NA; Hickok to Hopkins, February 14, 1934, and Elmer Scott to Hopkins, [April, 1934], in Hopkins Papers.

found that D. R. Coker, powerful planter, progressive agriculturalist and son-in-law of Commerce Secretary Dan Roper, insisted that relief be suspended statewide so that workers would be even more plentiful and cotton could be picked promptly. Gay B. Shepperson, Georgia ERA director, recalled that cotton farmers, and growers of other crops as well, were "quite brazen" in their demands for relief curtailment during crop seasons. Planters frequently complained of labor shortages to their congressmen. They in turn contacted Hopkins, and put him under considerable pressure in the fall of 1934. [8]

The relief establishment felt constrained to accommodate these demands, especially in the cotton belt. In September, 1934, Hopkins polled southern ERA directors and found without exception their policy was to release from their rolls persons offered employment in the fields. In numerous cases, however, planters, aware that relief clients had to accept their work offers, lowered wages even below customary levels. Therefore, the more conscientious administrators, such as Miss Shepperson, tried to ascertain that those cut from the rolls were offered bona fide employment of reasonable duration, paying at least the prevailing rate of fifty or sixty cents per day, which was still inferior to relief. [9] There is abundant evidence that FERA and its successor, the Works Progress Administration, continued throughout their existence discharging clients for low-wage cotton picking. [10]

8   Malcolm Miller to Hopkins, October 6, 1934, in RG 69, NA; Thad Holt to Hopkins, September 11, 1934, in Hopkins Papers; interview with Gay B. Shepperson, June 29, 1970.
9   Form letter, Hopkins to cotton states ERA directors, September 17, 1934, and replies from F. M. Baker of South Carolina (September 20), Thad Holt of Alabama (September 21), Mrs. Thomas O'Berry of North Carolina (September 21), Gay B. Shepperson of Georgia (September 21), Wallace Crossley of Missouri (September 25), George B. Power of Mississippi (September 26), and Walter L. Simpson of Tennessee (September 27), all in RG 69, NA; interview with Gay B. Shepperson.
10   For examples of continuing complaints against these policies under the WPA see Gardner Jackson to Franklin D. Roosevelt, September 12, 1936, Jackson to Hopkins, September 12, 1936, Roosevelt to Jackson, September 26, 1936, Jackson to Roosevelt, October 31, 1936, and Roosevelt to Jackson, December 16, 1936, all in Official File 444–C, Franklin D. Roosevelt Library. For a later protest from the Southern Tenant Farmers' Union, see D. A. Griffin and P. H. Benson to Hopkins, August 20, 1938, in Southern Tenant Farmers' Union Papers, Southern Historical Collection, University of North Carolina, Chapel Hill.

In the first year of the New Deal there were frequent cases in which southern state officials and ERA directors themselves were reluctant to extend adequate relief in rural areas. In the summer of 1933 Harper Gatton, the Kentucky administrator, told Hopkins that the 30 cents per hour recently specified for FERA work projects would "play havoc in our agricultural counties" where farmers had already protested a $1.50 daily wage. Gatton intimated that higher rates would not be paid in rural districts. Hopkins asserted that 30 cents per hour was "the lowest amount mentioned in the President's Reemployment Agreement," and federal standards would be maintained. He declared, "This business of [making relief conform to] a prevailing wage on the farms is a stall to pay miserable . . . wages for public work," and vowed "to have no part" in it. Furthermore, he told Gatton, "I am of the firm belief that in the long run the best thing that can happen to the South is a substantial increase in wage rates because I do not see how we are ever going to get any purchasing power into our new economy on a dollar a day."[11]

There were still other problems in Kentucky. The legislature refused to appropriate state money for relief after August 15, 1933. Gatton also declined, contrary to federal policy, to give relief to striking coal miners. Consequently, Hopkins, determined to fight out the issue of federal standards in Kentucky, cut off federal relief August 12. At the time 22 percent of the state's population was dependent on FERA. In early September Hopkins received a confidential report that at least 150,000 eastern Kentuckians, miners and subsistence farmers and their families, faced starvation.[12]

In August, 1933, Aubrey Williams met in Jackson, Mississippi, with Governor Sennett Conner and others, to discuss "the desirability of doing away with relief in this state September 1st," because of the objections of big tax payers and planters' opposition to work relief wage rates. Williams told the state officials they would have to assume full public responsibility for such action and that neither he nor FERA would justify or take part in it. This evidently ended the

11 Harper Gatton to Hopkins, July 31, 1933, Hopkins to Rowland Haynes, August 2, 1933, Hopkins to Gatton, August 3, 1933, all in Hopkins Papers.
12 Hickok to Hopkins, September 6, 1933, *ibid.*

discussion, although Williams did agree that relief could probably be suspended during cotton picking season for those offered work in the fields.[13]

In Georgia, where in September, 1933, 28 percent of the state's families were on relief, Governor Eugene Talmadge characterized the recipients as "bums and loafers" and decried the 30-cent-per-hour work project wages. Talmadge's obstruction of ERA operations finally led Hopkins to federalize all relief in Georgia on January 7, 1934.[14] Virginia state officials were not opposed to assisting the poor at federal expense, but were very reluctant throughout 1934 to provide state funds as requested by FERA. Senator Harry Byrd's organization reportedly would "resist [a state] appropriation for relief even to the extent of abandoning the relief program." On a more local level, planters and the county agent in Pulaski County, Arkansas, attempted in January, 1934, to persuade ERA officials there to consult landlords when their renters or laborers applied for relief and be governed by their recommendations. One planter strongly objected to the practice of providing Negro clients such "luxuries" as the tomato juice given to prevent rickets.[15]

Louisiana was a particularly striking example of reluctance to extend rural relief. Harry Early, the state director, told Hopkins that, contrary to usual practice, he had barred farmers, tenants, and croppers from FERA and CWA work projects because the farmer was a "proprietor," capable of self-support "would he but apply himself." In a further step, on February 10, 1934, the Louisiana administrator made them ineligible for direct relief, excepting only those in "dire need." He also complained that so long as CWA paid a 30-cent hourly wage, many regarded it as employment "which they feel [a] moral obligation if not patriotic duty to qualify for." Commenting to

13 Williams to Hopkins, August 14, 1933, *ibid.*
14 Alan Johnstone to Hopkins, September 18, 1933, *ibid.*; Michael Stephen Holmes, "The New Deal in Georgia: An Administrative History" (Ph.D. dissertation, University of Wisconsin, Madison, 1969), 64–66; Hopkins to Eugene Talmadge, January 7, 1934, quoted in its entirety in Talmadge to Roosevelt, January 10, 1934, and Roosevelt to Talmadge, January 22, 1934, all in Official File 444, Franklin D. Roosevelt Library.
15 Johnstone to Williams, March 7, 1934, Edith Foster to Hopkins, report for January 5–8, 1934, both in Hopkins Papers.

Aubrey Williams on ERA officials in Louisiana and surrounding states, a Tulane University social work professor found them "not far in advance of the rural thinking" in which "so few people care about the poor."[16]

In many other cases relief was inadequate when given. Sometimes this was due to temporary shortages of funds. During one such period, in July, 1933, the director of social services for the Alabama ERA reported that rolls were "ruthlessly cut" by dropping those with any opportunity of obtaining food, even in insufficient amounts. Aid per family was slashed to as little as 50 cents per week in some rural counties and completely stopped in others. By August, she estimated, the state relief load would include 101,000 families. Although this situation was extreme, usual conditions were little better. In September, 1933, Aubrey Williams informed Hopkins that Alabama relief was "far from adequate measured by any decent standards." The statewide average was then $8 or $9 monthly per family, but those figures were deceptively high because 20,000 Birmingham families received $17 or $18 per month. ERA grants per case in Georgia averaged only $5.48 in July, 1933, and $11.12 in January, 1934.[17] It was also true that FERA relief was lower in the South than elsewhere. This was frequently justified, occasionally even by Hopkins, with the claim that southern living costs were lower than those in the rest of the country.[18]

16 Harry J. Early to Hopkins, March 31, 1934, and November 15, 1934, in Hopkins Papers; Sytz to Williams, November 27, 1934, in Williams Papers. Louisiana is a good example of the degree of state independence in the decentralized FERA program. There was little the administration could do to force uniformity of policy, except to cut off a state's funds until it complied, as in Kentucky in 1933, or to federalize all relief operations, as in Georgia in 1934.

17 Mrs. A. M. Tunstall to Holt, July 28, 1933, in RG 69, NA; Williams to Hopkins, September 13, 1933, in Hopkins Papers; Holmes, "The New Deal in Georgia," 648.

18 Transcript of Harry Hopkins' testimony to the Bureau of the Budget, January 22, 1934, in Hopkins Papers. In 1935 the WPA continued regional differentials, paying as little as $19 and $21 per month in the rural South whereas other regions received a minimum of between $32 and $40. A defense of this system by Assistant Administrator Corrington Gill, based on the lower living costs argument, appeared in the New York *Times*, May 26, 1935, Sec. 4, p. 3, and a contrasting view by Jonathan Daniels in the Raleigh *News and Observer*, December 22, 1935. George B. Tindall argues cogently that "the differential . . . reflected differences not in the cost but in the standard of living." See his *The Emergence of the New South, 1913–1945* (Baton Rouge: Louisiana State University Press, 1967), Vol. X of 10 vols. in Wendell Holmes Stephenson and E. Merton Coulter (eds.), *A History of the South*, 483.

Despite its inadequacy, federal relief still had great impact in the rural South, especially during the winter of 1933–1934 when CWA injected unprecedented wages into the area. The effects of this were best recorded by FERA field representatives. The most important and perceptive of these observers was Lorena Hickok, a veteran newspaper woman for the Associated Press, friend and occasional traveling companion of Eleanor Roosevelt, and special investigator reporting directly to Hopkins. On several trips through the South Hickok attempted to assess public opinion and evaluate the federal program by interviewing people within and outside the relief bureaucracy.[19] During January and February, 1934, just as the dismantling of CWA was being planned for the spring, she toured the south Atlantic states.

Hickok found some outspoken supporters of CWA. Malcolm Miller, the South Carolina administrator, told her he was "strong for the federal wage scale," even though farmers paying their hands $3 per week could not compete with CWA, which paid them $9 per week. But he thought in the long run it was necessary to force wages up and make working conditions less exploitive. "For sixty-five years the South has been the sweatshop of the nation," he told her, because "we wanted to keep [the Negro] down—and did. But we dragged ourselves down too."[20] Around Moultrie, Georgia, an area of diversified farming, Hickok met local merchants who favored work relief because its wages enabled many to catch up in buying necessities, such as shoes, which they had needed for years. Several farmers, businessmen, and city officials commended the agency for employing surplus labor and "pour[ing] money in at the bottom."[21] She encountered similar warm support from the New Deal mayor of Charleston, Burnet Maybank, and editor Jonathan Daniels of the Raleigh *News and Observer*.[22]

---

19 Hopkins to Algernon Blair, January 5, 1934, in RG 69, NA. For an indication of the influence of Hickok's reports among New Dealers, including the president, see Rexford G. Tugwell Diary (Typescript in Rexford G. Tugwell Papers, Franklin D. Roosevelt Library), March 6, 1934.
20 Hickok to Hopkins, January 11, 1934, in Hopkins Papers.
21 Hickok to Hopkins, January 23 and 24, 1934, *ibid.*
22 Hickok to Hopkins, February 10 and 14, 1934, *ibid.*; Raleigh *News and Observer*, February 15, 1934.

Most opinion was unfavorable, however. The banker and chairman of the county commission in Jackson County, Georgia (a Bourbon "heart and soul," Hickok called him), condemned CWA as "charity" and its projects as useless, and thought it should pay no more than 12.5 cents per hour. Hickok thought he was representative of small town and rural reluctance to pay higher taxes or wages.[23] Racial antipathy also influenced feeling against CWA. In Savannah, among other places, Hickok encountered a concern that many rural blacks were crowding into the city for work relief, which they called "guv'ment easy money," and that the agency benefited them unduly. This opinion was rising among whites unable to obtain CWA employment after quotas were filled. One federal reemployment director told her, "Any nigger who gets over $8 a week is a spoiled nigger, that's all."[24]

Local relief administrators in Georgia and the Carolinas reported many cases of farmers wanting their surplus sharecroppers on CWA, but, as the 1934 planting season approached, there were increasing rumblings of discontent from farmers unable to reemploy their laborers. In other instances, CWA workers were still living rent free in shacks on their former employers' land. If their relief jobs continued after planting began, Hickok suspected, farmers would evict them and bring in other wage hands. In early January Georgia cotton planters bluntly told her they counted on CWA tapering off before planting time.[25]

Perhaps the most negative attitudes toward relief were those of Florida truck and citrus farmers. Like cotton planters, they complained that CWA lured away all their workers, although county relief figures demonstrated beyond question the existence of a labor surplus. In early January, citrus growers in Orlando met with local CWA officials and demanded that wages be reduced to prevailing agricultural levels, often 50 cents per day. The agency's field representative present regarded this as an unthinkable support for intolerable working conditions. The local administrators went to consid-

23　Hickok to Hopkins, January 14, 1934, in Hopkins Papers.
24　Hickok to Hopkins, January 16, 1934, *ibid.*
25　Hickok to Hopkins, January 11 and 14 and February 8, 10, and 14, 1934, *ibid.*

erable lengths to accommodate the growers, offering to remove from CWA, upon written request, any specific Negroes they claimed to need and could not induce to leave public work, provided they promise immediate and reasonably steady employment. Only five requests were received.[26]

Hickok thought Florida citrus growers were "irresponsible" because they made not even other planters' pretenses of supporting their workers during slack seasons. She also concluded they were dishonest in their claims that CWA caused a labor shortage. At the time of the Orlando meeting the local relief office employed 2,000 on CWA projects, but had 4,200 registered with the federal reemployment office and distributed direct relief to numerous others. Similar conditions prevailed around Lakeland and Tampa, and probably throughout the state.[27]

In Charleston Hickok conferred with a group that included Clemson College extension officials, cotton, tobacco, and truck farmers, relief administrators, social workers, Mayor Maybank, and the writer Julia Peterkin. The farmers, who wanted CWA ended, "did not have what you would call a social viewpoint. They were quite frank in their statements that they wanted to keep the price of labor down" to its usual level of 75 cents per day, or in the case of truck farmers, 40 cents per day. They wanted CWA discontinued in towns as well as in rural areas to prevent their Negroes from leaving farms to seek work relief. "There's a sort of enchanting naivete about these fellows," Hickok told Hopkins. "They take it for granted that their interests should be taken under consideration first and . . . then, if there is any consideration left, other people should have a chance." When she inquired how wage hands could subsist during slack seasons, one farmer replied, "Oh, they can fish"![28]

Later, Maybank and the ERA staff members stressed to Hickok that there was a labor scarcity only in terms of what most farmers

26 Owen R. Lovejoy to Johnstone, January 4, 1934, and Hickok to Hopkins, January 29, 1934, *ibid*. In the same place see Hickok to Hopkins, January 23, 1934, reporting a similar procedure with the same result in the cotton belt.
27 Hickok to Hopkins, January 29, 1934, *ibid*.
28 Hickok to Hopkins, February 8, 1934, *ibid*.

wanted to pay—a lack of farm workers who preferred 40 cents per day to CWA. They maintained that the shortage, if such existed, would disappear when employers paid a living wage. Maybank, discussing an outlook of some planters, told her that the truck farmers, especially, were "gamblers," thinking in terms of high-profit windfalls from a good season's crop, "up today and down tomorrow," never interested in "any ordinary, even income." Such attitudes were not conducive to steady employment of wage hands; rather, growers desired "plenty of cheap labor to grab on a moment's notice." Obviously, CWA disrupted this condition.[29]

Noting the tendency of relief to break down the sharecropping system, Hickok concluded that many farmers wanted the government to assume their old function of "carrying," or "keeping their peons alive during the slack season on pork and meal." But, she thought, both in the case of wage labor and tenancy, many farmers and planters expected relief to be ended prior to their work season "so these niggers will be good and hungry" and provide abundant cheap labor. Their opposition to CWA stemmed from the realization that it could force them to offer better terms to get and keep labor.[30]

In April, 1934, Hickok encountered in other parts of the South the irony of the rural poor finding better conditions on relief than in any agricultural work available to them. She observed the great numbers of blacks and Mexican-Americans, many no doubt of country origin, receiving aid in New Orleans, Houston, and San Antonio. In those places she found widespread opinion that they so saturated the rolls that funds were spread too thin, depressing the standards of public assistance for middle-class whites forced to seek it. Influenced by local ERA officials, she became half convinced that the government should force destitute Negroes and Mexican-Americans off the rolls and into agricultural labor, even though she recognized it as "peonage," on the assumption that they would be no worse off than usual. Then limited FERA money could provide work relief for the middle class without lowering their accustomed living conditions so

29 Hickok to Hopkins, February 10, 1934, *ibid.*
30 Hickok to Hopkins, February 10 and 14, 1934, *ibid.*

drastically. While Hickok admitted that a federal double standard of access to relief was hardly defensible, she had heard that such discrimination was quietly practiced in many areas anyway.[31]

By the beginning of 1934 FERA recognized still more problems in the rural South. The agency found its efforts complicated by acreage restriction. Dislocation of tenants and decreased need for wage hands enlarged an existing farm labor surplus and further overburdened relief rolls. In January, 1934, a cotton planter near Augusta, Georgia, bluntly told Hickok that as he curtailed his planting he would reduce his work force by 25 percent. Near Moultrie, Georgia, cropper displacement was already well advanced, not as a result of AAA, but because several years earlier progressive farmers had voluntarily diversified crops and introduced livestock, and in the process cut Colquitt County's cotton land from 90,000 to 45,000 acres. There was a corresponding increase in surplus laborers, many of whom were employed in 1934 by CWA. When Hickok met with South Carolina farmers and extension officials in February, they "insist[ed] that the reduction in acreage would NOT mean a reduction in employment," because their contracts required them to maintain their usual number of croppers and they "swore by all that was holy" they would observe that regulation. She told Hopkins she considered them less frank than Georgia planters.[32]

In eastern North Carolina, where surveys counted some 10,000 uprooted cotton and tobacco tenants, Hickok visited squatters living on farms in shacks and windowless tobacco barns, people without prospects of sharecropping who could expect early eviction by landlords who could not let them stay permanently. These people, she concluded, "are our relief load. Hundreds of them have moved to town [Wilson, North Carolina]. . . . Their number increases, due to the PRACTICAL results of AAA acreage reduction—I don't care HOW much the farmers talk about that agreement not to lay off hands."[33]

The effects of this displacement were well recognized in the

31 Hickok to Hopkins, April 13, 17, and 25, 1934, *ibid.*
32 Hickok to Hopkins, January 14 and 24 and February 8, 1934, *ibid.*
33 Hickok to Hopkins, February 14, 1934, *ibid.*

higher echelons of FERA. In hearings on January 22, 1934, Hopkins informed the budget bureau that "we will have to take care of tens of thousands of negro . . . and other farm laborers who have worked in the cotton fields, chopping, planting or picking . . . who will not be employed." Not that he welcomed the responsibility; he made clear that he thought it belonged elsewhere. "I have been over at the Agriculture Department," he said, "and tried to get them to put . . . a clause in this [pending Bankhead cotton control] legislation saying these people have to take care of their tenants."[34]

There was also an awareness within FERA that the rural South's labor surplus was not caused solely by acreage reduction, but was a long-standing condition. In Georgia, ERA administrator Shepperson estimated that the excess had been mounting for the last ten years. In North Carolina, Jonathan Daniels called it a permanent problem and suggested to Hickok that it would require more than emergency treatment. In February, 1934, near the end of her south Atlantic trip, Hickok summarized for Hopkins local administrators' opinions that "we are by no means through with this relief job in the South. Everywhere I hear the same thing. A tremendous labor surplus that is not an emergency surplus but CHRONIC [especially] in the rural areas among illiterate Negroes and poor whites." She continued, "Just how big this surplus is . . . can only be guessed at now . . . it might be a darned good idea to start finding out. That there IS going to be a [permanent] surplus, nobody doubts. And with the reduction in cotton acreage it's going to be greater."[35]

Not only did the depression direct attention to the rural labor surplus, but for some it also revealed the pervasive general poverty which had always existed. The Episcopal bishop of South Carolina confided to Hickok his suspicion "that even in good times things have been a whole lot worse in the South than we knew. If it hasn't done anything else, the federal emergency relief program has brought [poverty conditions] to our attention. And now, having had

34 Transcript of Harry Hopkins' testimony to the Bureau of the Budget, January 22, 1934, *ibid.*
35 Hickok to Hopkins, February 5, 1934, *ibid.* In the same place see Hickok's letters to Hopkins of January 23 and February 14, 1934.

them brought out into the open, we ought to clean them up." A New Orleans utility executive told another of Hopkins' representatives that federal relief had made visible the "accumulated dregs of human misery . . . which had been like sediment lying at the bottom and to [which] has been added all the wreckage of recent years."[36]

Throughout the South, FERA observers reached similar conclusions. Field reporter Edith Foster noted that Alabama sharecroppers crowded onto relief rolls because of "conditions [which] are the accumulation of many years of dwindling income." Likewise, she found local ERA directors in Arkansas concerned about the causes of dependency in a system which gave thousands a "starvation income." She discovered that many county relief officials considered it unnecessary to investigate applicants for aid because of their "uniform poverty." From Little Rock, Elmer Scott reported that "the product of fifty years' agricultural exploitation is a very large body of unskilled and . . . vagrant tenantry devoid of mental or material resources." E. J. Webster wrote from Dallas that "even more distressing than the low poverty level of many relief clients is the fact that it does not represent the consequences of an economic catastrophe. It is their usual state." A Florida administrator told of "wretched conditions of life" which had prevailed in the northwestern part of the state for ten years, since the decline of its lumber industry, and concluded, "This district has been little effected [*sic*] by the current depression."[37]

FERA administrators, who wrestled daily with the problem of dispensing relief to the unemployed in cities and towns, were in the best of all positions to appreciate that industry could not absorb the rural poor. The South Carolina and Georgia directors saw little

36 Hickok to Hopkins, February 5, 1934, and Scott to Hopkins, April 12, 1934, *ibid.* On the other hand, a field investigator telling Aubrey Williams of surveys made in 1926 that revealed widespread need in rural Virginia, thought the state's "conservative element" had been, and still was, indifferent. "Why should they be disturbed in 1934 and 1935 about those same people, plus a few more?" she wrote. See Gertrude Gates to Williams, December 11, 1934, *ibid.*

37 Edith Foster to Williams, reports for January 9–14 and February 12–15, 1934, Scott to Hopkins, [April, 1934], E. J. Webster to Hopkins, November 25, 1934, and Julius Stone to Hopkins, April 11, 1934, *ibid.*

likelihood of it. Malcolm Miller found textile mill managers skeptical of such suggestions, even though their factories were then increasing production. FERA continually received reports of destitution, appalling health conditions, squalid housing, and general misery among the "spare help" in Carolina mill villages, which were a problem for the agency in themselves.[38] Moreover, all the major southern cities Hickok visited in the first half of 1934 reported very large relief loads.[39]

Some within FERA also perceived that the declining cotton productiveness of the Southeast made it unlikely that the traditional staple crop economy could reabsorb its excess workers. Hickok encountered "a good deal of gloom about the economic future of the South" from Georgia and South Carolina administrators, who thought that their states, with much soil exhaustion and high fertilizer expenses, were finished as cotton growers, unable to compete with areas west of the Mississippi River. Thoughtful people might propose agricultural diversification, but to the extent that it had occurred, voluntarily or as a result of AAA, it had usually reduced the demand for hand labor.[40]

The most perceptive southern relief officials saw that attempting to support excess croppers and rural laborers would spread funds too thin to concentrate on depression unemployment. They recognized that to prevent continual expansion of its rural load, not to mention decreasing it, FERA would have to confront the problems of the impact of relief in an impoverished region, acreage reduction and tenant displacement, and chronic labor surplus. These concerns

38 Hickok to Hopkins, January 23, 1934, Malcolm Miller to Hopkins, April 3, 1934, Martha Gellhorn to Hopkins, November 5, 11, and 19, 1934, *ibid.*
39 Hickok to Hopkins, January 11, 16, and 31, March 29, April 8, 13, and 17, 1934, *ibid.* These reports cover Atlanta, Savannah, Miami, Montgomery, Birmingham, New Orleans, Houston, and San Antonio.
40 Hickok to Hopkins, January 11 and 24, 1934, *ibid.* For two contemporary scholarly views of the declining position of the Southeast see Arthur F. Raper, *Preface to Peasantry: A Tale of Two Black Belt Counties* (Chapel Hill: University of North Carolina Press, 1936), 171, 201–206, 216–22, 404–407, and Charles S. Johnson, Edwin R. Embree, and Will W. Alexander, *The Collapse of Cotton Tenancy: Summary of Field Studies and Statistical Surveys, 1933–1935* (Chapel Hill: University of North Carolina Press, 1935), 35–36, 39–43.

could put FERA into the business of providing some new means of self-support for the rural poor and raising their living standards to an acceptable level. Such a program would go far beyond the original objective of aiding the unemployed, yet such scope was necessary for its success.

The scheduled expiration of CWA, which threatened to return over a million cases to direct relief, made all these southern problems especially urgent. On January 24, 1934, Budget Director Lewis Douglas recommended to Roosevelt that he disband the agency by February 15, before the vested interests that many local governments were developing in it made that step increasingly difficult. Even if the president decided to continue the program, Douglas thought, it should be "materially diminished" in rural areas. Roosevelt, concerned about excessive spending and foreseeing creation of a permanent relief class, agreed. On February 17 Hopkins announced that CWA would be phased out. Industrial cities would maintain full quotas until late March, but 400,000 would be dropped within the week, beginning in the South.[41]

Those farmers and others who opposed work relief undoubtedly welcomed Hopkins' announcement. Some local ERA administrators also desired to end CWA because they thought they detected the spread of an improper belief among its employees that they were entitled by right to public jobs. Hickok reached this conclusion and found that many on the North Carolina staff agreed with her.[42] However, certain other state directors, notably Miss Shepperson in Atlanta, doubted that CWA could remedy any of the rural South's fundamental ills and therefore wanted to replace it with something of more lasting effectiveness and confine future FERA work relief to cities and towns.[43] Similarly, in February, 1934, Aubrey

---

41 Lewis Douglas to Roosevelt, January 24, 1934, memorandum in Hopkins Papers; Atlanta *Constitution*, February 17, 1934; William E. Leuchtenburg, *Franklin D. Roosevelt and the New Deal* (New York: Harper and Row, 1963), 122–23. Hopkins, concerned about moving too abruptly, influenced Roosevelt to reduce the pace of disbanding the Civil Works Administration. See Hopkins to Roosevelt, February 15, 1934, in Official File 444, Franklin D. Roosevelt Library.
42 Hickok to Hopkins, February 5 and 14, 1934, in Hopkins Papers.
43 Hickok to Hopkins, January 23 and February 14, 1934, *ibid.*

Williams, considering the deplorable standards of relief in the South, sensed a growing feeling in Washington that CWA could not simply be "choked off." But he also admitted that it could not permanently uplift the poor, even if continued indefinitely. If the FERA intended to get rural people on their feet, he wrote, other means would have to be found.[44]

Finding more appropriate means was a major problem, especially since there was general objection to direct relief or the "dole," which in any case would not be more effective than CWA in changing fundamental conditions. However, one fashionable idea of the early 1930s was that summed up by the phrase "back to the land." Some expected that large numbers of the unemployed could be moved to the country where they could subsist by growing their own food on small garden plots. This proposal, of course, failed to consider the existing excess of agricultural labor.[45] Among some in rural areas there was a corresponding and equally simplistic notion that displaced farmers could be absorbed by industry.

A somewhat more informed version of "back to the land" was the subsistence homesteading then being attempted by the Department of the Interior. Beginning in 1933, its subsistence homesteads division had established several "rural industrial" colonies for "stranded" workers (those left unemployed by the decline or failure of their area's only industry), providing them garden acreage and perhaps cows and chickens. Residents were to produce most of their own food and, if possible, secure part-time factory work for cash income. There were expectations, not well founded, that manufacturers would decentralize and locate near these subsistence communities. By early 1934 the FERA had created a few experimental projects, similar in concept. Among the most important was Woodlake, north of Houston, promoted by Lawrence Westbrook, the Texas ERA director.[46] Proposals to return the destitute to the land appealed to some southern businessmen. For example, an FERA field represen-

---

44   Williams to Foster, February 7, 1934, and to Early, February 26, 1934, in RG 69, NA.
45   Tindall, *Emergence of the New South*, 371–72.
46   Paul K. Conkin, *Tomorrow A New World: The New Deal Community Program* (Ithaca, N.Y.: Cornell University Press, 1959). See Chap. 5.

tative wrote from Houston that technological advances, NRA (National Recovery Administration) recognition of collective bargaining, and code provisions for minimum wages had given impetus in Texas to industrial plant modernization and elimination of labor in an effort to minimize costs. Accordingly, he reported, some industrialists, recognizing the displacement of workers, wanted subsistence homesteading to counteract it, absolving them of responsibility for increasing unemployment and allowing cost-cutting improvements to proceed as rapidly as possible.[47]

Another emerging idea, not to be confused with the subsistence communities, was that the rural poor, still located on land or only recently displaced from it, but in any case not adequately employed in agriculture, and perhaps on relief, could be reestablished as farmers on small individual acreages. There they could be made self-sustaining by a combination of credit and close supervision. By the beginning of 1934 this concept, which became known as rural rehabilitation, was fairly widespread in the South.

Possibly the earliest application of the idea was by a privately organized relief committee in Greenville, South Carolina. In 1930, its chairman, investment banker Robert W. Hudgens, who "had to sell the idea to himself," and Mrs. B. S. Hill, the committee's social worker, organized a farm project with many rehabilitative features. Administering Red Cross funds, they had been dispensing relief to unemployed mill hands, most of whom were of farm background and desired to return to the country. Accordingly, they selected recipients for possible reestablishment on the land, using as criteria farm experience, eagerness to work, intelligence, and adaptability.

Hudgens and Mrs. Hill had difficulty financing their program. Local churches and charities were uninterested. Extension officials at Clemson College told Hudgens that his relief clients had left farms in the first place because thay were basically "sorry," and derided his suggestion that they had failed for lack of farming knowledge. Hudgens was also unable to secure federal funds from the Hoover administration. Nevertheless they located land for their clients,

47   Scott to Hopkins, April 6, 1934, in Hopkins Papers.

thirty-two vacant farms near Greenville and a one-thousand-acre
tract in Abbeville County, foreclosed by a federal land bank. The
bank agreed to rent the land for $25 per family per year if the com-
mittee would supervise the tenants.

Meanwhile, Hudgens obtained $5,000 from the national Red
Cross with which to provide mules, wagons, plows, and simple tools
for the clients. Title to these goods remained with the Red Cross to
prevent sale or mortgage. In April, 1931, Hudgens and Mrs. Hill
settled thirty-two families on the individual farms and ten on portions of the Abbeville land. By June the latter were in difficulty and
the sponsors, primarily Mrs. Hill, applied more intensive supervision. "I stood over them the rest of the summer," she recalled.
"They were the most helpless people you ever saw. They wouldn't
even have their mules shod without advice!" As Red Cross funds ran
out she arranged $900 credit from local merchants. Under her guid-
ance the families were able to repay the advance and divide $840
cotton income and large quantities of garden produce. In 1932 Mrs.
Hill secured federal seed loans for the rehabilitants and by 1934 they
had progressed to the point of arranging this financing for themselves.[48]

The Abbeville project attracted considerable attention, including
that of Rexford G. Tugwell, who in 1935 offered Hudgens a position
in the recently organized Resettlement Administration. In the
summer of 1935 Hudgens accepted and began his career with the
agency, ultimately becoming an assistant administrator of the Farm
Security Administration.[49]

By the beginning of 1934 many within the FERA had concluded

---

48   This account of the Abbeville project is drawn from Hickok to Hopkins, February 7,
     1934, *ibid.*, and interview with Robert W. Hudgens, July 8 and 9, 1970. Hudgens
     stressed the need to supervise clients who had experienced such prolonged privation
     that "their recuperative powers were impaired." Although the Abbeville project was a
     community operating on a crop division basis, it differed significantly from subsistence
     homesteading (of which Mrs. Hill was a critic). Clients had to have farm backgrounds.
     No part-time industrial work was contemplated—the goal was self-sustaining farming.
     Although acreage per family was small and there was great emphasis on producing food,
     a cash crop was grown. Moreover, 32 families, of higher ability levels than the Abbeville
     clients, were placed on individual farms.
49   Interview with Robert W. Hudgens.

that a policy of reestablishing poor farmers on land through supervised credit would be an effective program in itself and a convenient replacement for CWA. Discussing the matter with Lorena Hickok, Miss Shepperson and Lincoln McConnell, the federal reemployment director for Georgia, expressed grave concern about the persistent surplus of ignorant and backward country people, often afflicted with debilitating diseases and not assimilable by industry. The administrators considered city and town unemployment a true depression emergency requiring maximum relief efforts. But they did not regard rural impoverishment as merely an emergency; it was a fundamental condition, which, though worsened by the depression, was not caused by it. For this reason, in Shepperson's opinion, the $7 million per month FERA and CWA spent in Georgia was wasted, except in the cities, since it effected no basic changes.[50]

Shepperson and McConnell, and members of the South Carolina relief staff as well, thought the solution was "subsistence" farming with intensive supervision. They did not regard availability of land as an insurmountable problem since their information was that the federal government owned extensive tracts in the South on which landless farmers could grow their food and small amounts of cotton for cash. Clients could repair, or if necessary build, their own cabins. Only the simplest equipment and facilities would have to be furnished them. Hickok reported that the administrators' advice was "don't try to start them off with bath tubs and mattresses. . . . Bring those things in one at a time. But first . . . get them out of those hovels [and] into weather proof cabins. That would be enough to start with."[51]

Despite references to this proposal as "subsistence farming," Hickok stressed that it differed from the Interior Department's project she had observed in 1933 at Arthurdale, West Virginia. There was no intention of moving stranded industrial workers into rural colonies, she pointed out, but rather of "taking people who are al-

50 Hickok to Hopkins, January 23 and February 5 and 14, 1934, in Hopkins Papers. By March Hopkins was making public remarks nearly identical to Miss Shepperson's. See Atlanta *Constitution*, March 14, 1934.
51 Hickok to Hopkins, January 23 and February 5 and 14, 1934, in Hopkins Papers.

ready on the land—thousands of share-croppers, tenant farmers, farm hands, who are existing in tumbledown shacks . . . cluttering up farms where there is no employment for them," and giving them the necessary supervision to raise their living standards, however modestly.[52]

The administrators emphasized that maximum supervision would be the key to any rehabilitative program's success, along with attention to the most serious of the clients' health problems. Such guidance might have to be permanent for the present generation of the poor, they thought, but with health care and education, their children might become self-sustaining. Hickok anticipated that some would object that the contemplated small-scale farming offered at best a subsistence with no chance for advancement, but she asserted that impoverished Negroes and poor whites were already a "wretched lot" without ambitions to blunt or morale to ruin. Moreover, she thought, they were docile enough to accept a supervision which might seem paternalistic to northern critics.[53]

Hickok informed Hopkins that he could probably expect Miss Shepperson to begin strongly advocating rehabilitative measures. However, the Georgia administrators were hardly the only ones thinking in these terms. Hickok found similar interest at the local level in Moultrie, Georgia, and in the state relief offices in the Carolinas. Later she discovered that the principle had been considered within the Alabama ERA since before her discussions with Miss Shepperson in January. In Raleigh, on February 15, 1934, Jonathan Daniels editorialized in general terms on the need to replace CWA with a permanent program of "human reconstruction." Meanwhile, at Fisk University, the distinguished black sociologist Charles S. Johnson outlined a plan for "Rehabilitation of Landless Rural Families" which included the essential features later adopted by the FERA. On February 19, with the idea gaining some currency, Lincoln McConnell publicly called for rehabilitation of at least 75,000 of the rural poor as the only solution to Georgia's unemployment prob-

52   Hickok to Hopkins, February 5, 1934, *ibid.* The Arthurdale project, a rural industrial settlement for unemployed miners, was of special interest to Mrs. Roosevelt.
53   Hickok to Hopkins, January 23 and February 5, 1934, *ibid.*

lem and summarized the ERA's expectation that "once back on the farm again, these farmers will be permanently removed from the relief rolls."[54]

Thus by February, 1934, the idea of rural rehabilitation was at hand and gaining acceptance within the FERA. It had, in fact, penetrated to the highest levels of the relief establishment. As early as December, 1933, Hopkins told the president that FERA and CWA had benefited "millions of working people and farmers, who even in 'prosperous' times never got much of a break" and had suffered more than anyone else since 1929. But he was concerned that "at the end of Civil Works this spring there will still be millions without work, heavily in debt and terribly discouraged," for whom provision would have to be made. A little more than one month later it became clear that he included destitute rural southerners in that number. Early in February, 1934, Hopkins brought Lawrence Westbrook, the Texas ERA director, to Washington to devise measures for reestablishing poor families on the land, including those displaced by production control policies. And by the end of February Aubrey Williams could inform the Louisiana administrator that Hopkins planned to replace CWA in part with a new rural program and add that he expected its announcement soon.[55]

54 Hickok to Hopkins, January 23 and 24, February 5, and April 7, 1934, *ibid;* Raleigh *News and Observer,* February 15, 1934; Charles S. Johnson, "Rehabilitation of Landless Rural Families" (Typescript in Charles S. Johnson Papers, Fisk University); Atlanta *Constitution,* February 19, 1934.
55 Hopkins to Roosevelt, December 29, 1933, in Official File 444, Franklin D. Roosevelt Library; Hopkins to Lawrence Westbrook, February 1, 1934, Westbrook to Holt, February 14, 1934, Williams to Early, February 26, 1934, all in RG 69, NA.

CHAPTER IV

Rural Rehabilitation
and the FERA's Farmers

EVEN AS early as the beginning of 1934 it was clear to Federal Emergency Relief Administration officials, though perhaps not to the Agriculture Department, that so far New Deal programs, the Agricultural Adjustment Act in particular, had not benefited the most destitute people of the rural South. On March 4, 1934, the Atlanta *Constitution* reviewed recent federal announcements concerning relief policy and commented:

It would appear that it has finally been discovered that measures taken to relieve farm distress through acreage curtailment, paying rental for idle acres, processing taxes, and other similar expedients do not reach the underlying trouble, and that practical and lasting recovery will not begin until former farm families are removed from temporary relief lists . . . and placed in homes on land where they may adequately care for themselves and begin to build for the future.

The paper noted that Georgia had 75,000 displaced farmers on public rolls who had not been helped by current agricultural policies, but saw indications that the government was finally seeking their permanent rather than temporary relief.[1]

The *Constitution* had read FERA intent accurately. After an-

---

1 Atlanta *Constitution*, March 4, 1934.

nouncing the end of the Civil Works Administration, Hopkins and Roosevelt proposed to reorganize federal relief to concentrate on three problems: providing work for the urban unemployed, assisting certain "stranded" industrial populations, and rural rehabilitation.[2] Accordingly, Hopkins assigned Lawrence Westbrook to plan the latter. By March 7, Westbrook, advised by Lorena Hickok, had outlined a program that he and Hopkins expected to replace direct relief completely in rural areas. The basic plan was for state relief administrations to locate unused or available land, such as acreage rented by the AAA or farms foreclosed by federal land banks or private mortgage holders. An ERA could arrange for landless farmers on relief, or surplus tenants still on the land, to work small plots for family subsistence. Preliminary investigation indicated that ample acreage, with numerous tenant houses, was available. Clients could work out land rental by repairing cabins and fences, terracing and erosion control work, or labor on the farm owners' crops. All of this would be done under ERA supervision, at a rate of exchange agreed upon by the relief administration and the landowners.[3]

After placing its rehabilitants on land, the ERA could furnish them, on credit, essentials for farming, such as the implements and workstock which nearly all of them lacked. The ERA might also provide cows and pigs (perhaps acquired from AAA surplus), poultry, stock feed, and crop and garden seed. It could even advance groceries to the clients until they could produce their own food. Rehabilitants would be expected to pay for livestock, equipment and advances with a share of their garden produce, eggs, milk, and the like, which the ERA could distribute to nonfarm reliefers.[4] This plan

2 New York *Times*, March 1, 1934, pp. 1, 14.
3 U.S. Federal Emergency Relief Administration, "Suggested Rural Program (as amended)," typescript, March 7, 1934, enclosed in Howard Odum to Will Alexander, March 7, 1934, in Commission on Interracial Cooperation Papers, Atlanta University, hereinafter cited as CIC Papers; transcript of minutes of FERA Regional Conference on Rural Rehabilitation, Atlanta, March 12–13, 1934, in "Records of the Work Projects Administration," Record Group 69, National Archives. Evidence of Hickok's contributions appears in Lorena Hickok to Harry Hopkins, July 1, 1934, in Harry Hopkins Papers, Franklin D. Roosevelt Library, Hyde Park, N.Y.
4 Federal Emergency Relief Administration, "Suggested Rural Program," in CIC Papers; minutes of Regional Conference on Rural Rehabilitation, March 12–13, 1934, in RG 69, NA.

proposed, in effect, that the ERA assume the traditional "furnishing" of the landless poor, as well as their supervision. Thus, in two important functions it would substitute for the landlord.

Hopkins and Westbrook realized that FERA's farmers would need a minimal cash income for living expenses and repayment of advances. But rehabilitants could not cultivate a money crop; to avoid running afoul of AAA's control of staple production they would have to be restricted to food and feed crops. Accordingly, clients would be permitted to earn supplementary cash by part-time work on relief projects, such as building community parks, repairing country schools, road work, and construction of cooperative produce markets and food canning facilities. Many of these suggested projects were actually the unfinished work of CWA. The planners also hoped that as clients progressed in rehabilitation farming, some might eventually achieve steady enough incomes to become potential buyers of any small acreages which planters, land banks, or corporate mortgage holders wished to sell.[5]

To coordinate the new undertaking, Westbrook proposed a rural rehabilitation division within FERA. But in keeping with the agency's decentralization, state relief administrations would conduct the new program, acting through special committees employing state rehabilitation directors. Hopkins and Westbrook intended to allow states great latitude in developing their own procedures, so long as they aimed to uplift poor farmers permanently. At the local level they envisioned county or community committees selecting clients and providing for their supervision. However, since FERA had no staff of trained agriculturalists to oversee its new farmers, it would have to borrow personnel from the Department of Agriculture's Extension division.[6]

---

5 Federal Emergency Relief Administration, "Suggested Rural Program," in CIC Papers; minutes of Regional Conference on Rural Rehabilitation, March 12–13, 1934, in RG 69, NA; Harry Hopkins, "Rural Program: Statement of Policy," directive to all ERAs, March 22, 1934, in Herman Clarence Nixon Papers, in possession of the Nixon family, Nashville.

6 Federal Emergency Relief Administration, "Suggested Rural Program," in CIC Papers; minutes of Regional Conference on Rural Rehabilitation, March 12–13, 1934, in RG 69, NA.

The plan was hastily devised, partly because of the need for a quick replacement for CWA and also because a rural operation, to be effective, would have to start before the South's crop season began. Westbrook suggested that Hopkins organize the new FERA rehabilitation division immediately and outline the program to state ERA directors. Accordingly, Hopkins scheduled a conference of southern relief staffs and Extension Service officials for March 12–13 in Atlanta.[7]

One indication of FERA's hurried planning was that Secretary of Agriculture Henry Wallace, whose cooperation would be essential, was apparently not consulted until Hopkins sent him a draft of the proposal one week before the Atlanta conference. Anticipating one major objection from the secretary, and aware of FERA's dependence on Extension Service supervision of clients' farming, Hopkins stressed that the whole program would conform to AAA crop control. He even argued that rehabilitation farming would further reduce the acreage planted in cash crops. He also told Wallace the plan would enable clients to subsist on their own, get them off relief rolls, and make them potential purchasers of small acreages.[8]

Wallace took issue with Hopkins' assumption that placing reliefers on land to produce food and feed could help curtail planting of staples. In his opinion, clients could not make adequate incomes from subsistence farming and would almost be forced to grow a money crop. At best, he contended, they could produce part of their food and fuel, but no meat or clothing. Even if they raised all their food, he thought, they still would need cash for clothing, health care, minimum furniture and household goods. He pointed out that even in the Department of Agriculture's proposed modest living standard budget of $2,000 per year, nonfood items comprised 70 percent of family expenses. Furthermore, Wallace considered it even more unlikely that FERA's farmers, without cash incomes, could ever purchase small acreages.[9]

7 Federal Emergency Relief Administration, "Suggested Rural Program," in CIC Papers; Atlanta *Constitution*, March 10, 1934.
8 Henry Wallace to Hopkins, March 12, 1934, in RG 69, NA. This letter outlines Hopkins' letter to Wallace of March 5, 1934.
9 *Ibid.*

Wallace observed that rehabilitants could earn cash incomes in only three ways: by growing and marketing a staple crop and thus interfering with production control, by work relief which would leave them as partial public charges, or by part-time industrial employment wherever it could be arranged. Resolutely opposed to the first alternative and assuming the second to be undesirable, Wallace suggested that FERA confine rehabilitation efforts to selected areas where some industrial work was available. There clients could be settled on five-acre plots and, the secretary proposed, gain two-thirds of their support from nonagricultural work. This was, of course, the program of the Interior Department's subsistence homesteads division and had not noticeably reduced rural poverty. Wallace hoped that expansion and decentralization of industry might provide more widespread work opportunities in rural areas, but he admitted that the prospect was remote.[10]

Thus, despite Hopkins' assurances, Wallace perceived that FERA's entry into farm affairs might disrupt crop control. He consented to the rural rehabilitation plan most reluctantly, stating that his department could not support any expansion of agricultural production except for home consumption or free distribution through relief channels. Having detailed these limitations, he then said perfunctorily that the department would be glad to cooperate with FERA in developing the program and that he would send representatives to the Atlanta conference.[11]

Although the secretary's arguments had some force, it is possible that impoverished rural southerners might have benefited more from farming for home use than Wallace supposed. Certainly the incomes of the landless farmers and laborers on relief were normally far below the $2,000 per year that Wallace referred to as supporting a modest living. Therefore they might not require 70 percent or any such substantial part of their incomes in money to improve their living conditions. Later research by the Works Progress Administration suggested that, whereas landowners' cash receipts increased in

10   *Ibid.* Wallace also feared rehabilitation farming would bring back into production much of the marginal land retired under the AAA.
11   *Ibid.*

direct proportion to the percentage of their land planted to staple crops, the real living standards of tenants and sharecroppers, at the very bottom of the scale to begin with, could be increased significantly by production for home consumption.[12]

On March 12, at the Biltmore Hotel in Atlanta, Westbrook outlined the new program to FERA's conference of southern relief directors and their staffs, representatives of the Extension Service, and other interested persons. He defined the first priority as placing rural relief recipients on land and in houses. He thought land was readily obtainable from landlords who had AAA "rented acres" available, and insurance companies, commercial banks and federal land banks, all of which held foreclosed farms. He expected these owners to provide acreage willingly if it were made clear to them that they would benefit from farm improvements made by expertly supervised tenants. Indeed, Westbrook asserted, this was the only way in which FERA could reasonably expect to enlist their cooperation.[13]

Westbrook thought the simplest arrangement would be to obtain land from private landlords. Because most of their unused land was "rented" under AAA contracts, no cotton could be grown on it and therefore clients could raise only food and feed crops. Rehabilitants, he emphasized, should have assurances, preferably written, of at least one year's tenure on the land. He also recommended that if funds became available tenants who proved successful under supervision might be assisted to purchase their small acreages.[14]

The Agriculture Department was represented in Atlanta by Louis Bean of the Bureau of Agricultural Economics, who restated the views Wallace had expressed to Hopkins. Like the secretary, he stressed the need for nonagricultural work to provide clients most of their incomes in lieu of cash cropping. Westbrook assured him that rehabilitation farming would not interfere with production control, but would help cut the output of staples by requiring crop diversifi-

12 Thomas Jackson Woofter, Jr., *Rural Planning for More Workers* (Washington: Farm Security Administration, mimeographed, 1940).
13 Minutes of Regional Conference on Rural Rehabilitation, March 12–13, 1934, in RG 69, NA; Atlanta *Constitution*, March 12 and 13, 1934.
14 Minutes of Regional Conference on Rural Rehabilitation, March 12–13, 1934, in RG 69, NA.

cation. Since Wallace had reluctantly agreed that the department would cooperate in devising the new program, Bean indicated one substantial contribution it could make. He informed the conference that AAA could furnish state relief administrations with surplus cattle, from other areas, for use by rehabilitation families.[15]

Most of the state relief officials present responded favorably to Westbrook's outline. The Georgia ERA, under Miss Shepperson's guidance, had already considered ways to implement the FERA proposal. Alabama relief officials (who would, during 1934, develop the country's largest rural rehabilitation operations) were enthusiastic about the new plan. They hoped it would develop into a broad, long-term credit program. But they thought it would be useful even on an emergency basis for the current year because immediate measures were needed to care for 30,000 rural relief families in their state.[16]

Others, however, were skeptical about some of the plan's features. A Virginia administrator pointed out that landlords were accustomed to paying wages lower than relief rates and predicted they would refuse to participate if FERA expected them to observe a minimum standard of thirty cents per hour for rehabilitants working part time on their farms to repay advances of equipment or rent. Westbrook hastened to assure him that this was not contemplated. FERA, he said, would continue its minimum wage for work relief, including that performed for settlement of advances it made. But it would not attempt to impose rates of labor exchange upon planters who furnished acreage or equipment. Fully aware of FERA's dependence on landlords' cooperation in allowing access to the land, Westbrook stated that the new program simply could not be instituted under any other policy.[17]

Several relief administrators wanted FERA to concentrate on encouraging small farm ownership. The North Carolinians said they had experienced in the eastern part of the state massive AAA displacement of cotton and tobacco tenants who then had to be taken

15 *Ibid.*
16 *Ibid.*
17 *Ibid.*

on relief. They doubted that rural rehabilitation could be of more than supplementary use in reestablishing them on land. For several months they had contemplated forming a nonprofit lending agency which would locate displaced tenants on land, equip them, and allow them to pay for their small acreages and implements on extended contracts. Malcolm Miller, the South Carolina director, feared that the new policy might only increase the tenant population and he predicted failure for any plan not aimed at ultimate ownership. Similarly, the Mississippi administrator thought it would be most economical to have clients buy land outright, on long terms with supervision. Relying on his consultations with the state Extension Service, he estimated that a reliefer could acquire a small farm with a house and barn, as well as a mule, plow, wagon, cow, and other minimum stock and equipment for about $1,080, repayable over a period of years.[18] But clearly he was not thinking of terms that could be met by the most impoverished in his state.

Malcolm Miller also questioned Westbrook's assumption of the ready availability of farms foreclosed by federal land banks. He reported that of 737 farms comprising 162,000 acres held by the land bank in Columbia, South Carolina, only 231, averaging about 70 cultivable acres each, were not already rented out. He suspected that these were among the least productive foreclosed properties in the state, and therefore not of the type on which clients should be settled.[19]

The most negative views at the conference were those of two spokesmen from Louisiana. N. C. Williamson, planter, president of the American Cotton Association, and advocate of government assistance through AAA, spoke "as a farmer myself," and declared:

I do not believe these enormous numbers of people need permanent ... or temporary relief.... As far as Louisiana is concerned, we would like to see ... this meeting ... report that there will not be any relief program next year for agriculture.... The general attitude of people is that if they can get relief ... they will get all they can. I do not believe that the southern states are in anything like as dire distress as we have

18 *Ibid.*
19 *Ibid.*

pictured them. . . . I do know that whenever you begin . . . any kind of relief [it] will grow as it is continued. . . . I think we should consider a program of educating our people to relying on themselves again . . . . The quicker our farming people know they are going to have to rely on their own resources, the better off they will be. . . . The people are supposed to support the government, not the government the people.

Another Louisiana planter concurred: "I do not feel that we need a continuation of relief. I believe we can get along without it as we did in years past." He neglected to inform the conference whether just planters or the whole rural population of Louisiana got along so well without FERA assistance.[20]

Hopkins arrived in Atlanta on the afternoon of March 12, as the conference recessed for the day. That evening he talked with reporters about the objectives of rehabilitation. He envisioned a broad alternative to direct relief in rural areas. He thought state directors should "forget emergencies" and seek to make the poor permanently self-supporting. This would require a long-term program; Hopkins thought it would be "remarkable," in fact, "if we even get started this year getting them used to working on their own piece of land, or if we can get it underway with the kind of supervision we need." Concerning the probable size of the new undertaking, he commented that he had available for immediate use in the spring of 1934 between $250 million and $350 million, of which an "appreciable amount" would be spent in the South. The FERA then counted 765,472 families (or 3,498,832 persons), the majority of them rural, receiving direct relief in twelve southern states; Hopkins estimated that about 120,000 southern families would be included in the new program.[21]

Alabama, Georgia, and Louisiana initiated rural operations

20 *Ibid.*
21 Atlanta *Constitution*, March 13 and 14, 1934; Montgomery *Advertiser*, March 13 and 14, 1934; "Suggestions for Mr. Harry Hopkins' Statement," undated typescript [before March 7, 1934] in RG 69, NA. For relief figures see U.S. Federal Emergency Relief Administration, *Monthly Report, March 1–31, 1934* (Washington: Government Printing Office, 1934), 23–24, and *Monthly Report, January 1–31, 1934*, p. 9. The national average of rural families in the relief load was 36.3 percent. Only two southern states, Virginia and Texas, were below that average, whereas the others ranged between 45.8 percent (Florida) and 81.5 percent (Kentucky).

within several weeks after the Atlanta conference. Their programs were the only ones which really functioned during the 1934 crop season. Most other southern relief administrations were slow in planning and began work near the end of 1934 or in 1935.[22] Although FERA intended ultimately to expand rehabilitation into a nationwide undertaking, its efforts were always concentrated in the South. By February, 1935, only 87,350 families received loans and guidance. More than half of these were in Alabama (20,813) and Louisiana (25,584), while Arkansas and Georgia had 9,942 and 6,978, respectively. Moreover, 93 percent of the recipients were in the South and only six other states aided as many as 100. By June, 1935, when the new Resettlement Administration absorbed FERA's farmers, the South still had 60 percent of the 203,000 cases in the country. This predominance was due to the tenancy system, in which the poor were already on the land or only recently removed from it, and landlords were either unable or disinclined to furnish them.[23]

Even after the Atlanta conference Henry Wallace still had reservations about rural rehabilitation. On March 21 chairman Donald Comer of the Alabama rehabilitation committee wrote Westbrook about a discussion with Wallace in which the secretary wondered "why his Department should turn over to us land which he had rented away from cotton farmers... so clients can raise truck... for sale in competition with what ever truck the neighboring farmers might be... raising." In May, after the program had started on a limited scale in the South, Wallace received a favorable assessment

22 Lawrence Westbrook to Hopkins, April 9, 1934, in RG 69, NA. For reports on state programs see Malcolm Miller to Hopkins, November 30, 1934 (on Texas), Loula Dunn to Josephine C. Brown, January 8, 1935, and field report from William Watson, June 15, 1935 (on Arkansas), all in RG 69, NA. In the Hopkins Papers see T. P. Lee to Hopkins, November 3, 10, and 26, 1934, and January 17, 1935 (on Mississippi), A. H. Ward to Westbrook, December 22, 1934 (on Florida), Miller to Hopkins, February 7, 1935 (on Arkansas), J. R. Allgyer to Hopkins, February 9, 1935 (on Tennessee), and Alan Johnstone to Hopkins, January 19, 1935 (on North Carolina). For the difficulties in starting the Tennessee program see Grace E. Falke to Rexford G. Tugwell, June 6, 1934, in Rexford G. Tugwell Papers, Franklin D. Roosevelt Library.

23 Berta Asch and A. R. Mangus, *Farmers on Relief and Rehabilitation*, Works Progress Administration Research Monographs, VIII (Washington: Works Progress Administration, 1937), 17–21.

of it from Calvin B. Hoover, the department's leading authority on the displacement of tenants by the AAA. Hoover implied that FERA's attempts to stabilize the rural poor would actually help fulfill one part of the AAA contract by counteracting the reduction of the number of sharecroppers on the land. He pointed out that rehabilitation families were most frequently settled by arrangement with landlords, often those who had previously cut their normal number of tenants. Hoover also assured the secretary that "this work is being carried on in close cooperation with our extension agents and every effort is being made to see to it that the program does not interfere with our acreage reduction... and... does not result in any improper use of 'rented acres.'"[24]

Wallace was never wholly convinced. On July 25 he told Aubrey Williams he doubted "subsistence farming" could be kept completely noncommercial. Reluctantly he said that "established agriculture" would accept rural rehabilitation because it desired to help solve the nation's relief problems. But he feared that "we may not couple subsistence-farming with adequate part-time employment," and FERA's farmers might enter commercial channels and affect AAA's benefits to landowners. "In that event," he wrote, "agriculture will pay more than its share of the relief bill."[25]

Because of Wallace's reservations and FERA's need for Extension Service supervision of rehabilitants, the relief administration, the Extension Service, and the AAA signed an agreement in the summer of 1934 which not only specified coordination with AAA crop control, but also gave the Agriculture Department a potential check on rehabilitation operations. The agreement stated that only "trained specialists in agriculture and home economics," assisted by capable local farmers, would supervise clients; ERA caseworkers were specifically excluded from this role. Furthermore, the department created its own rehabilitation coordinating committee to which

24 Donald Comer to Westbrook, March 21, 1934, in RG 69, NA; Calvin B. Hoover to Wallace, May 2, 1934, in "Records of the Office of the Secretary of Agriculture," Record Group 16, National Archives.
25 Draft pages of secretary of agriculture's annual report enclosed in Wallace to Aubrey Williams, July 25, 1934, in RG 69, NA.

all its personnel assigned to FERA would report. Thus the price FERA paid for Extension Service assistance was partial surrender of direct client supervision.[26]

The Agriculture Department also exercised great influence in selecting administrators for the program. All state rehabilitation directors were to have Extension Service's endorsement. In Georgia, for example, Miss Shepperson and the state rehabilitation committee appointed Robert L. Vansant, a county agent. The Alabama ERA chose Robert K. Greene, a prominent planter and graduate of the state's land grant college at Auburn. At the local level the agreement recommended that county committees include the agricultural and home demonstration agents as well as relief directors. It was generally expected that these committees would play a major role in selecting clients. They were also to employ rehabilitation supervisors who had the qualifications of the "more mature county agricultural agents" as well as the Extension Service's recommendation. These officials, in turn, were to have staffs of assistants, outstanding farmers of the area, to supervise rehabilitants directly for a per diem compensation. Parallel staffs of women assistants would supervise clients' wives in homemaking.[27]

The pervasive influence of the Extension Service in the new program was important because of the considerable divergence of outlook between county agents and relief administrators, a difference acknowledged by both sides. As part of the Department of Agriculture, Extension was preoccupied with the needs of landowning commercial farmers. It was also administered through the land grant

26 U.S. Federal Emergency Relief Administration, "Objectives and Suggested Procedure for Rural Rehabilitation," directive, June 27, 1934, and "Memorandum of Understanding," June 7, 1934, both in RG 69, NA. The latter was signed by Westbrook, H. R. Tolley of the AAA program planning division, and C. W. Warburton, head of the Extension division.

27 Federal Emergency Relief Administration, "Objectives and Suggested Procedure for Rural Rehabilitation," June 27, 1934, and "Memorandum of Understanding," June 7, 1934, in RG 69, NA; interviews with Gay B. Shepperson, June 29, 1970, and Robert L. Vansant, July 16, 1970; "Field Notes," in *Rural Rehabilitation*, I (November 15, 1934), 16. No state seems to have accepted FERA suggestions that established tenants or some of the clients themselves be included on local committees, but most included area farm owners and businessmen.

colleges and staffed by professional scientific agriculturalists who were greatly concerned with improving farm technology. Understandably, the county agents were often closely associated with those progressive and usually prosperous landowners most receptive to their advice. Robert L. Vansant, the Georgia rehabilitation director, recalled a general opinion in the 1930s that Extension Service men were "old-line conservatives" and admitted that they were mainly concerned with successful farmers.[28]

The agriculturalists tended to conceive rehabilitation as extending credit according to sound financial principles and saw supervision as instruction in the best technical methods. As Alabama operations began in late April, the state rehabilitation office advised its supervisors, concerning the guidance of clients, "above all, do not lose your sense of proportion and let's make this a sound and sensible program that will be an example of good business practice under adverse conditions."[29] When Vansant agreed to head the new effort in Georgia he wanted it understood that he would conduct an "agricultural program, not a social work program." He consistently maintained that only sound loans for which repayment could reasonably be expected should be made and that borrowers should be supervised by "practical, technical, agricultural men." But as an official of the FERA, and later the Resettlement and Farm Security administrations, Vansant became convinced that chronic poverty was rooted in lack of opportunity, ignorance, and ill health. He was "converted" to an appreciation of the need to improve the abilities of the poor. After this realization many of his Extension Service acquaintances concluded that he had "gone over completely to social work."[30]

In contrast to the agriculturalists, relief administrators were mostly former social workers who saw their function as helping needy people. They saw rural rehabilitation as an experiment in improving the farming skills and general living habits of their clients,

28 Interview with Robert L. Vansant. For a critical appraisal of the Extension Service see Gladys Baker, *The County Agent* (Chicago: University of Chicago Press, 1939).
29 Montgomery *Advertiser*, April 22, 1934.
30 Interview with Robert L. Vansant.

encouraging their self-direction and lessening their dependence on both government and landlords. Miss Shepperson recalled that the Extension Service in Georgia was very cooperative in providing supervision and technical assistance. But she also remembered that one could "tell these agriculturalists that our purpose was the re-habilitation of people, not land, and they would agree 100 per cent." However, in the application of the program she regarded them as overly concerned with technical methods and thought they lacked understanding of efforts to increase the general competence of the poor.[31]

Late in April, 1934, as Alabama rehabilitation work was getting underway, Lorena Hickok visited Montgomery and traveled through the black belt. She found that the relief staff had little use for Extension Service officials and doubted the value of their assis-tance. Relief administrators thought Extension was too "political minded" and convinced Hickok that in choosing local supervisors the agriculturalists would probably look for men with superior tech-nical qualifications, bypassing those who could deal sympathetically with poor families. Hickok had previously observed that county agents were usually uninterested in people on relief. They preferred to work with big, successful farmers, she reported, and were too "silo-minded." If Hickok was critical of the agriculturalists, she was caustic in her assessment of the home demonstration agents. They "spend most of their time fooling around with girls' clubs," and have a "Chautauqua slant on life," she wrote. She suspected they would "shudder at the idea of walking into a tenant farmer's shack and teaching the wife how to clean the place up."[32]

How each state administration determined reliefers' eligibility for rehabilitation had much to do with whether the program reached those in greatest need. Hopkins had suggested that ERAs clear their relief rolls of all rural cases having any other means of support and consider those remaining as possible clients. The candidates should be required to show that they had no access to any employment at a

31 Interview with Gay B. Shepperson.
32 Hickok to Hopkins, April 7, 1934, in Hopkins Papers.

living wage (including available work in spring plowing and planting), no jobs in local business, industry, or public projects such as
roadwork. Moreover, they should demonstrate that they could not
arrange for use of land on any terms, could not obtain government or
private credit, and had no AAA benefits due.[33]

In Georgia, county directors certified relief families who had a
physically fit male of at least eighteen years of age with farm experience. In the spring of 1934 they assigned priority to those already
located on land and requiring the smallest cash advance to start farming. Miss Shepperson announced that the first 1,000 clients would
be former farm owners who had lost their land. By August Georgia
had a more detailed system which divided relievers into three
groups. Class A consisted of 25,200 destitute families in the open
country, of whom 6,700 had no acreage to work. Of the remaining
18,500 about half owned no equipment. Class B families were those
farmers on ERA rolls in towns—about 1,000 landowners and 3,100
tenants and laborers. There were also about 7,500 class C families,
not yet on relief but probably needing rehabilitation. A state directive gave preference to the "A" category.[34]

In Louisiana, where most farmer clients had already been removed from the relief rolls, the state office reviewed all rural applicants and considered those without prospects for public or private
jobs or credit eligible for rehabilitation. These cases were classified
as owners, tenants (with equipment), croppers (without equipment),
wage hands, and squatters. The Louisiana plan gave first attention to
those who could be made self-sustaining with a "reasonable expendi-
ture," especially those who with some help could qualify for a government crop loan. Since the latter credit went only to those who
grew staples, these beneficiaries, due to AAA contracts, would be
landowners. Other selection criteria included the client's attitude,
experience, and, remarkably, his "standing in the community."
Tenants and croppers were considered only if they had secured a

33 Harry Hopkins, "Rural Program: Statement of Policy," and Hopkins to all ERAs, April
    2, 1934, in Nixon Papers.
34 Report on Georgia program by W. T. Bennett, August, 1934, in RG 69, NA; Atlanta
    Constitution, May 11 and 23, 1934.

year's lease. Wage hands had to meet the same standard and were therefore effectively excluded.[35] There is little evidence of how the Louisiana program actually operated, but it seems clear that these requirements prevented it from reaching the state's worst levels of poverty.

The Alabama ERA accepted reliefers for rehabilitation only if they had exhausted all possibilities of credit. But it regarded share-cropping as one of those possibilities and was determined to force landlords to assume as much of their old furnishing burden as possible. Therefore, the ERA refused to accept as rehabilitants persons it thought farm owners could support. It even went one step further and ruled, on April 17, that tenants would be denied relief of any kind unless their landlords certified by affidavit that they could not furnish them. Likewise the relief administration rejected as re-habilitants qualified persons whose landlords would not waive back debts. This was to prevent creditors from taking over equipment and goods which the ERA helped its clients acquire. Thus one's acceptance for the program depended in part upon a planter's cooperation, a factor unrelated to need. Finally, Lorena Hickok reported that the ERA withheld even general relief from persons eligible for rehabilitation if their landlords refused to sign debt waivers. She considered this policy "a bit harsh," but relief officials defended it as an attempt to force farmers either to give tenants credit or cooperate with rehabilitation. Administrators counted on public opinion to bring recalcitrant planters in line, but Hickok doubted the tactic would work.[36]

The application of such criteria greatly reduced the relief rolls, and therefore the number who could hope to be chosen as rehabilitants. In late March 30,000 rural Alabama families were on relief, but by April 22, as the program started, there remained only 17,200

35 "Plan for Rural Rehabilitation in Louisiana" and "Initial Steps in Rural Rehabilitation" (Typescripts from April, 1934, in Nixon Papers).
36 Montgomery *Advertiser*, March 21, and April 15 and 17, 1934; Hickok to Hopkins, June 7, 1934, in Hopkins Papers. It should be noted that FERA had to rely on persuasion and public opinion to influence planters since, unlike the AAA, it had no economic leverage to force them to help support the rural poor.

from whom the first selections were made. Between March and June one black belt county reduced its clientele from 456 families to 53, while accepting only 70 as rehabilitants and 20 on work projects. Some of those cut were being carried by planters but others were completely dropped from relief because landlords declined to waive old debts. In June Aubrey Williams commented privately that in shifting to rural rehabilitation, Alabama and Louisiana had taken "arbitrary actions" to slash relief loads. "I strongly suspect this is the cause of considerable suffering," he wrote.[37]

Another major factor determining the effectiveness of the program was the amount and kind of help clients received in getting equipment, livestock, and use of land. FERA defined two kinds of credit for rehabilitants. One was subsistence loans for food, clothing, fuel, and essential medical care—things usually provided by relief. The other type was rehabilitation, or capital, credit to purchase or lease tools, domestic livestock, work animals, feed, seed, and fertilizer. All advances were to be secured by notes held by the ERA. The state relief administration would retain title to all chattel goods until farmers paid in full, to prevent their selling or mortgaging equipment before its complete amortization. Likewise, no client should receive title until the ERA had assisted him to settle his back debts, lest creditors take over capital goods as soon as he acquired them. Most equipment was to be paid for within a time equal to its useful life. FERA suggested two or three years for livestock and one year for consumable subsistence items. In the few cases in which land was sold the repayment period was about thirty-five years.[38]

In April the Georgia relief administration sent the FERA an outline of the assistance it intended to give its farmers. The plan anticipated that each rehabilitant would cultivate no more than ten or fifteen acres, although he might have more for pasture. Clients could produce no cotton, but would grow various soil builders, corn,

37 Montgomery *Advertiser*, March 22, April 22, and June 9, 1934; Williams to George B. Power, June 4, 1934, in Aubrey Williams Papers, Franklin D. Roosevelt Library.
38 Lawrence Westbrook and Corrington Gill, "Rural Rehabilitation Program: Financial Policies and Procedures," FERA directive, December 26, 1934, in AAA legal office files in RG 16, NA.

peas, beans, peanuts, sorghum, vegetables, and melons. The ERA figured that an average family advance would provide land rental ($50 per year), house repair ($50), fertilizer (300 pounds per acre averaging $51.75), food ($92.40 for flour, meal, lard, meat, sugar, and coffee) for the six months when gardens could not be grown, clothing ($60), and medicine ($12). Mules would be rented at first to cut expenses. The ERA expected that its charges could own capital goods eventually. The agency planned to advance to cost-sharing pairs of families half interests each in a mule, harness, wagon, and implements for $130. In addition individual families might acquire a cow ($25), hogs ($20), and chickens ($10). At first these items could be lent by the relief administration in return for the farmer's pledge to "keep, use and protect" them. Later, as they made some profits, they could amortize equipment and livestock, and perhaps land as well.[39]

Alabama's rehabilitation plan was the first submitted to the FERA and some of its procedures were regarded as models for other states.[40] Robert Greene, the state director, had been an outspoken critic of FERA's previous rural operations. Aided by Extension Service consultants, he outlined an "economy program" designed to cost no more annually than direct relief. In the spring and summer of 1934 the average advance per family was only $94.11. As in other states, clients were expected to repay everything in full. By November 15, 1934, $650,000 had been loaned and $500,000 repaid either in work or produce. Among cost-saving techniques was a requirement that families preserve their garden vegetables by drying, rather than canning, since the former method was cheaper and simpler and therefore more likely to be continued by the poor.[41]

But the most publicized expense-cutting was in providing work-

39 Plan for rural rehabilitation in Georgia enclosed in Count D. Gibson to Shepperson, April 17, 1934, in "Records of the Farmers Home Administration," Record Group 96, National Archives; Atlanta *Constitution*, May 24, 1934. The plan estimated that there were 6,800 vacant tenant houses and 251,000 unused acres available for rehabilitants in 126 rural counties.
40 Miller to Williams, October 15, 1934, in Hopkins Papers; Montgomery *Advertiser*, March 21 and July 10, 1934.
41 "Field Notes," 16; Montgomery *Advertiser*, April 22, 1934.

stock, which gave Alabama operations popular notoriety as the
"steer program." If clients lacked work animals, the relief administration furnished cattle or oxen, on credit. Sometimes these were
AAA surplus animals, but usually local scrub "piney woods steers"
were found more satisfactory for plowing. The ERA was emphatic
that it would not supply mules because their ownership and care
were major financial burdens for poor farmers. Mules were expensive in Alabama, costing at least $100–$150 apiece and consuming
about $120 worth of feed per year. "You can see," the ERA told its
clients in an unintentional comment on its relief standards, "that it
costs almost as much to feed a mule for a year as it costs to feed a
whole family." But steers cost only about $24 per year to feed be-
cause they could graze for their subsistence.[42]

Lorena Hickok was in the Alabama black belt in April, 1934, as
the steer program began. She encountered much public skepticism
about it among small-town whites. One critic exploded, "Hell! This
ain't no New Deal if we . . . gotta go back plowin' steers!" He told her
the cattle were difficult to break to a plow. Furthermore, they would
not work in the heat, but "jest lay right down—or wander off to the
swamp, draggin' the nigger with 'em, if he ain't leadin' 'em!" But
such detractors, she observed, were mostly nonfarmers. She also
talked with some rehabilitants who were plowing satisfactorily with
steers. A black farmer assured her, "Anybody c'n git along alright
wid a steer."[43]

Other critics contended the program was starting too late for the
crop season in southern Alabama, but Extension Service experts dis-
agreed. Various others thought the FERA was going to entirely too
much trouble for the benefit of "pore white trash an' niggers."
There was similar skepticism in Georgia, where the state director
recalled numerous "doubting Thomases." But Hickok found that the
Alabama relief staff was confident of good results and the more
thoughtful local businessmen and planters expected that perhaps

42 Hickok to Hopkins, April 7, 1934, and Alabama Relief Administration, "Instructions for
    Rehabilitation Subscribers in Group I," December, 1934, both in Hopkins Papers;
    Montgomery *Advertiser*, June 4, 1934.
43 Hickok to Hopkins, April 7, 1934, in Hopkins Papers.

half the clients could be permanently rehabilitated. But all agreed that close supervision was essential. "You just gotta stand right over 'em," they told her. [44]

In June, 1934, Hickok returned to Alabama and traveled through the northern part of the state. Near Florence she observed clients supplied with seed, fertilizer, tools, and draft animals (mules in this area, unlike the rest of the state). Advances ranged from $49 to $165 and averaged $80. The relief administration bought no land but located families on landlords' AAA "rented acres." Rehabilitants grew no cotton unless they turned it over to FERA for relief use. The ERA applied their surplus produce to their indebtedness and gave them preference for local road work. Hickok discovered that most landlords were quite willing to waive debts and otherwise co-operate, apparently convinced that land improvement and super-vised repair of cabins and fences were adequate compensation. In the matter of client selection Hickok noted that, although those chosen were unquestionably needy, there was some tendency to bypass the most destitute and dependent. "The idea is to start out this year with those most likely to succeed," she wrote. "These will be given further opportunities next year, if they make good ... and ... if the program goes on, less likely candidates may be taken on. It's all experimental this year ... and they want the best possible material to work with." [45]

Hickok was surprised to find that rehabilitation supervisors with Extension Service backgrounds were contributing more to the pro-gram than relief officials had originally expected. These "farm fore-men" handled about eight families each and several were sufficiently interested to work overtime with their wards. Hickok made the rounds with one foreman who was quite proud of his clients' prog-ress and confident of their success, although he did admit personal difficulty with one "smart nigger who don't like to take advice." Another conscientious supervisor told her that most rehabilitants were illiterate and had great need for someone to advise them in

44 *Ibid.*; interview with Robert L. Vansant.
45 Hickok to Hopkins, June 7, 1934, in Hopkins Papers.

business affairs, since landlords had always kept their accounts. "Now our job is to see that they get a new start, with someone to protect them," he said.[46]

Although Hickok admitted that the Alabama program, with its steers, $40 mules, borrowed land, and minimal loans, might seem "niggardly" to some, she thought it had an essential practicability. "Instead of starting out with $2,500 homes . . . brand new expensive equipment and stock" and excessive indebtedness, she observed, "these people are being given the things they actually need to get started—and on terms they can meet." Other improvements in their living standards "will come in time," she added.[47]

Hickok's observations underscore the important question of the effectiveness of FERA rehabilitation in reaching the South's worst poverty. It is true that it aided only reliefers who had no prospects of jobs or credit, but it was less than comprehensive in this. As the program progressed in 1935 it tended to become more selective as state administrations, as Hickok noted, placed only the "best material" on land with guidance and credit. Beginning rehabilitation in 1935, Arkansas applied the selection criteria of farming experience, ability to manage capital advances, possession of some livestock and equipment, and sufficiency of family labor. By these standards 17 percent of the clients were classed as "best risks" and 56 percent as secondary "good prospects." Nearly 92 percent of the former and 65 percent of the latter had been small landowners or cash or share tenants. Although the Arkansas program accepted about 18,000 cases (6.7 percent of the state's rural population) by mid-1935, few of these were chronic dependents; about 60 percent had been on relief less than six months and 85 percent less than a year.[48] A similar trend prevailed in the Southeast. One investigator found that only about one-fifth of the rehabilitants in a seven-state area were wage hands, and of the others, only about a third were sharecroppers. He concluded, "Those farm families who were presumably in a better

---

46 *Ibid.*
47 *Ibid.*
48 E. L. Kirkpatrick, *Analysis of 70,000 Rural Rehabilitation Families* (Washington: Farm Security Administration and Bureau of Agricultural Economics, 1938), 19–21, 30–31.

financial situation . . .were more often taken on the . . .program than were croppers and farm laborers."[49]

The Alabama program also became increasingly selective. By September, 1934, the ERA had placed 60.9 percent of it's clients in a category reserved for those, mostly former farm owners and share tenants, able to manage capital advances and farm with little supervision. Furthermore, considerable self-direction was expected of these top rehabilitants. In its instructions for 1935 the Montgomery office required them to find their own places to farm, make rental agreements with landlords, preferably for more than one year and, if possible, with an option to purchase the land they worked.[50] Arrangements such as these were clearly more than the most impoverished and dependent reliefers could negotiate. Throughout the South the poorest rural dwellers, if accepted in the program, were usually given limited assistance. Two WPA researchers, writing in 1936, concluded that great numbers of rehabilitants, presumably the most destitute, received little more than general relief.[51]

The extent to which impoverished rural Negroes shared the benefits of the FERA program varied throughout the region. Official policy, of course, prohibited racial discrimination and some states did have large numbers of black clients. In April, 1935, a National Emergency Council official reported that one-third of Alabama's 10,000 rehabilitants were Negroes. In Arkansas, on the other hand, blacks accounted for only 8 percent of the clients, whereas they were 26.5 percent of the state's rural population. There is evidence that Negroes, to be accepted, had to be relatively well off; of those approved in Arkansas 22.5 percent were farm owners, compared to only 16 percent of the state's black farmers who owned land. There were also disparities in black and white clients' loans. By June, 1935, 4,028 whites surveyed in seven southeastern states had received av-

49 Thomas Jackson Woofter, Jr., *Landlord and Tenant on the Cotton Plantation*, Works Progress Administration Research Monographs, V (Washington: Works Progress Administration, 1936), 174.

50 Kirkpatrick, *Analysis of 70,000 Rural Rehabilitation Families*, 5, 7; Alabama Relief Administration, "Instructions for Rehabilitation Subscribers in Group I," December, 1934, in Hopkins Papers.

51 Asch and Mangus, *Farmers on Relief and Rehabilitation*, 18–19.

erage advances of $205 since acceptance in the program, while the figure for 2,260 blacks was only $122.[52]

Some localities may also have exerted subtle pressures to discourage black applicants. A study sponsored by the Arkansas rehabilitation director stated that blacks were "less inclined" than whites to apply for the program and were "not accepted in as high a proportion" since few were farm owners or share tenants, and besides, "their needs were often met by plantation landlords." In December, 1934, the Georgia relief administration reported that many presumably eligible blacks were afraid to apply because they doubted FERA could provide any "measure of economic and social protection... in the rural areas." However, the report continued, black rehabilitants had progressed as well as the whites and there was "no evidence of racial antipathy" to them in the communities. The writer concluded that the agency should strive to overcome unfounded black apprehensions about the program.[53]

In October, 1935, Alfred Edgar Smith, a researcher for FERA's race relations unit, found rural rehabilitation "effective enough in its limited scope," but inadequate for the needs of blacks. In a later report Smith concluded, "Apparently Negroes shared in every phase of emergency relief but were definitely discriminated against in one or more detail of administration."[54] No doubt his general assessment applied to rural rehabilitation.

FERA's rural operations were hastily conceived and conducted with little central direction. Rehabilitation reached limited numbers, 209,951 cases in its peak month of April, 1935,[55] and then bypassed the most impoverished. But its idea of combining credit and guidance was sound. It fit the experience of the South's rural

52 John D. Petree to Eugene S. Leggett, April 2, 1935, in "Records of the Office of Government Reports," Record Group 44, Federal Records Center, Suitland, Maryland; Kirkpatrick, *Analysis of 70,000 Rural Rehabilitation Families*, 20; Woofter, *Landlord and Tenant*, 173.
53 Kirkpatrick, *Analysis of 70,000 Rural Rehabilitation Families*, 20; Shepperson to Hopkins, December 5, 1934, in Hopkins Papers.
54 Alfred Edgar Smith, "Negro Labor and Unemployment Relief," October, 1935, and "Report-Summary, 1935, Negro Clients on Federal Unemployment Relief," December 31, 1935, both in RG 69, NA.
55 Asch and Mangus, *Farmers on Relief and Rehabilitation*, 17–18.

poor, who had always received advances and supervision from the same source, their landlords. FERA assumed these functions with the intent of encouraging and improving the competence of destitute and landless country folk, and without charging planters' interest rates. By supplying workstock and implements it provided some propertyless croppers a chance to raise their status to that of share tenants.[56] The New Deal continued and refined this rehabilitative idea in its Resettlement and Farm Security administrations.

Harry Hopkins was convinced of the worth of rural rehabilitation and wanted to expand it as part of the relief effort. On December 14, 1934, he proposed to Roosevelt a complete reorganization of federal relief for 1935 and assigned the rural program a place in his new design. He told the president that FERA then gave direct aid to 4.3 million families and 700,000 single persons. Of these 5 million cases, a million were unemployable because of age, illness, or disabilities. Another 3.5 million were unemployed and simply needed jobs. But about 500,000 needed rehabilitation as farmers. Hopkins proposed to abolish direct relief and turn unemployables over to the care of the states. For the jobless he favored a new federally administered and financed work relief agency. To complete the plan he wanted to expand rehabilitation to cover a half million cases, and at the same time, resettle "stranded" farm families from submarginal lands to more fertile acres.[57]

Finally, throughout 1934 many associated the rehabilitation idea with the encouragement of landownership. Some regarded purchase of small acreage as an essential step in uplifting the poor. Even before the Atlanta meeting Hopkins had suggested to Wallace that rehabilitants could be potential land buyers. At the conference itself several of the state relief officials urged the idea upon Westbrook. By the middle of 1934 FERA began listing among its goals assisting

---

56 Woofter, *Landlord and Tenant*, 189.
57 Hopkins to Roosevelt, confidential memorandum, December 14, 1934, in Official File 444-C, Franklin D. Roosevelt Library, and Hopkins' press conference of December 27, 1934, in Official File 444. The new work relief agency was, of course, the Works Progress Administration. The reorganization was carried out in April, 1935, but rural rehabilitation was transferred to the new Resettlement Administration.

clients to own small tracts.[58] Many of the state plans affirmed the
same intention. The Georgia ERA proposed that its best farmers be
located "at once on lands which they shall eventually amortize for
themselves." At the end of 1934 the Alabama ERA instructed its top
clients to attempt to arrange with landlords leases with options to
buy. In June, 1935, the Arkansas program contemplated land acquisition by clients because "home ownership is the ultimate aim in
every case." And by the latter part of 1934 most state administrations
had established rehabilitation finance corporations to fulfill legal requirements in obtaining, leasing, and selling real estate.[59]

Landownership as a means of rehabilitating the poor was in fact
an emerging idea, among both critics and supporters of FERA's
rural policy. In June, 1934, T. J. Woofter, a researcher of farm problems for the relief agency, advised Will Alexander, executive director of the Commission on Interracial Cooperation, of his latest
findings. Woofter was convinced of the need for a "long time plan
looking to the reduction of tenancy to the status of a way station to
ownership." He thought FERA's "recent hurried attempt at rural
rehabilitation" was no substitute for a farm ownership program, since
it was mainly a scheme to get country families off relief and dealt
with "the most depressed tenant class." The elimination of tenancy,
in his opinion, would necessitate "working first with the better class
of tenant" in an "evolutionary" plan which would "open . . . wide the
door of land ownership" for them.[60] Woofter knew Alexander was
then involved in investigations of the South's rural poverty. But he
could not foresee that Alexander would soon help promote federal
legislation to accomplish rehabilitation through land redistribution.

58 U.S. Federal Emergency Relief Administration, "Objectives and Suggested Procedure
    for Rural Rehabilitation," directive, June 7, 1934, in RG 69, NA.
59 Georgia plan enclosed in Gibson to Shepperson, April 17, 1934, in RG 96, NA;
    Alabama Relief Administration, "Instructions to Rehabilitation Subscribers in Group
    I," December, 1934, in Hopkins Papers; FERA field report by William Watson for
    two weeks ending June 15, 1935, in RG 69, NA; Lawrence Westbrook and Cor-
    rington Gill, "Rural Rehabilitation Program: Financial Policies and Procedures," De-
    cember 26, 1934, in AAA legal office files, in RG 16, NA.
60 Draft of introduction to tenancy study, enclosed in T. J. Woofter to Will Alexander,
    June 20, 1934, in CIC Papers.

CHAPTER V

The Bankhead Bill and the Resettlement Administration

THE MOVE for antipoverty legislation began late in January, 1934. Stacy May of the Rockefeller Foundation telephoned Will Alexander in Atlanta, and suggested that as the New Deal neared its first anniversary, it was time for serious investigation of the impact of federal recovery efforts upon Negroes. May told Alexander that the foundation could provide $50,000 for research on the subject, but desired no publicity. Accordingly, he proposed to channel the money through the Julius Rosenwald Fund, which had a long interest in the problems of Negroes, to the Commission on Interracial Cooperation which would conduct the inquiry. May requested that Alexander, with Edwin R. Embree, executive director of the Rosenwald Fund, and Charles S. Johnson, a Fisk University sociologist, accept responsibility for the study. Alexander agreed, and in late March, 1934, the board of the interracial commission formally approved his participation.[1]

1 "Reminiscences of Will W. Alexander" (Typescript, 1952, in Oral History Collection, Columbia University), 372; Edwin R. Embree to William P. Beazell, February 15, 1935, and minutes of executive committee, Commission on Interracial Cooperation, March 30, 1934, in Commission on Interracial Cooperation Papers, Atlanta University; hereinafter cited as CIC Papers. This chapter has benefited generally from a good secondary account of the origins of the Bankhead tenancy bill and the Resettlement Administration, Sidney Baldwin's *Poverty and Politics: The Rise and Decline of the Farm*

Alexander, Embree, and Johnson designated themselves the Committee on Minority Groups in the Economic Recovery, and on the last weekend in January met in Nashville to organize the study. They assumed the task of examining New Deal agricultural policies. As Alexander informed Howard Odum, "It was decided to make some sort of effort to discover an intelligent basis for a long-time program for Negroes on the farm, particularly those who will be uprooted by crop reduction and the withdrawal of marginal lands."[2] Significantly, even at this early date, there was consideration of the need for long-range policies.

Johnson directed the study of the AAA. By June, 1934, he had sent a staff of investigators into the Deep South. He took special pains to assure his biracial group of field men personal "security and confidence" in potentially hostile plantation districts where they might be regarded as meddling outsiders. He attempted to obtain credentials for them from the Interior Department through Clark Foreman, Secretary Harold Ickes' advisor on Negro affairs. Failing in this, he made the best possible local arrangements. In Mississippi for example, Johnson secured the cooperation of the state director of the Extension Service, who instructed county agents to provide assistance. Johnson procured letters of introduction from the state commissioner of agriculture, and Oscar Johnston, president of the Delta and Pine Land Company, granted full access to that plantation. As a final precaution, the field staff received the written sanction of at least one sheriff.[3]

Most of the field investigations were concluded by October, 1934. The voluminous evidence confirmed the deterioration of the cotton tenancy system, that crop restriction had compounded the difficulties, and that AAA's reputed inequities for tenants were real enough and widespread in the cotton belt. These findings compelled

Security Administration (Chapel Hill: University of North Carolina Press, 1968), Chaps. 4 and 5. Another useful work is Wilma Dykeman and James Stokely, *Seeds of Southern Change: The Life of Will Alexander* (Chicago: University of Chicago Press, 1962).

2 Will Alexander to Howard Odum, February 15, 1934, in CIC Papers; "Reminiscences of Will W. Alexander," 373–75.

3 Charles S. Johnson to Alexander, June 14, 20, 23, and 25, 1934, in Charles S. Johnson Papers, Fisk University.

the committee to shift its concentration from exclusive concern with the condition of rural blacks to the deplorable plight of all the landless farmers of the South.[4]

The committee believed its purposes included arousing public opinion and inspiring congressional action. To influence the public they determined to publish a brief report rather than the voluminous results of the field studies. To prepare this, the committee hired Frank Tannenbaum, an historian with considerable reputation in Latin American studies. Tannenbaum, then employed at the Brookings Institution in Washington, was well versed in the history of foreign land-reform movements, particularly those of Mexico. He also knew the South; in 1924 he had written *Darker Phases of the South*, a perceptive book about the section's social and economic deficiencies. He had not, however, been in the region since that time.[5]

In the early fall of 1934, Alexander, Embree, Johnson, and Tannenbaum met at Alexander's home in Atlanta to review the committee's findings. They concluded that the AAA cotton program had been an "unforeseen calamity" for sharecroppers and tenants, reducing and even destroying the minimal security afforded by the crop lien system. Landowners now found it profitable to reduce the number of their tenants and demote those remaining to wage laborers. Those displaced were forced on relief, "with all that means in purposelessness, in futility, in the absence of self-governance, in the destruction of ambition and the devastation of a dream that 'next year'" would promise better conditions. The committee was by no means the first to make such observations, but after considering the results of Johnson's studies it clearly perceived the trend in the South.[6]

Discussion turned to the proposal of some minimum program. "The problem as we visualized it," Tannenbaum wrote, "is to find an

4 Embree to Beazell, February 15, 1935, in CIC Papers; "Reminiscences of Will W. Alexander," 373–75.
5 "Reminiscences of Will W. Alexander," 375–77.
6 Frank Tannenbaum to Alexander, October 13, 1934, in Frank Tannenbaum Papers, Columbia University.

immediate way out for the poorest and most nearly forgotten group in our rural population." But despite this affirmation, the conference sought no sweeping plans for the eradication of poverty. Instead, the four searched for some program which could be achieved quickly and at relatively low cost to the government. They maintained that the aim should be to *restore* tenants and croppers to something like their past condition rather than raise them to any ideal status. This would provide a sense of security and renew the ambition of the poor.[7]

The four men developed only one tentative recommendation—a pilot project in which three hundred rural relief cases would be provided half-acre homes in a government-supervised farm community settlement. These clients would be expected to build their own homes, of logs if necessary, and to achieve self-sufficiency in gardening. The community might own land collectively, or permit residents to hold acreages individually. Cash cropping would be de-emphasized but probably not eliminated completely.[8] This vague proposal seems to have drawn upon the example of the Interior Department's subsistence homesteads and the FERA's rural communities.

This "meagre program," the committee thought, realistically recognized the chronic impoverishment and marginal abilities of those it sought to help. It wisely refused to idealize the poor by overestimating their capabilities, providing elaborate cooperative projects which they could not manage for themselves, or expecting rapid or dramatic changes in their living standards. The committee did expect its approach, if widely applied, to get rural people off relief and care for some of those displaced and "set adrift." The plan's chief limitation was also mentioned by the committee, but as a virtue: it aimed only to relieve emergency conditions and contemplated no broad permanent reconstruction of rural life. The committee assumed that fundamental improvement in the lives of the poor had to await the return of general prosperity.[9] This recom-

7 *Ibid.*
8 *Ibid.*
9 *Ibid.*

mendation illustrates that even the thinking of these men, who were well informed and sincerely concerned about the poor, was restricted by timidity and lack of imagination in the face of an overwhelming problem.

It was probably at this meeting that the committee asked Tannenbaum to tour the South and observe conditions firsthand before writing the report. About mid-December, 1934, Tannenbaum began an itinerary suggested by Johnson through Arkansas, Mississippi, Alabama, and Georgia. He originally intended to take ninety days for the trip but cut it short after only ten, declaring that he had seen enough to convince him that the tenancy system had collapsed under the weight of its own inadequacies and the depression, and could not be restored or made to support masses of landless people. Either the committee or the New Deal, he asserted, had to do something about it.[10]

Tannenbaum's brief excursion was a turning point for him and the committee. He had not been south since before the Great Depression. Although he had been well acquainted with the region's poverty in the early 1920s, he apparently was unprepared for the destitution he witnessed ten years later. Alexander's recollections suggest that Tannenbaum had been appalled by what he saw. At the same time, Tannenbaum's sense of shock evidently altered his colleagues' thinking. The following March Alexander recalled that at the end of 1934 "our committee was of the opinion that the tenant system could never be patched up, that at its best it was an impossible system, that its breakdown is complete."[11]

Between October, 1934, and the end of the year the committee's outlook had changed dramatically. The community pilot project was never mentioned again, nor was there further talk of restoring the former position of the poor, or of the impracticability of basic reform during hard times. By December the committee was formulating a plan to end tenancy and reduce poverty permanently by promoting

10 Johnson to Alexander, December 10, 1934, in CIC Papers; "Reminiscences of Will W. Alexander," 377.

11 "Reminiscences of Will W. Alexander," 373–77; Alexander to Bruce Bliven, March 9, 1935, in CIC Papers.

small landownership. Alexander emphatically told Embree that any program which aimed at less than this was "temporizing."[12] Thus, by the beginning of 1935 the committee had abandoned palliative measures and shifted its attack to the southern land tenure system. It now thought in broader and more fundamental terms than it had dared in October, 1934. But as later experience revealed, the emphasis on land ownership also meant an increasingly narrower concern with only those among the poor who had sufficient ability and resources to become small owners.

At the end of 1934, Tannenbaum returned to Washington, where the committee had provided him an office and where he was to write the report and circulate the findings among New Deal officials. But since the committee also intended to promote public policy, he assumed the extra duty of trying to stir the administration to action. Tannenbaum's essential proposal, traceable to his studies of Mexico, was a massive government land-buying program which would create small farms for resale on easy terms to the rural poor. Shortly before the new year he discussed this idea with Assistant Secretary of Agriculture Paul Appleby, who was receptive and willing to convey the proposal to Henry Wallace. At the secretary's suggestion Tannenbaum then saw Chester Davis, who joined Appleby in recommending circulation of an outline within the department.[13]

In the last days of 1934 and the first month of 1935, Tannenbaum refined his proposal in four memoranda. On December 29 he submitted an outline to Appleby. On January 6 he conferred again with the committee in Atlanta and made notes for its use. Later in the month he helped prepare a comprehensive statement, in the name of the whole committee, for circulation within the Agriculture Department and the FERA. It traced what the committee probably then considered the ultimate dimensions of its program. Finally, Tannenbaum wrote a fourth memorandum, more cautious in tone than the third, which he probably intended to be the outline of a

12   Alexander to Embree, January 8, 1935, in CIC Papers.
13   "Reminiscences of Will W. Alexander," 378; Tannenbaum to Alexander, December 26, 1934, in Tannenbaum Papers.

bill. From these sources the thinking of Tannenbaum, the committee, and its sympathizers in the department can be reconstructed.[14]

In Tannenbaum's analysis, the plantation was normally deficient in providing adequate living standards for its workers. Since the 1920s, however, depression conditions had struck a mortal blow to the system. As landlords' incomes declined, so had their sense of responsibility for their dependents, and the old practice of furnishing had fallen off. Into this situation came federal programs. The presence of relief, for example, encouraged the abandonment of furnishing, since many planters saw FERA as a substitute for their own commissaries. Then AAA had further decreased tenants' security, speeded the trend to day labor, and promoted mechanization, which promised to displace tenants and wage hands alike.

The meaning of all this, Tannenbaum thought, was that the South could expect the dispossessed portion of its population to increase. As he considered the "peculiar character of the South, its persistent race feeling, and the temper which governs friction when it comes to a head," he concluded that "the social consequences of large groups of homeless and propertyless migrants, both white and colored, constitute the elements of a serious problem, which may prove beyond easy remedy in the not distant future."[15]

If the government acted promptly, Tannenbaum thought, a remedy was possible. But the solution assuredly did not lie in revised parity policies, or even in improved crop control contracts. A parity price for staple-producing landowners was distinctly different from an effort to reduce poverty. The real key to the problem was a comprehensive land settlement program, indeed, a new land tenure system for the South. As the committee's notes expressed it, "It is now apparent that . . . some fundamental change in the relationship

---

14 Tannenbaum to Paul Appleby, December 29, 1934, and "Notes on Conference of Messrs. Embree, Alexander, Johnson, Tannenbaum and Simon on Agricultural Rehabilitation," January 6, 1935, in Tannenbaum Papers; Will Alexander *et. al.*, "A Proposed Program for the Improvement of the Condition of the Tenant Farmer, Particularly in the Cotton Areas of the South," January, 1934 [1935], in CIC Papers; "A Program to Develop a New System of Rural Land Tenure," [January, 1935], in Tannenbaum Papers.

15 Tannenbaum to Appleby, December 29, 1934, in Tannenbaum Papers.

of tenants to the soil" is necessary, the only alternative being indefinite emergency relief.[16]

Having examined an immense and complex situation and prescribed land distribution as a general remedy, Tannenbaum then considered where the government should concentrate its resources. In his memorandum outlining legislation he proposed to direct government assistance to tenants, young farmers needing help in getting established, and some of the most capable and stable wage laborers. The government should strive to create a better tenure for these people without moving them. In encouraging small ownership, it should give preference to those still located on farms as tenants or croppers, and secondary attention to those already "set adrift." This policy was expected to prevent further displacement of people, but not necessarily restore all the dispossessed to the land.[17]

In the memorandum drafted for circulation within the Agriculture Department and the FERA, Tannenbaum envisioned a distinctly broader program than that in the bill-draft memorandum. In this document the committee traced its hopes for the ultimate scope of its program—hopes too broad to be written into a bill. It declared that the end should be "to establish in farm ownership a huge number of families now entirely cut off from ownership and even from tenancy or crop sharing arrangements."[18] Here was a suggestion that the government concern itself with people already "adrift," a more inclusive aim than that of concentrating on those who still had access to land on some terms.

To implement the program, Tannenbaum proposed to empower a special federal agency to purchase the extensive foreclosed lands held by banks, insurance companies, and federal land banks. He expected these corporate landholders to welcome a chance to sell and convert their assets to more liquid form. Acreage could also be purchased from individuals. The projected government agency

---

16   *Ibid.*; "Notes on Conference on Agricultural Rehabilitation," January 6, 1935, in Tannenbaum Papers.
17   "Program to Develop a New System of Rural Land Tenure," in Tannenbaum Papers.
18   Alexander *et al.*, "Proposed Program for the Improvement of the Condition of the Tenant Farmer," January [1935], in CIC Papers.

should retire any submarginal lands it acquired, and break up the rest into family-sized farms, varying according to the region, but probably forty-acre plots in cotton country. The land would then be sold on easy terms to tenants, croppers, and laborers, with preference to those already working it. The agency might also extend additional loans for buildings and livestock, and at least initially, provide some production credit.[19]

Tannenbaum and the committee recognized that merely extending credit to inexperienced and impoverished tenants would accomplish little. They thought credit should be minimized in favor of the supervision which they saw as most essential. The committee anticipated direction of tenant purchasers' crop selection (in conformance with the AAA program) and general operations for perhaps as long as ten years. Supervisors could also advise clients in marketing their crops and organizing cooperative associations.[20]

Even as early as 1935 rural community projects organized by the FERA and the subsistence homesteads division of the Interior Department were highly controversial. Therefore, Tannenbaum stated flatly in one memorandum that "in the main there would be no effort to create new communities." On the other hand, the committee's memorandum to the Agriculture Department and the FERA recommended experimentation with "carefully directed cooperative communities."[21] Far from ignoring the possibilities of cooperative agriculture, the backers of what would develop into the Bankhead-Jones tenancy bill had endorsed it as a useful experiment long before the Southern Tenant Farmers' Union formally suggested cooperative farming as a panacea in 1936. But knowing that Congress would be antagonistic to collectivist projects, the committee undoubtedly

---

19 "Program to Develop a New System of Rural Land Tenure," undated, and Tannenbaum to Appleby, December 29, 1934, both in Tannenbaum Papers; Alexander *et. al.*, "Proposed Program for the Improvement of the Condition of the Tenant Farmer," January [1935], in CIC Papers.

20 Alexander *et. al.*, "Proposed Program for the Improvement of the Condition of the Tenant Farmer," January [1935], in CIC Papers.

21 "Program to Develop a New System of Rural Land Tenure," undated, in Tannenbaum Papers; Alexander *et. al.*, "Proposed Program for the Improvement of the Condition of the Tenant Farmer," January [1935], in CIC Papers.

considered it politically unwise to ask for specific authorization for such communities. The tenancy legislation, when introduced, was silent on this point.

Finally, Tannenbaum considered ways of financing the program. The simplest method would be a congressional appropriation for the proposed land-buying agency. An alternate method would establish the agency as a government corporation authorized to sell federally guaranteed bonds, using the proceeds to buy land and resell it to tenants on credit. The bonds, of course, would be secured by mortgages on the land. Tannenbaum saw disadvantages in the latter plan. He thought it would be administratively complicated. More importantly, he feared that the corporation, to safeguard the value of its bonds, might lend only to relatively good risks, thus subordinating social purposes to financial considerations in its credit policies. But even though he preferred direct appropriation, Tannenbaum thought congressional and public opinion might support the creation of a bond-issuing corporation. As always, expense would be a major factor in congressional thinking. A land program large enough to be effective would cost, in the committee's estimation, several billion dollars during the next few years. Congress would probably balk at such direct expenditures, but it might approve a mortgage-bond program.[22]

Tannenbaum's memoranda were important landmarks in the formation of tenancy legislation. Brought together, they reveal a broad concept of credit for land purchase and acquisition of implements and livestock, as well as for production needs and even subsistence. Moreover, the credit would be combined with supervision of borrowers. Here was the outline of a sweeping program of rehabilitation by promoting landownership, which the committee hoped could follow the passage of proper legislation.

During the first six weeks of 1935 the committee contacted several important officials of the Agriculture Department. Alexander and Embree met with Wallace, who seemed uninterested in their

22 "Program to Develop a New System of Rural Land Tenure," undated, in Tannenbaum
    Papers.

findings. Shortly afterward, however, the secretary put them in touch with Rexford G. Tugwell and land-use expert L. C. Gray. Meanwhile, Tannenbaum worked closely with the departmental establishment. He conferred with Undersecretary M. L. Wilson and discovered that they "talk[ed] ultimately the same language on basic issues." Paul Appleby showed special interest in the memoranda Tannenbaum submitted to him and suggested that he take a desk in the department "to work on the problem from the inside." Tannenbaum accepted, and by February was working with Wilson and Gray to develop a bill.[23]

Also in January, 1935, the committee attempted to approach the president with its findings and plans. Alexander's contact with the White House was George Foster Peabody, an 83-year-old philanthropist and long-time acquaintance of Roosevelt's.[24] Alexander knew Peabody through the interracial commission's dealings with educational foundations; the Peabody Fund had been instrumental for years in uplifting public instruction for both races in the South. Peabody was sympathetic to efforts to deal with tenancy and agreed to try to get Alexander and Embree an appointment with Roosevelt. On January 10 he wired Presidential Appointments Secretary Marvin McIntyre, stating that Alexander and Embree had reliable new data on the breakdown of tenancy, as well as a policy proposal consistent with Roosevelt's general ideas as Peabody understood them from previous conversations. Peabody urged Roosevelt to see them. For the moment the president was uninterested. He told McIntyre to suggest that the committee discuss the matter with Hopkins.[25] Thus the first effort to gain presidential support for tenancy legislation failed.

23 "Reminiscences of Will W. Alexander," 381–84; Tannenbaum to Alexander, December 26, 1934, Tannenbaum to Alexander, Embree, and Johnson, January 11 and February 2, 1935, in Tannenbaum Papers.

24 "Reminiscences of Will W. Alexander," 274; Baldwin, *Poverty and Politics*, 131. Peabody had introduced Roosevelt to Warm Springs, Georgia, as a therapeutic center.

25 Alexander to Tannenbaum, January 10, 1935, in Tannenbaum Papers; George Foster Peabody to Marvin McIntyre, January 10, 1935, and McIntyre to Peabody, January 17, 1935, in Official File 1650, Franklin D. Roosevelt Library, Hyde Park, N.Y. A copy of Peabody's January 10 telegram in CIC Papers is charged to Alexander, who evidently

Meanwhile, with guidance from Tannenbaum and Gray, a department lawyer drafted a bill. It was broadly drawn, to allow great latitude in dealing with tenancy. Senator Josiah Bailey of North Carolina, who opposed it, later complained that it was "as wide open at both ends as a barrel with both heads knocked out." It provided for a government corporation authorized to issue $1 billion worth of federally guaranteed bonds. With the money it raised, the corporation could purchase and resell land to tenants on long repayment terms. Borrowers would pay as low an interest rate as possible, depending on what the corporation had to pay to market bonds. The new agency could buy and resell farm equipment in the same manner. Eligible purchasers would be limited to tenants, croppers, and laborers. The bill made no mention of the supervision of clients described in the committee's memoranda; nor did it even contain a clause preventing purchasers from alienating their land to speculators. But the drafters had provided that the corporation would keep formal title until the tenant's debt was completely amortized. This would prevent alienation and give the corporation leverage for supervision to protect its loan.[26]

The bill was written by February 3, but needed a sponsor. Tannenbaum originally thought of calling on Senator Theodore G. Bilbo of Mississippi but discarded the idea. As early as mid-January, M. L. Wilson had begun to sound out Senator John Hollis Bankhead of Alabama, who was then asked to introduce the bill. Bankhead had played no part in conceiving the measure, but agreed to present it.[27]

wrote it. Harry Hopkins to McIntyre, January 17, 1935, in Official File 1650, Franklin D. Roosevelt Library, indicates that Hopkins saw Embree on January 18. All available evidence indicates that Alexander did not have a private appointment with Roosevelt to discuss tenancy until December, 1935, after he had become assistant administrator of the Resettlement Administration. See Alexander to Embree, December 5, 1935, in CIC Papers.

26   "Reminiscences of Will W. Alexander," 390; Tannenbaum to Alexander, Embree and Johnson, February 2, 1935, in Tannenbaum Papers; *Congressional Record*, 74th Cong., 1st Sess., 6121. The text of the bill appears in *To Create the Farm Tenant Homes Corporation, Hearings before a Subcommittee of the Committee on Agriculture and Forestry*, Senate, 74th Cong., 1st Sess., 1–5.

27   "Reminiscences of Will W. Alexander," 378–79; Tannenbaum to Alexander, Embree and Johnson, January 11, 1935, in Tannenbaum Papers; Alexander to Bliven, March 9, 1935, in CIC Papers; Rexford G. Tugwell Diary (Typescript in Rexford G. Tugwell

The bill's supporters knew that Bankhead's name was an important asset. The senator was an influential member of the Agriculture and Forestry Committee. Since the chairman of that committee, Ellison D. "Cotton Ed" Smith of South Carolina, was an ardent foe of the New Deal, the administration was accustomed to working with Bankhead on southern agricultural matters. Bankhead was intimately connected with price parity policies. He had sponsored the Cotton Control Act of 1934, which increased the effectiveness of the AAA cotton program by adding to it an element of compulsion. With Roosevelt's authorization in 1933 he had also introduced the legislation which established the subsistence homesteads division in the Interior Department.[28]

Although the Senator was fundamentally conservative (Will Alexander once referred to him as a Bourbon), he was committed to most New Deal policies. He had a reputation as an effective legislator when properly motivated. Alexander, who worked closely with him, thought he was pompous and vain. He later recalled that in promoting the bill he flattered the Alabamian and "massaged his ego" to encourage his efforts. At any rate, the bill met Bankhead's approval and when he introduced it on February 11, it "had become his idea."[29]

As he introduced the bill Bankhead had it referred to the Agriculture and Forestry Committee, and from there directly to a subcommittee headed by himself. On February 15 he spoke over radio from Washington, outlining the bill and stating that its intention was to check the increase of tenancy, open homeownership oppor-

Papers, Franklin D. Roosevelt Library), January 23, 1935. The first public disclosure that Bankhead would sponsor the bill appeared in Birmingham *News*, February 3, 1935.

28 Baldwin, *Poverty and Politics*, 132–33; John H. Bankhead to Harold Ickes, March 8, 1933, in Agricultural History Office, Economic Research Service, U.S. Department of Agriculture.

29 "Reminiscences of Will W. Alexander, 597–98. Baldwin, *Poverty and Politics*, 132, has a good description of Bankhead as "one of that breed of southern politicians in the 1930s who helped bridge the gap between the conservative agrarian ideals . . . of an age that was dying, and the new needs of a changing South" and who could "balance his allegiance to a conservative southern constituency [with] the liberal goals of the New Deal."

tunities to tenants, and lessen the waste of soil resources by retirement of submarginal lands. He added that establishment of farm communities was not contemplated.[30]

The bill's proponents were optimistic about its chances. Tannenbaum informed Charles S. Johnson that, although it lacked certain desirable features, it was "satisfactory" and "a good start." In the Agriculture Department M. L. Wilson became coordinator of efforts for the measure and L. C. Gray began arranging favorable testimony for congressional hearings, expected within a few weeks.[31]

During February, 1935, there were two incongruous developments in the Agriculture Department. On February 5 Jerome Frank and other liberals in the AAA legal division were fired in the dispute over sharecropper policy. But at the same time a tenancy bill had been prepared within the department and was about to be introduced in Congress by Bankhead. Thus while the AAA tried to rid itself of the tenancy issue and succeeded only in arousing more controversy, others in the department were developing legislation which they expected to contribute to the elimination of tenancy and poverty.

The Bankhead bill was not an administration measure at first. It was written and introduced without Roosevelt's direct knowledge; indeed he had avoided Peabody's and Alexander's attempt to familiarize him with their general program. At a press conference two days after the legislation's introduction the president was asked to comment on it. He declined, saying he had only read about it in the newspapers. Roosevelt's interest had been aroused, however. Within another day or two he had discussed the matter with Tugwell and by February 15 he had received copies of the bill and asked Hopkins and William I. Myers of the Farm Credit Administration (FCA) for their opinions of it.[32]

30 *Congressional Record*, 74th Cong., 1st Sess., 1782; typescript of radio speech by Bankhead, February 15, 1935, in CIC Papers.
31 Tannenbaum to Johnson, February 26, 1934 [1935], in Johnson Papers; L. C. Gray to Carl C. Taylor, March 2, 1935, in "Records of the Office of the Secretary of Agriculture," Record Group 16, National Archives.
32 Roosevelt Press Conferences, V, 106, in Franklin D. Roosevelt Library; Tugwell Diary, February 16, 1935; Roosevelt to Hopkins and William I. Myers, February 15, 1935, in Official File 444, Franklin D. Roosevelt Library.

Myers' response, written after consultation with Hopkins, was unfavorable. Desiring to forestall any new rural lending agency, he argued that the proposed corporation would duplicate the credit programs of both the FCA and FERA's rural rehabilitation, especially since Congress was considering liberalizing FCA lending rules. He also asserted that since most good lands in the South were already being worked by tenants, little acreage was available for relocating the landless. Probably with Hopkins' concurrence, Myers proposed instead to use funds from the pending Emergency Relief bill of 1935 to develop a coordinated program in which FERA's rural rehabilitation assisted a greatly increased number of clients, while a liberalized FCA financed the most able and risk-worthy tenants in farm ownership.[33]

The bill's supporters in the Agriculture Department firmly rejected loan procedures such as Myers advocated. Outlining administrative policies for M. L. Wilson, L. C. Gray stressed that because the aim was to promote the social and economic progress of the poor, the tenancy program should not be confined by customary banking methods which sanctioned loans only to good risks. He noted that the FCA sought legislation to permit it to lend up to 75 percent of the value of real estate on long terms at low interest. But a program no more liberal than that would help few southern tenants. On the other hand, more favorable extensions of credit could only be justified by requiring a "paternalistic" supervision of borrowers to protect the loans. Moreover, most southern tenants and sharecroppers were not competent to select and buy farms in the first place without considerable guidance. Therefore a federal agency should not merely lend them money, but should acquire and improve land and resell it on extended contracts which prohibited alienation by the buyer. Finally, to avoid overloading clients with credit and debt, Gray thought the value of land and improvements sold to a southern purchaser should not exceed $2,500.[34]

Gray's recommendations are a good example of the intention of the bill's framers to stretch its general language into the broad pro-

33   Myers to Roosevelt, March 1, 1935, in Official File 503, Franklin D. Roosevelt Library.
34   L. C. Gray to M. L. Wilson, February 18, 1935, in Tannenbaum Papers.

gram of credit and supervision that was later basic to the Farm Security Administration's program. But Gray also anticipated some later problems of the FSA's farm purchase operations. He recognized that in the effort to reach the destitute and dependent, political expediencies would probably compel the extension of aid to some farmers who were relatively well off. Gray also saw that the cost considerations would be politically important and suggested a gradual expansion of the program, from total loans of about $15 million in the first year to some $250 million by the third.[35]

Throughout early 1935 the committee tried to generate public support for the bill. Alexander, whose interracial work had given him access to liberal, business, and philanthropic circles in the South, began by contacting influential friends, such as Edgar Stern, a wealthy New Orleans cotton broker. Stern then secured the support of W. L. Clayton of Houston, one of the nation's largest cotton exporters. Alexander, meanwhile, talked with Peter Molyneaux, editor of an important farm journal, the *Texas Weekly*, and critic of crop restriction, who agreed to promote the bill among his readers.[36]

Whether by design or not, Alexander was drawing upon a major stream of opposition to the AAA in seeking support for the bill. Cotton brokers and allied editors like Molyneaux were interested in handling a large volume of cotton in international trade and had little concern for its price per pound. Therefore they opposed AAA crop restriction. These men were disposed to support the Bankhead bill, perhaps reasoning that if a small ownership policy resolved the tenancy crisis, large planters could end sharecropping altogether and mechanize their operations. The government could then end crop controls, and the planters, freed from furnishing responsibilities and fully mechanized, could plant unlimited acreages and still profit, even if prices dropped to 1932 levels. Meanwhile, the brokers and

---

35 *Ibid.* To hold down costs Gray proposed to lease some lands from landlords with a government guarantee of rent and supervision.
36 Alexander to Tannenbaum, two letters of February 18, 1935, in Tannenbaum Papers; Alexander to Johnson, February 18, 1935, Edgar Stern to Alexander, March 21, 1935, and Stern to W. L. Clayton, March 21, 1935, in CIC Papers.

exporters could, by handling larger amounts of cotton, recapture world markets, lost since American cotton prices had risen under the AAA.[37]

The bill's promoters did not overlook academicians and journalists in their search for support. Alexander enlisted Herman Clarence Nixon of Tulane University, who later became a major advocate of the measure, and approached Clarence Poe of Raleigh, North Carolina, editor of the *Progressive Farmer*, the South's most influential farm periodical. Other press support came from Jonathan Daniels of the Raleigh *News and Observer*, who editorialized that the new relative prosperity of agriculture made an "ugly irony" of tenant destitution. North Carolina desperately needed a bill, Daniels said, which, by "ending the procession toward peasantry in American agriculture [would] be a bargain at a billion dollars" and a major New Deal achievement.[38]

In advocating the measure the committee determined that race should not be discussed unnecessarily. Johnson's research had shown that although most southern blacks were desperately poor, tenancy was not exclusively or even predominantly a Negro problem. There were more than 1 million white tenant families in the cotton belt, compared to slightly less than 700,000 black tenant families. The committee had long since expanded its interest to include all the landless. Any public suggestion that the bill's chief purpose was to benefit Negroes could have repelled important supporters. Consequently, the committee resolved to stress landlessness as a serious economic problem and minimize race.

With this approach in mind, Tannenbaum suggested to Johnson that he ask the National Association for the Advancement of Colored People to contact influential northern friends in the measure's be-

---

37 For a later argument that the Bankhead small farm ownership plan *must* be coordinated with a revival of American exports, see Peter Molyneaux, "Displaced Tenants and World Trade," *Texas Weekly* (October 12, 1935), 4–7.

38 Alexander to Tannenbaum, two letters of February 18, 1935, in Tannenbaum Papers; Alexander to Johnson, February 18, 1935, in CIC Papers; Jonathan Daniels to R. B. Eleazer, March 22, 1935, and to George Foster Peabody, April 16, 1935, in Jonathan Daniels Papers, Southern Historical Collection, University of North Carolina, Chapel Hill; Raleigh *News and Observer*, March 10, 1935.

half. But he warned that this should be done discretely or not at all. When the executive director of the Federal Council of Churches criticized the bill for failing to include a specific ban on discrimination, Tannenbaum cautioned against direct mention of race. He considered nondiscrimination requirements ineffective anyway, he said, and preferred to rely on sympathetic administration of the program once the legislation was enacted. Tannenbaum also had little patience with open criticism of the bill by prominent blacks. He privately complained that recent comments by John P. Davis of the National Negro Congress, concerning lack of a nondiscrimination clause, were "uninformed if not in bad taste."[39]

In addition to influencing individuals, the supporters obtained endorsements for the bill from religious and reform organizations. The Federal Council of Churches publicly favored it, but otherwise gave little support. Tannenbaum, through acquaintances in the Catholic hierarchy, secured more vigorous aid from the National Catholic Welfare Conference. Not surprisingly, the Commission on Interracial Cooperation also officially urged passage of the measure.[40]

Alexander also hoped to receive the backing of organized labor. To George Googe, southeastern representative of the American Federation of Labor (AFL), and A. Steve Nance of the Atlanta Federation of Trades, he argued that tenancy legislation would benefit industrial workers by stabilizing the great reservoir of cheap rural labor which continually dragged down southern wage standards. This reasoning impressed the AFL national leadership and on April 15 William Green announced that the federation was in "hearty accord" with the bill. The endorsement was unprecedented since the

---

39 Tannenbaum to Johnson, March 6, 1935, in Johnson Papers; George E. Haynes to Tannenbaum, March 15, 1935, and Tannenbaum to Haynes, March 18, 1935, in Tannenbaum Papers.

40 "Reminiscences of Will W. Alexander," 388–89, 591–92; transcript of report by Will Alexander to the board of the interracial commission, April 16, 1936, and commission press release, April 26, 1935, in CIC Papers; Tannenbaum to Alexander and Embree, March 23, 1935, and Tannenbaum to Alexander, April 24, 1935, in Tannenbaum Papers; *Congressional Record*, 74th Cong., 1st Sess., 5755; Baldwin, *Poverty and Politics*, 148–49.

AFL had never taken a position on a measure not immediately affecting union labor.[41]

Even more essential for the bill's future than all the endorsements, however, was the neutrality of the American Farm Bureau Federation (AFBF). Alexander, then a novice in agricultural politics, quickly learned of the federation's power and of the apprehension in the Agriculture Department that it might oppose the bill. But in late March a relieved Tannenbaum reported that AFBF officials had agreed not to impede it. It is possible that this resulted from Tugwell's efforts. On March 14 the undersecretary had discussed with the president the "unexpected opposition" to the measure by leaders of farm organizations. He suggested that Roosevelt, as he saw those leaders about other matters, try to obtain their support for it. But although Roosevelt said he would do so, there is no conclusive evidence that he influenced the AFBF's position.[42]

The supporters adopted the common lobbying tactic of forming a front organization to endorse their aims. During March and April they organized the National Committee on Small Farm Ownership, which drew upon the bill's clerical support, southern educators and journalists, black leaders, organized labor, and national farm organizations. Under Peabody's nominal chairmanship the committee met in Washington on April 19, heard a speech by Bankhead, and endorsed the bill. It also published a pamphlet outlining the measure.[43]

41 Alexander to Embree, March 12, 1935, in CIC Papers; Alexander to Tannenbaum, March 12, 1935, Tannenbaum to Alexander, April 13, 1935, Charlton Ogburn to John H. Bankhead, April 9, 1935, in Tannenbaum Papers; New York *Times,* April 15, 1935, p. 6–L; Baldwin, *Poverty and Politics,* 149.

42 Alexander to Embree, March 12, 1935, in CIC Papers; Tannenbaum to Alexander and Embree, March 23, 1935, in Tannenbaum Papers; Tugwell Diary, March 14, 1935. Alexander later recalled that the AFBF could have blocked the legislation had it so desired. See "Reminiscences of Will W. Alexander," 586–87.

43 Alexander to Tannenbaum, two letters of April 9, 1935, and statement and membership list of National Committee on Small Farm Ownership, April 19, 1935, in Tannenbaum Papers; *Farm Tenancy –the Remedy: Twenty Questions Asked and Answered* (Washington: National Committee on Small Farm Ownership, n.d.). Committee members included the Reverend John A. Ryan of the National Catholic Welfare Conference, Dr. Ivan Lee Holt of the Federal Council of Churches, Edgar Stern, Howard Odum, W. E. B. DuBois, President Robert R. Moton of Tuskegee Institute, publisher Clark

While the bill was being developed, its original backers had not lost sight of the need for a report on the AAA's effects on tenants. Tannenbaum, who was supposed to produce it, lost interest in writing as he became confident of the bill's passage. Charles S. Johnson then assumed the task. Meanwhile, on March 21, Alexander had the preliminary findings released with much press coverage. By mid-April Johnson finished a draft of the whole report. Embree and Alexander edited it, and the result was a thin volume, *The Collapse of Cotton Tenancy*.[44] This concise summary of Johnson's field studies of 1934 and other investigations of southern rural life was factual and moderate in tone but firmly indicted the AAA. In the fall of 1935 it was published by the University of North Carolina Press and is still recognized as the best brief survey of the tenancy crisis of the 1930s.

Senator Bankhead wasted no time starting the bill toward the Senate floor. He scheduled hearings for March 5, sooner than its supporters had expected, leaving them no opportunity to call favorable witnesses from throughout the South.[45] But in the hearings Wallace and Gray spoke for the Agriculture Department. Both endorsed the bill, observing that tenancy was a problem of staggering magnitude. Gray offered his opinion that the bill would be effective nevertheless, because it was aimed primarily at those regions where tenancy was most severe—a clear indication of its southern orientation.[46]

Both Wallace and Gray presented the same analysis of the causes of poverty in the rural South. They stated that it resulted from the de-

---

Howell of the Atlanta *Constitution,* farm editors Clarence Poe and B. Kirk Rankin, William Green and counsel Charlton Ogburn of the AFL, Birmingham industrialist Donald Comer, M. W. Thatcher of the Farmers' Union and the Grange's Louis Taber.

44 "Reminiscences of Will W. Alexander," 391–92; Embree to Beazell, February 4 and 15, 1935, Beazell to Embree, February 12, 1935, "Forward and Conclusion of a Study of Agricultural, Economic and Social Conditions in the South," press release, March 21, 1935, in CIC Papers.

45 Tannenbaum to Johnson, March 6, 1935, in Johnson Papers.

46 Unless otherwise cited, discussion of the hearings is taken from *To Create the Farm Tenant Homes Corporation, Hearings Before a Subcommittee of the Committee on Agriculture and Forestry,* Senate, 74th Cong., 1st Sess. Wallace's testimony appears on pp. 5–14, and Gray's on pp. 14–28. Although Wallace's endorsement gave the bill some New Deal support, it still lacked the president's open acknowledgment and thus could not be considered an administration measure.

terioration of the tenancy and credit system since the World War. This decline had had multiple causes. For one thing, cotton production was steadily becoming mechanized as more tractors were introduced into the Southwest and the alluvial plains. Meanwhile, the Southeast had special problems. It suffered from the competition of fertile trans-Mississippi areas which grew cotton at minimum cost. Soil exhaustion, erosion, and depletion of timber resources were additional hardships in the eastern cotton belt. In addition, Wallace emphasized that the unfavorable price situation since World War I had impaired the ability of landowners and supply merchants to continue furnishing tenants. Finally, some southern rural laborers had been attracted to industrial centers before 1929, only to come streaming back to the country as unemployment increased, adding themselves to the rural labor surplus.

All these conditions, the officials stressed, meant that displacement of tenants was already a severe problem when the New Deal began. Both Gray and the secretary admitted that crop controls had made the situation worse. But they maintained that the presence of federal relief had also undermined furnishing by encouraging landlords to dump their workers on the public rolls during slack seasons. Gray went so far as to assert that relief had regrettably become an integral part of the cotton belt's labor system. But even though crop restriction and relief aggravated the general situation, neither the AAA nor any relief program, in their opinion, could come to grips with the breakdown of tenancy. Indeed, Gray noted, despite attempted safeguards, the more favorable the cotton contract was for tenants, the more inducement there was for landlords to displace them and avoid dividing benefit payments.

The solution, then, was the policy of the Bankhead bill, which Wallace expected to reverse the unfavorable trends and start large numbers of farmers toward ownership. For maximum effectiveness, he thought, the program should include guidance in land selection and management advice for clients. Special care should be taken to ensure that the tenants' new farms would be sufficient to provide them with adequate cash incomes.

A careful reading of Wallace's and Gray's testimony reveals the reasons they supported the bill. Wallace, obviously referring to the Southern Tenant Farmers' Union, remarked that current conditions in the South provided a fertile field for "socialist and communist agitation," which he deplored. The remedy for this, however, was not suppression of radicalism, but ownership opportunities for the dispossessed.

Secondly, the legislation was based to a certain extent on observations of successful foreign land reforms. The original bill's statement of purpose referred to creating a "democratic system of land tenure" in "accordance with the example of many other civilized countries." Tannenbaum used his knowledge of Mexican land redistribution in shaping the bill. More importantly, the authors of the bill had been interested in the landownership programs of Europe, especially those in Ireland and Denmark, where tenancy had been virtually eliminated since the late nineteenth century.[47] In the hearings Wallace traced his approval of these foreign programs to 1912, when he had been part of a congressionally sponsored delegation which traveled to Europe to study systems of land tenure, rural credit and cooperative enterprise. Other American farm leaders had also been members of the delegation and the tour left a significant impression upon their generation of agriculturalists. Many of them, like Wallace and Clarence Poe, approved the Bankhead bill partly because they saw in it an American version of those European programs they admired. They also regarded it as an extension to poorer farmers of benefits like those of the most significant outgrowth of the European journey, the Rural Credits Act of 1916, which had established the federal land bank system but which had aided mainly the more affluent producers.[48]

If the bill drew upon foreign precedents, it was even more consistent with the American family farm tradition. Wallace praised the wisdom of the nineteenth-century homestead policy, but regretted that it had lacked safeguards to preserve the farmer's hold on his land and prevent the rise of tenancy. He thought the Bankhead bill

47   Wilson to A. R. Mann, April 12, 1935, in RG 16, NA.
48   *To Create the Farm Tenant Homes Corporation, Hearings Before a Subcommittee of the Committee on Agriculture and Forestry,* Senate, 74th Cong., 1st Sess., 73–75.

would restore this sound traditional policy of family farming, but with the necessary protections. As a midwesterner, Wallace tended to see tenancy resulting from the loss of farms by small owners, rather than in southern terms as a dependent condition in which masses of poor people had always found themselves. Gray observed that other nations had dealt with tenancy by one of three methods: accepting it and working for maximum security for tenants, reducing or eliminating it by promoting small ownership, or state tenancy as in the Soviet Union. He noted approvingly that the Bankhead bill was clearly an example of the second alternative, the one most in accord with American ideals.

Probably the most important reason that Wallace and Gray found to support the bill was that it was not contrary to their main agricultural policy. Among its stated aims was "contributing to agricultural adjustment."[49] Wallace declared that it would start an evolutionary trend toward ownership, and at the same time complement the AAA and aid national recovery. In other words, the bill promised an ultimate solution to intolerable rural poverty, which the AAA had admittedly aggravated, but would demand no changes in the parity policies to which the whole administration was committed. Its great virtue was that it offered a plausible plan for the relief of poverty without directly implying criticism of the New Deal or the Department of Agriculture. For this reason it was not coincidental that some of the most ardent advocates of the bill, notably Bankhead himself, were also staunch supporters of the general administration farm policy.

Finally, Gray suggested that prompt action on the bill was desirable because the time was ripe for it. The year 1935 was an opportune moment for poor men to buy farm homes because, he said, land prices were still at low depression levels, whereas crop prices, upon which the earning power of the land was based, were increasing.

Bankhead's subcommittee heard more favorable testimony from Lawrence Westbrook, editor B. Kirk Rankin of the *Southern Agriculturalist* of Nashville, rural sociologist C. Horace Hamilton, Carl

49 *Ibid.*, 1. Text of the bill.

C. Taylor, southeastern director of the AAA land policy section, and Hugh MacRae, the North Carolina promoter of farm colony schemes and crop diversification. Clarence Poe endorsed the bill by letter. The subcommittee received this evidence and then adjourned, having met for only one day.[50] Later, March 13–17 and April 16, the House Agriculture Committee conducted brief hearings on a companion bill sponsored by its chairman, Marvin Jones of Texas.[51]

Shortly after the hearings the president's influence was felt for the first time in these matters. Sometime just before March 22, Bankhead, Jones, and Hopkins met with Roosevelt to discuss differences between the Senate and House versions of the bill and the relief administrator's views on tenancy policy. There may have been considerable discord in the meeting. Hopkins' presence suggests that one disagreement may have been over which agency should administer a new tenancy program. Hopkins may have argued that the credit should be extended through the FERA rural rehabilitation program. Whatever the dissensions, Roosevelt was noncommittal. He merely requested the three to meet privately and compose their differences. Accordingly they reached a compromise and Bankhead rewrote the bill.[52]

On March 26 Bankhead introduced his revised measure. There had been two substantive changes. In the original bill the secretary of agriculture could appoint and remove the directors of the land-buying corporation and conduct all its operations. In the new version it would be completely independent of the Agriculture Department and run by a board of three presidential appointees, with the secretary of agriculture and governor of the FCA serving ex officio. The other difference was in the corporation's initial financing, necessary before it could begin issuing bonds. The old bill provided for a

50   *Ibid.*, testimony of Westbrook, 41–48, Rankin, 33–37, Hamilton, 37–41, MacRae, 48–67, Taylor, 67–71, and Poe, 73–75.
51   The House committee published no proceedings. Excerpts from the testimony appear in the appendix of *Farm Tenancy, Hearings Before the Committee on Agriculture, House of Representatives*, 75th Cong., 1st Sess., 323–362.
52   Charles B. Crow to Hugh MacRae, March 28, 1935, in Herman Clarence Nixon Papers, in possession of the Nixon family, Nashville; Tannenbaum to Alexander and Embree, March 23, 1935, in Tannenbaum Papers. These letters suggest that others attended, but that Tannenbaum, Wilson, and Tugwell were not present.

capital stock of up to $100 million drawn from the funds of the Reconstruction Finance Corporation. The new bill allowed the president, *at his discretion*, to transfer $50 million from the 1935 relief appropriation to vitalize the corporation.[53]

Tannenbaum, Tugwell, and M. L. Wilson thought these changes were unsatisfactory. But they decided to continue pushing the bill and work for restoration of its old form later. They were concerned that the revised measure might give control of the tenancy program to the FERA, which they considered inadequate for fundamental land redistribution. Tannenbaum wrote Alexander that due to the recent changes Colonel Westbrook might "steal the show."[54] Indeed, the compromise among Bankhead, Jones, and Hopkins, by removing the corporation from Agriculture Department control and making its initial financing dependent upon Roosevelt's discretionary use of relief funds, left the door ajar for possible administration of tenancy matters by the FERA. These concerns were further increased by the fact that in early 1935 federal relief policies were being completely renovated.

In January, 1935, Roosevelt had proposed the Emergency Relief bill and asked Congress for $4.8 billion, the largest peacetime appropriation in American history to that time. The pending measure would give the president broad discretion to allot and spend the money. Under these circumstances it was not surprising that all agencies concerned in any way with relief or economic recovery developed claims on the anticipated revenues and sought to prevail upon Roosevelt to channel money to their programs. The best example of this was the rivalry between Hopkins and Harold Ickes of the Public Works Administration for the lion's share of the appropriation.[55]

This unprecedented spending bill was actually part of Hopkin's plan for general reorganization of federal relief. He proposed to re-

53 *Congressional Record*, 74th Cong., 1st Sess., 4418. For Bankhead's analysis of the changes see 5748–59.
54 Tannenbaum to Alexander and Embree, March 23, 1935, in Tannenbaum Papers.
55 William E. Leuchtenburg, *Franklin D. Roosevelt and the New Deal* (New York: Harper and Row, 1963), 124–25.

turn to the states responsibility for care of unemployables—those who needed public assistance even in normal times—while the federal government enrolled those who were jobless because of the depression in a new national work relief program. The third element in Hopkins' plan was rural rehabilitation, which many in the FERA thought should help clients acquire land. If no changes were made, that program would continue as part of FERA or a successor agency and receive an allocation from the relief appropriation.[56]

On February 18, 1935, during debate on the relief bill, the Senate approved an amendment by Richard Russell of Georgia which permitted lending of funds from the appropriation to tenants, croppers, and laborers for purchase of land and farm equipment. Russell said the intent was to promote home ownership for the landless and to reach those not then eligible for FCA credit. The Russell amendment allowed the president to determine how much, if any, relief money should be used in this manner, to prescribe the terms of loans, and to designate which agency should make them.[57] This was recognized in subsequent debate on the Bankhead bill which, as revised, permitted the president to transfer $50 million from relief funds, consistent with the Russell amendment, to the proposed Farm Tenant Homes Corporation to initiate its program. But, as Bankhead admitted, the president would not be compelled to make the transfer and vitalize the corporation. Thus, Roosevelt would have complete flexibility under both the relief act and the Bankhead bill, to use part of the relief appropriation for tenant purchase loans by assigning the money to the FCA or the Farm Tenant Homes Corporation, or by leaving it with the FERA.[58]

Not only was federal relief being reordered in the spring of 1935, but a new administration related to agriculture was being formed. In part this development was due to Tugwell's dissatisfaction with the Agriculture Department and his dwindling influence within it. Tugwell's general complaint against the department was that it did

---

56   Typescript of Hopkins' press conference, December 27, 1934, in Official File 444, Franklin D. Roosevelt Library.
57   *Congressional Record*, 74th Cong., 1st Sess., 2099–2104.
58   *Ibid.*, 5750–51.

too little about poor land and needy people, which he regarded as two aspects of the same problem. Alexander recalled that the undersecretary perceived the basic American agricultural problem as haphazard and unscientific use of land. He was convinced that most of the rural poor were in their deplorable condition because they were located on marginal lands, trying to scratch livings from acreages never suited to farming in the first place. Later he stressed to Roosevelt, "It is poor land which makes poor people, usually." Tugwell had accepted production control as an emergency measure to reduce surpluses. But the permanent answer to farm problems was better land use under government planning and relocation of those on submarginal acres.[59]

The AAA purge was a turning point for Tugwell. The undersecretary, who had been antagonistic to Chester Davis and sympathetic to Jerome Frank on numerous issues, was in Florida when the AAA liberals were fired and was not consulted about the matter. Convinced that Secretary Wallace was excluding him from agricultural policy making and listening instead to Davis, Tugwell's "first impulse was to resign at once." But after talking with the president on February 13 he agreed not to leave the administration. Roosevelt, however, did not insist that Tugwell stay in the Agriculture Department if he regarded the situation as intolerable, and agreed to consider his request for new responsibilities, possibly including direction of a land-use planning program funded by the pending relief bill. On February 18 the president asked Tugwell to consider heading a new agency.[60]

Although the scope of the projected agency was still undefined in March, 1935, Roosevelt and Tugwell intended to consolidate such new or existing activities as housing programs (at first urban as well

59 Bernard Sternsher, *Rexford Tugwell and the New Deal* (New Brunswick: Rutgers University Press, 1964), 262–64; "Reminiscences of Will W. Alexander," 384–86, 432; Baldwin, *Poverty and Politics*, 87–88, 104–105. The quotation is from Rexford G. Tugwell to Franklin D. Roosevelt [November, 1936], in President's Secretary's File, Agriculture: Tugwell, Franklin D. Roosevelt Library. For examples of Tugwell's views on the possibilities of a more effective production control through government direction of land use, see Tugwell Diary, December 6, 10 and 13, 1934.

60 Tugwell Diary, February 10, 13, 16, and 19, 1935; Sternsher, *Tugwell*, 264.

as rural), suburban resettlement, submarginal land retirement, and farmer relocation. With the exception of urban housing, which was soon deleted, these were the programs Tugwell was most eager to manage. He had no compelling interest in rural rehabilitation as conducted by the FERA, and of all the components which would soon make up his Resettlement Administration he wanted experimental farm communities least. Likewise he had no particular desire to direct lending for tenant land purchases. Although Tugwell generally supported the proposal for small ownership loans, Alexander remembered that, concerning his and Tannenbaum's efforts for the Bankhead bill, the undersecretary "thought we were a lot of amateurs who would pretty well mix things up.... He never thought much of what we were doing."[61]

Rural rehabilitation, the FERA communities, and the small ownership ideas of the Bankhead bill were, however, unavoidably related to the core of Tugwell's concerns. Coordination of all these programs would be necessary. Removal of submarginal land from cultivation, for instance, raised the problem of resettling the people either in new communities or on more fertile small farms. Federal encouragement of scientific land use obviously could not progress far in the South's soil-mining, land-ruining tenancy system. And if Tugwell believed that poor land produced poor people, some rehabilitative process seemed an appropriate part of land-use planning. At the same time, massive programs of rural rehabilitation or sale of farms to tenants could, if not coordinated with the new agency, actually interfere with federal guidance of land use. Furthermore, in their first conversation on the Bankhead legislation, Roosevelt had pointed out to Tugwell the probable relationship of the bill to FERA's rural rehabilitation.[62]

Over a period of several weeks in March and April, 1935, Tugwell gradually concluded that the new administration would have to be more inclusive than he had originally planned. Lending for ten-

---

61 Tugwell Diary, February 16, 19, and 24 and March 3, 1935; Sternsher, *Tugwell*, 264–65; "Reminiscences of Will W. Alexander," 387.
62 Indeed, Roosevelt seems to have been the first to grasp the important connection between the two programs. See Tugwell Diary, February 16, 1935.

ants' purchases and perhaps even FERA's rural rehabilitation might have to be attached to the new agency. As Alexander remembered it, the undersecretary began to see the Bankhead bill, particularly, as another approach to what he wanted to do. Accordingly, Alexander thought, Tugwell determined to "take us into camp" in order to get everything "under one tent."[63]

Nevertheless, Tugwell was still reluctant to assume responsibility for tenancy programs unless he could find a subordinate to take charge of them. In late March, after some preliminary searching, he turned to Alexander, telephoning him in Atlanta. Alexander was taken by surprise but agreed "at Tugwell's earnest request" to come to Washington and discuss the matter. In Washington Tugwell asked him to oversee tenancy and related affairs for the projected agency, but not even the undersecretary was precisely sure what would be included in the program.[64]

Apparently Tugwell and Alexander discussed the possibilities of financing a tenancy program with relief funds. Tugwell was aware that the Russell amendment to the relief bill would permit the transfer of money for tenant purchase lending to his new administration as well as to any other, provided he could persuade Roosevelt to make the change. After lengthy discussion, however, Alexander concluded that such prospects were too indefinite to warrant his final commitment to Tugwell. But he agreed to discuss the undersecretary's proposal later, preferably after the presently expected passage of the relief bill. Alexander then returned to Atlanta.[65]

Having failed initially to enlist Alexander, Tugwell sought to reach him through Tannenbaum. He told Tannenbaum he wanted Alexander to conduct a tenancy program under him and that, while Tugwell would "be the boss," Alexander would have policy-making power to the extent that he could influence his superior. Tannenbaum wrote to Alexander that, although the decision was his, "that

63 "Reminiscences of Will W. Alexander," 387, 396–98.
64 Tugwell Diary, March 3, 14, and 31, 1935; Alexander to Embree, April 1, 1935, in CIC Papers; interview with Arthur F. Raper, December 27, 1969. Raper was in Alexander's office when Tugwell called.
65 Alexander to Embree, April 1, 1935, in CIC Papers.

you must not forego an opportunity to influence the tenancy program through a direct inside pressure seems to me perfectly clear."
Furthermore, Tannenbaum advised, "Working with Tugwell you
would probably find yourself having influence on a great many
things that are close to your heart, and I should certainly want to see
you give it a try, as occasions of this sort to influence major national
policy directly don't come every day to people like you, who have
fought for the underdog most of their lives."[66] Alexander, soon to
make his decision, was undoubtedly moved by such encouragement.

Tugwell had always given general support to the Bankhead bill,
particularly since he anticipated that its program could be liberally
administered to transcend mere lending and become a lever for
land-use reform.[67] On the other hand, as his approach to Alexander
shows, he had become convinced that tenant purchase credit should
be coordinated with his new RA and possibly be made part of it.
Therefore Tugwell disapproved of certain features of the legislation;
he thought the proposed Farm Tenant Homes Corporation with its
independent administrative board would hinder the general oversight he envisioned for the RA.[68] For this reason Tugwell may not
have been pushing the Bankhead bill with full vigor. Aware that
relief funds might be channeled to his agency, he had assured Tannenbaum that even if the measure failed, a considerable number of
tenant purchase loans might still be made under his auspices.[69]

As Congress passed the relief bill on April 6 and the Senate
began debate on the Bankhead measure on April 16, there was considerable confusion about the location of responsibility for programs
affecting the South's rural poor. Uncertainty revolved about the administration of loans to tenant purchasers. The Bankhead bill proposed a corporation but left the initiation of its efforts to the president, who could decide whether to assign relief funds to it. By

66 Tannenbaum to Alexander, April 4, 1935, in Tannenbaum Papers.
67 Tugwell Diary, January 23 and February 16, 1935.
68 For a slightly later expression of Tugwell's disapproval see *ibid.*, May 7, 1935.
69 Tannenbaum to Alexander, April 4, 1935, in Tannenbaum Papers. Tugwell probably
    stretched this point. Any farm purchase program conducted under his RA would be
    limited by the amount of money he could obtain from the relief appropriation—and
    there were already many claims on those funds. A billion-dollar bond program under
    the Bankhead bill would undoubtedly have been larger in the long run.

another choice Roosevelt could allow Westbrook to lend through the FERA. And Tugwell, as mentioned, may have preferred to tap the relief appropriation to carry out a credit program under the RA, rather than enact the Bankhead bill.

There was similar confusion about rural rehabilitation. That activity could remain under the FERA, perhaps with expanded financing under the new relief appropriation, or it could be transferred to the contemplated RA. By late April Hopkins and Tugwell had generally agreed that FERA's experimental farm communities, at least, should be attached to the new agency. But they were undecided about the rest of the rehabilitation program, having received no indication of the president's wishes on the matter.[70]

The probable inclusion of rehabilitation in the RA increased the value of Alexander's services to Tugwell. It is not certain that Tugwell and Alexander discussed rehabilitation in their March conference. But Alexander was, by that time, an advocate of the concept. This had not always been his position. As late as January, 1935, he had criticized the FERA program for caring only for those on relief while ignoring dispossessed tenants not on the public rolls. He also thought the relief administration was "temporizing" because it usually arranged for its clients to rent land, rather than encouraging small-farm ownership. Furthermore, Alexander had long thought that the routine procedures of relief were shot through with racial discrimination. Because of these shortcomings he had dismissed FERA's efforts as inadequate.[71]

But Alexander had recently been converted to the rehabilitation idea. In February he informed Tannenbaum that he had become a member of the board of directors of the Georgia rural rehabilitation corporation. Through this involvement he had observed the program and concluded that, despite its shortcomings, much could be accomplished through its methods.[72] Significantly, Alexander was beginning to see rural rehabilitation and promotion of small owner-

70 Tugwell Diary, April 27, 1935.
71 *Ibid.*, April 29 and May 2, 1935; Alexander to Embree, January 8, 1935, to James H. Dillard, May 18, 1933, and to Clark Foreman, January 16, 1934, in CIC Papers.
72 Alexander to Tannenbaum, February 18, 1935, in Tannenbaum Papers; "Reminiscences of Will W. Alexander," 398, 653–54.

ship as complementary policies.

On April 24, 1935, Roosevelt announced that several existing programs would be consolidated into a Resettlement Administration, separate from the Agriculture Department and headed by Tugwell. The RA would relocate people affected by retirement of submarginal lands and would have charge of several types of rural and suburban planned communities, as well as the land-planning undertakings which had been Tugwell's original concern. The president stated that no decision had been reached as to whether rural rehabilitation would be included or remain with the FERA, but he regarded that problem as a "very small thing" which could be adjusted later.[73]

Since the full dimensions of the RA were still undefined, Tugwell redoubled his efforts to persuade Alexander to administer a tenancy program under his auspices. On the day after the president's announcement Tannenbaum wrote to Alexander of his latest discussion with the undersecretary:

I have just talked to Tugwell, and I said to him, "Tugwell, are you going to get all rural rehabilitation or just [FERA] communities? For mercy's sake don't take the communities alone." To which he replied, "If I took the whole thing, will Alexander come up and help? That is one thing that is bothering me." I said, "Yes, if you take the whole thing, Alexander will have to come up and help . . . ." He said, "Well, I am glad to know that. I will let you know."[74]

Thus assurance of Alexander's commitment would overcome Tugwell's last reservations about rural rehabilitation and help determine the scope of the RA. As Alexander later remembered it, he became

73   Roosevelt Press Conferences, V, 235–36, in Franklin D. Roosevelt Library. The consolidated agencies included the USDA Land Planning Division, AAA Land Policy Section, all land planning functions of the National Resources Board, the Interior Department's Subsistence Homesteads Division, and the FCA's farm debt adjustment program. For a secondary account see Baldwin, *Poverty and Politics*, 92–93.
74   Tannenbaum to Alexander, April 25, 1935, in Tannenbaum Papers. Just after this conversation Tugwell noted privately that he had concluded "some time ago" that the only satisfactory course, even though he might "prefer . . . it another way," would be to "take over the whole business." Nevertheless, "this whole problem still remains to be settled," partly because of uncertainty about the president's wishes. See Tugwell Diary, April 27, 1935.

assistant administrator because it seemed the best way to "get Rex interested in the rehabilitation program. . . . I thought it was awfully sound . . . . I wanted to help save that if I could."[75]

The final decision on rural rehabilitation was made soon after Tugwell's conversation with Tannenbaum. On April 29 Roosevelt and Tugwell agreed that the whole program should be attached to the RA.[76] On April 27 Roosevelt created by executive order the Works Progress Administration, the work relief agency which replaced the FERA. Four days later, on May 1, he established the RA by another proclamation. The new organization included all of rural rehabilitation except for a few FERA communities transferred to the WPA.[77]

On May 2 Tugwell conferred again with Alexander, and by the middle of May Alexander was back in Washington committed to working with the RA. For several weeks he acted informally as assistant administrator before officially taking the position, and devoted half his time to lobbying for the Bankhead bill. Alexander and Tugwell were still uncertain about what could be done to buy land and resell it to tenants through the RA using relief money. Under these circumstances they planned land purchase and tenant-lending activities within the RA as they continued to work for the Bankhead measure.[78]

Just after his arrival in Washington Alexander reported to Embree and Johnson that despite setbacks in the Senate he and Tugwell thought the Bankhead bill's prospects were good, and besides, the president was understood to be sympathetic. With the establishment of his RA, Tugwell's own commitment to the legislation appeared to increase, prompting Tannenbaum to comment to Alexander that "we can count on Tugwell's straight support for this measure after this." But the undersecretary's support was actually conditional. He

75 "Reminiscences of Will W. Alexander," 653.
76 Tugwell Diary, April 29, 1935.
77 New York *Times*, April 27, 1935, p. 1, and May 2, 1935, p. 8.
78 Alexander to Embree and Johnson, May 27, 1935, in CIC Papers; Tugwell Diary, May 2, 5, and 19, 1935. Until early May, Tugwell had tried to enlist Lawrence Westbrook as director of rural rehabilitation under Assistant Administrator Alexander. But Hopkins retained Westbrook to manage several rural communities which were kept in the WPA.

still had reservations concerning the independent board of the proposed Farm Tenant Homes Corporation. He advised Senator Bankhead that he preferred to have the bill amended to place the tenant purchase program exclusively under the RA.[79]

More important than these jurisdictional problems, however, was the emergence of a concept within the RA that its functions, including rural rehabilitation, could be combined with the small ownership aims of the Bankhead bill in a concerted attack on rural poverty. During the spring Tugwell, whatever his reservations about the legislation, had recognized the desirability of coordinating it with his agency. At the time of the formation of the RA Tannenbaum had remarked to Tugwell that if in addition "we get the bill through . . . we will have a swell instrument," and Tugwell had agreed. And as Alexander began work in Washington he intended to help manage the new administration in such a way as to "lay foundations for the program contemplated under the Bankhead bill."[80]

When the RA acquired rural rehabilitation from the FERA it moved directly and deeply into the problem of rural poverty. This is at least evident in retrospect since rehabilitation became the RA's largest single operation. At the same time, as Tugwell secured the services of Alexander, a major proponent of the Bankhead legislation, there occurred a coalescence of the small ownership objective and the rehabilitation idea. The close association of those two policies would be perfected during the summer and fall of 1935 and from that juncture would emerge the basis of the Farm Security Administration (FSA) of 1937. Thus the general outlines of the FSA were present in the minds of the RA's administrators in the spring of 1935.

Enacting the Bankhead legislation, however, was the obvious step yet to be taken. And in the meantime the bill had encountered heavy attack in the Senate.

79 Alexander to Embree and Johnson, May 6 and 27, 1935, inCIC Papers; Tannenbaum to Alexander, April 26, 1935, in Tannenbaum Papers; Tugwell Diary, May 7, 1935.
80 Tugwell Diary, April 29, 1935; Tannenbaum to Alexander, April 25, 1935, in Tannenbaum Papers; Alexander to Embree and Johnson, May 27, 1935, in CIC Papers.

CHAPTER VI

The Bankhead Bill
in the Senate, 1935

T HE BANKHEAD tenancy bill was introduced in the Senate on February 11, 1935, and brief hearings were held on March 5. Then, because of differing opinions concerning the administration of its tenant purchase loan program, the measure was redrafted, with the encouragement but not the supervision of the president. The new version was introduced on March 26 and referred to the Agriculture and Forestry Committee, which reported it favorably on April 11. On April 16 the majority leader, Joseph T. Robinson of Arkansas, brought the bill to the floor for debate.

The revised legislation provided for an independent farmers' home corporation with an executive board of three presidential appointees, and the secretary of agriculture and the governor of the Farm Credit Administration as ex officio members. The president could, at his discretion, vitalize the agency by providing $50 million of initial capital from the 1935 relief appropriation. Once in operation, the corporation could issue $1 billion worth of federally guaranteed bonds and use the proceeds to buy land, farm equipment, and livestock for resale to tenants, sharecroppers, and laborers on liberal credit terms.

The debate which began April 16 lasted only until the twenty-fourth, when the bill was temporarily returned to committee. Discussion did not resume until June 21, but the Senate passed the legislation three days later. During the three months of intermittent debate Bankhead and Robinson were the chief advocates of the bill, with substantial help at times from Senators Robert LaFollette of Wisconsin, George Norris of Nebraska, and Hugo Black of Alabama. Their interpretations of the legislation, scattered through the *Congressional Record*, reveal their perception of poverty and their ideas of what should be done about it.

Bankhead and Robinson, partly because of their own inclinations, but also to win support from conservative colleagues, stressed the proposal's moderation. Bankhead emphasized that it did not propose directly to spend $1 billion, but would establish a self-liquidating credit program in which nearly all the money loaned would be recoverable. Furthermore, the extension of aid would be selective. LaFollette observed that the bill not only provided for present tenants, but also for those who had lost their places on the land and were unable to make even sharecropping arrangements. Bankhead agreed, but reiterated that priority would be assigned to those who were, or recently had been, tenants, croppers, or laborers, and that preferred applicants would have to have families, "good character," and farming experience. The intention was to aid those "who have had that sort of experience which would lead us to believe they are more likely to be able to retain ownership." In other words, credit was meant for those who were relatively good risks.

Early in the debate Bankhead underscored the assumption that encouragement of small ownership was an adequate remedy for much of the nation's poverty. When one critic envisioned the corporation accumulating property and creating a "vast federal overlordship" of land resources, Bankhead assured him that the goal was widespread private landholding. "What we need is more individual home ownership," he declared. "We have 6,500,000 farmers in the United States, nearly half of them drifting from year to year, hunting a place to roost . . . at the end of the year. Farm ownership is what we need. . . . That is my philosophy. . . . I have looked upon this . . . as a program in favor of the under dog in agriculture." To Bankhead and those of like mind, credit for purchase of land and equipment was the major means of rehabilitating the poor.[1]

The original language permitted the corporation to "sell or lease" properties it acquired. So strong was the emphasis on private ownership, however, that Bankhead, at Robinson's urging, agreed to delete the word "lease." The majority leader apprehended that the bill might "put the government into the landlord business," and that some "wild-eyed person who might get on the board [would] influence the corporation to embark upon a practice of leasing out lands to tenants and sharecroppers," all of which he thought inconsistent with the aim of ending tenancy through promoting small farm ownership. With the concurrence of Bankhead, Robinson, and Norris, the measure was later amended to restrict leasing of land.[2]

The proponents moved quickly to quash any notion that they contemplated land redistribution through confiscation. When Senator William E. Borah of Idaho inquired whether the corporation would acquire property through eminent domain, Bankhead stressed that land would be obtained only through voluntary sale and accepted an amendment to clarify the point. Similarly, Bankhead and Robinson, in order to distinguish the bill from the Resettlement Administration program then being established, stated that there was no thought of a "general shifting of populations" in the process of settling tenants on new lands of their own. Wherever possible the corporation would sell to those already working as tenants.[3]

Finally, the two advocates reassured supporters of price parity policies that the proposed program would comport with the AAA. Without mentioning any contemplated supervision of tenant purchasers, they indicated that the corporation would prevent its clients from expanding the production of controlled commodities.[4]

Perhaps Robinson best expressed the bill's fundamental conser-

1 *Congressional Record,* 74th Cong., 1st Sess., 5751, 5754.
2 *Ibid.,* 5758–59, 5762.
3 *Ibid.,* 5751–52.
4 *Ibid.,* 5752.

vatism in a remark on June 22, just before its passage by the Senate. Responding to the fears of Senator Thomas P. Gore of Oklahoma that the measure threatened destruction of the South's existing land tenure system, the majority leader stated that he hoped the measure would indeed destroy some of the features of southern tenancy. But he added: "I do not expect revolutionary results from this bill. . . . I think there are some who have an erroneous opinion as to what may be expected . . . who think it is contemplated that all persons who are not owners of homes shall be afforded an opportunity to acquire farm homes. Manifestly, that is . . . impracticable . . . . The object . . . is to afford a process of selection under which those who are believed to possess the capacity . . . to build and maintain homes may have an opportunity of doing so."[5]

Although providing landownership opportunities for a large number of the most able tenants was a limited goal, the bill was, within the bounds of that purpose, broadly drawn. At the same time that the measure's advocates stressed its moderation, they also called attention to the potential breadth and flexibility of its coverage. They maintained that their tenancy program would be national in scope, by no means useful for the cotton belt alone, but also applicable in the West, the North Central states and the Plains region.[6] When Huey Long questioned whether the legislation could reach significant numbers of the poor, Bankhead estimated that, although the program would develop gradually, it could ultimately aid approximately 500,000 families with average loans of $2,000.[7]

Answering suggestions that currently operating programs could meet the credit needs of landless farmers, the proponents pointed out that the new corporation's lending policies were intended to be broader, and in fact fundamentally different, from those of the Farm Credit Administration, the most liberal of existing agencies. Robinson stressed that the FCA lent only to those who had title to farms,

5 *Ibid.*, 9917.
6 *Ibid.*, 5752. Despite statements of this type, there was a sort of underlying assumption that the bill's orientation was toward the South. Most of the examples which proponents and opponents used in their discussion of how the program might work were taken from the southern tenancy system.
7 *Ibid.*, 6135.

thus excluding tenants from its benefits. It was also legally limited at that time to lending 50 percent of the value of the land offered as collateral. But the new corporation would advance funds for the purchase of homesteads, lending, if necessary, 100 percent of the land's price, and furnishing still more money for livestock and equipment. Robinson declared that arbitrary credit limits should be avoided because the "purpose of this act is to get genuine assistance to a class that has no resources, that can offer no security."[8]

Another example of the measure's adaptability was that it purposely placed no restrictions on the size or value of farms which the corporation could sell to clients. The advocates regarded this as essential to assure applicability of the program throughout the United States, since both land values and the definition of an adequate family-sized farm differed in each section, and since the corporation would have to be free to lend the full amount necessary in any area of the country. Not surprisingly, this broad provision provoked criticism. Some saw a danger of extravagant extensions of credit. Senator Joseph O'Mahoney of Wyoming suggested that the corporation might consider that the "sky is the limit" in its lending. Bankhead, underlining the bill's flexibility, replied, "I think so...the sky and the cellar, both."[9]

The proposed agency was also expected to protect clients in their new ownership. LaFollette stated that he understood that tenant purchasers would not be permitted to mortgage or alienate their lands. Bankhead agreed that such a policy was fundamental. Later he explained that the corporation could prevent liens from being taken against the land by formally holding title until the purchaser had completely amortized his debt, which in many cases could be as long as sixty years.[10]

During the course of debate several amendments broadened the bill. One specifically safeguarded the purchasers' possession of their farms by exempting their land, up to a value of $2,500, from encumbrances by liens, mortgages, or other debt obligations. Thus the prevention of alienation of land was made statutory, rather than an administrative procedure. Another change required that individual farms sold by the corporation be of a size and fertility and sufficiently stocked and equipped to enable purchasers to meet their obligations and maintain a "decent standard of living." A third important liberalization, introduced by LaFollette, empowered the agency to assist its clients in establishing cooperative associations.[11]

Throughout the debate, Bankhead and Robinson construed the bill narrowly and soft-pedaled its more innovative features, such as government initiative in purchase and resale of land, and lending for equipment and livestock. They said nothing about the supervision of borrowers which Tannenbaum and Gray had stressed in their memoranda. They presented the bill as a standard credit plan, modified to extend better terms to tenants who had no assets to offer as collateral. Even as they expected it to help large numbers, they admitted that it could not provide for all the landless. Both senators, however, affirmed on several occasions the necessity of aiding a poorer class of farmers than the government then reached. Both probably recognized that the flexible provisions of the bill and its ample bond issue would permit considerable distribution of its benefits, expecially in the hands of sympathetic administrators.[12] In fact, the measure was about as broadly conceived as a land purchase credit program could be. But its opponents made clear that it was also about as much as the Senate could be expected to approve.

The attack on the Bankhead bill came from three sides. One part of the opposition was made up of influential Republicans such as Borah, Arthur Vandenburg of Michigan, and L. J. Dickenson of Iowa, as well as conservative Democrats William H. King of Utah and Alva Adams of Colorado. A closely associated group included several southerners who had already emerged as consistent anti–New Dealers: Josiah Bailey of North Carolina, "Cotton Ed" Smith of South Carolina, Virginians Harry Byrd and Carter Glass, and

---

11 *Ibid.*, 6194–95, 6207.
12 For Bankhead's remarks on the need for sympathetic administration see *ibid.*, 5757–58, and for Robinson's observations see 5761.

Thomas P. Gore of Oklahoma. The third part of the opposition consisted of only one senator, Huey Long of Louisiana, who was then challenging the administration from the left and whose emphasis differed from that of other opponents. Like the proponents of the bill, these critics revealed in their statements examples of current thinking on the causes of poverty and remedies for it.

Several senators argued that tenancy was not a serious enough problem to warrant government action. Dickenson quoted with approval a South Carolina newsman who branded as a "false assumption" the proposition that tenant farming was an evil. According to this source, many farmers found it profitable to avoid ownership with its heavy payments for taxes, upkeep, insurance, and the like. Josiah Bailey thought landlords provided necessary security for sharecroppers and he identified farm debt and lagging income as the major rural problems. "If we can find some way whereby we can get the farm income... above the present [level] we shall not have a tenant problem, for they will be buying land," Bailey declared. Cotton Ed Smith informed his colleagues that because of overhead expenses the landlord was no better off than his tenants, and besides, "no thrifty, saving, provident individual has ever lacked the opportunity of owning his own farm." [13]

A second assertion was that lending money to tenants would create debt. Bankhead had maintained that sharecroppers buying land from the corporation would acquire equity while making annual payments no larger than the customary interest charges on goods advanced to them. But Bailey diagnosed the farm problem as one of excessive indebtedness and doubted that tenants could improve themselves by contracting obligations to a government agency. According to Vandenburg, the government was moving "too haphazardly" in extending credit. He equated the proposed program with those of the FCA, federal land banks, Commodity Credit Corporation, and emergency seed loans as ways to get farmers into debt. [14]

13 *Ibid.*, 6128, 5945, 6126.
14 *Ibid.*, 5938, 5945.

Since the bill's proposed bond issue was very large, expense was another ground for criticism. Vandenburg, who had opposed the huge 1935 relief appropriation, complained that a small portion of that money, transferred to the corporation, would be used as a "springboard" for a supplementary billion-dollar program. He insisted that federally guaranteed bonds constituted a liability against the public credit. Others saw the bill as a continuation of an unwelcome trend of big expenditures. Bailey called the measure "the culmination of a . . . process of taking up to the Treasury one group after another of the American people," which had begun with the Reconstruction Finance Corporation's aid to business. Predicting that the government's credit would be ruined, he lamented that "we are victims of our own precedent . . . [of] 1932." Still others regarded the bill as an opening wedge for more spending as demand grew for expansion of its benefits. Byrd described it as "simply the beginning of many appropriations which must be made for the same purpose." [15]

At times proponents replied vigorously to the expense argument. When Bailey maintained that the corporation, before lending, should determine the solvency of its borrowers, Hugo Black declared that in 1932 he had opposed the RFC bill for the very reason that it had proposed to lend millions to banks and businesses generally known to be insolvent. But, he indignantly observed, cost considerations were raised against a suggestion to lend money to "the forgotten tenant farmers and sharecroppers, those little men, few of whom vote . . . who live upon the fringe and the border line of subsistence." [16]

Several senators wanted limitations placed on the amount loaned and the acreage acquired for individuals. Senator Gore thought the traditional 160-acre homestead should be the maximum unit. He sarcastically suggested that if purchasers could not be satisfied with that acreage, "then let Congress make provision for the imperial estates on which such tenants may be content." He also

15 *Ibid.*, 5937, 5942, 5947.
16 *Ibid.*, 6129–31.

noted the lack of a statutory limit on the size of loans to borrowers he thought would be poor risks. Accordingly, Gore and others made a strong effort to set definite figures ($5,000 and $15,000 were suggested) on the value of farms sold. Bankhead, Black, and LaFollette managed to modify the critics' amendment so that the individual's credit could not exceed the value of an average-sized farm in his locality, as determined by the 1930 census.[17]

Inevitably there were charges that the measure was socialistic or foreign inspired. Senator Dickenson, who thought government credit would compete with private lending, attributed the bill to Tannenbaum and other "social planners in the AAA and the FERA" and claimed they contemplated the destruction of large landholdings as in the agrarian programs of "Russia, Mexico and Spain." Bailey repeatedly referred to the bill as "federal socialism." At one point, Harry Byrd warned his colleagues that by purchasing and leasing land the corporation would accomplish "the same thing that is now being done in Russia, to carry out the idea of collective ownership or operation which Dr. Tugwell has advocated in his speeches."[18]

Some detractors claimed the program was too inadequately funded to reach many tenants and would benefit chiefly corporations and planters who had excess land to sell. Although few conservatives made this charge, Huey Long used the argument vigorously. He questioned whether the proposed amount of money could reach more than 5 or 10 percent of the nation's landless farmers. Furthermore, in his opinion the bill was "designedly drawn" to aid those who wanted to dispose of land. The Kingfish asserted:

This is what the owners of those plantations are going to do: they want to sell out to the government, and . . . will take a poor colored man and a poor white man and sell him part of the plantation on which he is working. . . . So they will call in poor old colored "Mose", or an old white man . . . who is worn out and broken down and has about three more years to live, and he will sign a 60-year mortgage and move on the farm and that will be the last to be heard of him. . . . [His] condition will be worse instead of better.

17 *Ibid.*, 5763, 6197–6204.
18 *Ibid.*, 6008, 6128, 6185. Byrd was unaware that the bill had already been amended to prevent almost all leasing by the corporation.

What do you mean when your tears are streaming because of the pity you have for the [tenant] farmer?... I can almost see the tears of the landlords down on Red River... as they weep over the condition of the tenants, and about their going to make a sale of some of their mortgaged lands, upon which they cannot make any profit in this day and time.[19]

Long's remarks were later echoed by the Southern Tenant Farmers' Union and the Socialist party in their attacks on the bill.

Hugo Black countered this general line of criticism by admitting that the bill did indeed give landowners a favorable chance to sell property. But, he demanded, "how else can a [tenant] farmer get land? We have [private] ownership of land in this country and unless we... socialize all the land, there is no earthly chance for a tenant to get land except by buying it... from those who own it." And that, he declared, would necessitate government assistance.[20]

A final important feature of the debate was that it illustrated the attitudes of both supporters and enemies of the tenancy bill toward the administration's price parity goals. Alexander, Embree, Tannenbaum, and others originally promoted the legislation partly because they disapproved of the AAA's effects on the rural poor. During this time their criticism was quite explicit. They were, for example, preparing their forthright statement, *The Collapse of Cotton Tenancy*. At the same time, Department of Agriculture and congressional friends of the bill supported price parity policies. They ignored the anti-AAA inclinations of the Alexander-Tannenbaum group and viewed the Bankhead proposal and crop control as complementary. The tenancy bill suggested a way to alleviate rural poverty, which all admitted the AAA had exacerbated, but without changing the parity concept to which they were committed. On the other hand, opponents of the bill were, for the most part, critics of the AAA. They used the debate as an occasion to attack the administration's general agricultural policies. In doing so they used two arguments: that the Bankhead proposal and the AAA were contradictory, and that the tenancy measure was a misguided attempt to repair some of the social damage done by New Deal crop control.

19 *Ibid.*, 6279–80.
20 *Ibid.*, 6131.

Of these arguments, the first was the weaker. The contention was that at the very time that the government attempted to curtail cotton growing, the bill would furnish land and equipment to set up tenants in cotton production, thus defeating the main policy. As Long put it: "One day here we vote an appropriation of several . . . billion dollars . . . to take land out of cultivation, and the next day we vote a few billion dollars to get it back in cultivation. One day we vote a few billion to kill all the hogs, and then the next day we vote a few billion dollars to raise hogs. A bill is brought in here . . . [to give credit to tenant purchasers]. We have two agencies of farm relief, one to hire a man not raise, and the other to [enable] him to buy land on which to raise. Where in the hell are we going?" Cotton Ed Smith agreed that "on the one hand we are restricting, curtailing, licensing, regimenting, and on the other hand we are throwing the door wide open with a billion to increase the number of farmers." These attacks were answered with little difficulty. Bankhead merely pointed out that his bill would not increase the number of tenants, the acreage they already farmed, or overall cotton production. It merely proposed to improve their relation to the land and enable them to produce for themselves rather than for landlords.[21]

The charge that the legislation was an attempt to compensate for the AAA's bad effects on tenants was less easily answered, since it involved the bill's friends in a defense of the administration's cotton program. Long stated that crop restriction had put many Louisiana tenants off the land and on relief, but the bill would, according to his calculations, benefit only about one fourth of 1 percent of them. Furthermore, crop restrictions would prevent clients from producing enough on their small acreages "to support themselves in anything like respectable poverty." Likewise, Bailey claimed that since the 1934 Cotton Control Act would prevent tenants from raising more than two bales of tax-free cotton per season they could not hope to pay debts or buy land. One-third of all southern farmers, he noted, were two-bale producers. Bankhead, the father of the control act, retorted that because poor farmers had always produced small

21 *Ibid.*, 6137, 6272–73, 6276.

amounts anyway, the law's two-bale tax exemption was not a limitation for them. Besides, he said, no one expected tenant purchasers to depend completely on cotton for their incomes.[22]

At times the supporters were hard pressed to defend the AAA. They avoided discussion of its effects on the poor by simply asserting that administration policies had increased farm prosperity. For example, when Gore branded the tenancy bill as an attempt to correct the mistakes of crop restriction policies, especially tenant displacement, Hugo Black replied, not precisely to the point, that he had recently observed conditions in Alabama and could speak from "absolute knowledge of the way those farmers live and what has happened to them" and could "deny that . . . they have been sent to the relief rolls on 12-cent cotton when they were rolling in luxury in the good old days of 5-cent cotton."[23]

Although the Bankhead bill's billion-dollar bond feature disturbed fiscal conservatives, it was otherwise a moderate proposal. Its ultimate aim, the promotion of small farm ownership, was hardly revolutionary. Those who conceived the bill and those who pushed it in Congress were not radicals. Moreover, they never really claimed that it was a full answer to rural poverty. Both Bankhead and Robinson described it as a selective program to aid worthy and capable clients. But moderate as the bill was, it encountered formidable opposition which succeeded in preventing its full passage in 1935. These facts should be taken into account before hasty judgments are made that the Bankhead proposal of 1935 (or of 1937 for that matter) failed to attack the roots of rural poverty or make sweeping reforms in the southern land system. Alexander later suggested that the bill was probably as much as Congress would accept at that time.[24] The course of the measure in the spring and summer of 1935 supports his opinion.

22　*Ibid.*, 9939–42, 5946–47.
23　*Ibid.*, 9938.
24　"Reminiscences of Will W. Alexander" (Typescript, 1952, in Oral History Collection, Columbia University), 414–15. In retrospect Alexander remarked that belief in the desirability of landownership is so deep in the United States that one cannot maintain a contrary policy, especially in Congress. "Congress was ready to go that far [i.e., accept

The opposition made repeated attempts to emasculate or side-track the bill. On April 22 Harry Byrd moved to send it to the Banking and Currency Committee on the grounds that the corporation, since it extended credit, had most of the attributes of a bank. Byrd withdrew his motion at Borah's suggestion and substituted one to recommit the measure to the Agriculture and Forestry Committee for more hearings. The effort was defeated. On the same day Bailey proposed to eliminate the corporation's bond-issuing powers. This was a clear attempt to kill the program by reducing the corporation's financial resources to the $50 million that Roosevelt could transfer from relief funds for its initial operations. That attempt was also unsuccessful. On the twenty-fourth a similar motion by Bailey to cut the authorization for bonds to $100 million failed.[25]

The tactic which finally succeeded in delaying Senate action was that of returning the bill temporarily to the Agriculture and Forestry Committee. On April 24 Senator Royal S. Copeland of New York and William E. Borah successfully moved for recommitment, ostensibly for restudy, and with instructions to the committee to report the bill by May 12.[26] Although the recommitment was temporary, it was a serious blow to the bill's prospects. Bankhead judged that it would be difficult to bring the measure back to the Senate floor because the calendar was already so crowded with major bills that the legislative logjam would prevent action on it.[27] The bill was not finally stopped in the Senate, but because of the delay it was stalled in the House in the summer of 1935.

This development dismayed the bill's supporters. Some expressed resentment against the senators who had engineered the recommitment. George Foster Peabody said privately that the whole thing merely confirmed his long-held opinion that Borah was "without the essentials of character respecting public welfare." But Tan-

---

the Bankhead bill] and I was always convinced that they were not ready to go any farther. I know now they weren't."

25 *Congressional Record*, 74th Cong., 1st Sess., 6121, 6126, 6132, 6194, 6272.

26 *Ibid.*, 6278, 6290.

27 *Ibid.*, 6126. Bankhead was speaking of an earlier attempt to recommit, but his remarks were applicable to all such motions.

nenbaum placed the responsibility on several "liberals" who had been expected to support the measure but had been "misled by some of our extreme leftist friends."[28] As he unburdened himself to Alexander, he indicated who these "leftists" were. He complained bitterly that "in part Roger Baldwin's crowd in Washington was responsible for the recommitment... for reasons that God only knows [because of their] complete political irresponsibility, and [their] messing in things that they know nothing about." Identifying still more critics, he remarked that "I don't see why [we should] leave it to Walter White and Gardner Jackson and Ben Marsh to mislead and misinform a group of people who by every instinct and tradition would be for us."[29]

As Tannenbaum suggested, there had been objections to the bill from liberal and radical critics of the New Deal. On May 5, for example, Norman Thomas wrote to the editor of the New York *Times* to deplore the condition of Arkansas sharecroppers. The Socialist leader described administration tenancy policy as ranging from "swivel chair liberalism" at best to the "hypocrisy" of paragraph 7 of the AAA cotton contract. He rejected the Bankhead bill as a solution for tenancy because successful cotton farming could not be carried on by the "subsidized peasants," which he claimed the measure would create. This would be especially true, he thought, because recent progress in the development of a cotton picking

28 George Foster Peabody to Frank Tannenbaum, April 26, 1935, Tannenbaum to Will Alexander, April 25, 1935, in Frank Tannenbaum Papers, Columbia University. The "liberal" Senators were not identified, but Tannenbaum probably referred to several who had aided the bill on key votes and then switched to vote for recommitment. Possibly these included Bronson Cutting of New Mexico, Thomas D. Schall and Henrik Shipstead of Minnesota, and perhaps Harry Truman of Missouri and others. For a secondary account see Sidney Baldwin, *Poverty and Politics: The Rise and Decline of the Farm Security Administration* (Chapel Hill: University of North Carolina Press, 1968), 151–53.

29 Tannenbaum to Alexander, April 26, 1935, in Tannenbaum Papers. Tannenbaum referred to Roger Baldwin, chairman of the American Civil Liberties Union; Walter White, head of the National Association for the Advancement of Colored People; Gardner Jackson, recently fired from the AAA consumers' counsel staff and then organizing the National Committee on Rural Social Planning, which later became the Washington publicity outlet for the Southern Tenant Farmers' Union; and Ben Marsh, executive secretary of the Peopole's Lobby, a liberal pressure group under the presidency of John Dewey.

machine promised to make large mechanized operations imperative for profitable farming. Like Huey Long, Thomas also claimed the bill would "bail out" land-poor planters and holders of foreclosed property. He concluded that the real key to improving sharecroppers' conditions was their right to organize a union.[30]

Another attack came from Ben Marsh, head of the People's Lobby, who charged in a letter to the editor of the *New Republic* that the bill would aid those who wanted to sell land, including "land-speculating and 'deserving' Democrats." Probably unaware of the intent to supervise clients through the proposed corporation, he declared that it was "folly to assume that most tenant farmers and sharecroppers can run their own show. Many . . . of them can work only under direction." Because he considered credit for land purchase a mere palliative, Marsh summarized the Bankhead measure as an "effort to have [the] government evade its responsibility to find a real solution for the agricultural problem."[31]

Although the Southern Tenant Farmers' Union was later a severe critic of nearly all New Deal attempts to deal with tenancy, it was not very outspoken in opposition to the Bankhead bill in the spring of 1935. At that time the STFU was struggling to organize, and indeed fighting for its life, in eastern Arkansas. It was then more concerned with the relatively narrow issue of securing equitable treatment for sharecroppers under the AAA cotton contract, and with stopping the suppression of its members' and sympathizers' civil liberties, than with broad pronouncements on pending legislation.[32]

Finally, it should be noted that opponents of differing political persuasions used many of the same arguments against the bill. The attacks by Thomas and Marsh had much in common with those of

---

30 New York *Times,* May 5, 1935, Sec. 4, p. 9.
31 Ben Marsh, "Dangers in the Bankhead Plan," *New Republic,* April 10, 1935, p. 246. Marsh did not reveal what should be done but he did hint that confiscatory taxation would be more effective than a bond program in acquiring and redistributing land.
32 See generally David E. Conrad, *The Forgotten Farmers: The Story of Sharecroppers in the New Deal* (Urbana: University of Illinois Press, 1965), Chap. 5, and Donald H. Grubbs, *Cry from the Cotton: The Southern Tenant Farmers' Union and the New Deal* (Chapel Hill: University of North Carolina Press, 1971), Chap. 4.

Huey Long. More surprising than this, however, was the similarity of their arguments to those of some conservatives. For example, Stanley Morse, a South Carolina editor who praised the southern land tenure system and considered the Bankhead measure a "revolutionary" attack upon it, charged, like the critics of the left, that the bill attempted to offset AAA's effects on tenants, and would establish an inefficient "subsidized peasantry" which could not produce major commodities economically. He questioned whether most tenants could operate their own farms and maintained that the bill would benefit those looking for a chance to unload land on the government. The latter charge was also made by the Liberty League, and occasionally by conservative senators in congressional debate.[33]

Thus, by the spring of 1935 the following situation had developed. The New Deal had reorganized its relief efforts, created the Resettlement Administration, and determined that rural rehabilitation activities, formerly part of the old FERA, would be attached to the new agency. The Bankhead tenancy legislation had been introduced and the idea had emerged within the RA that its rehabilitation program and the bill were complementary and ought to be coordinated in some way. Alexander, about to become assistant administrator of the RA, was working vigorously for the measure. There was general optimism that it would be enacted. On April 17 the New York *Times* reported that Senate passage was "certain" on the next day.[34] But on April 24 the bill was sidetracked and all efforts turned to getting it out of committee and before the Senate again.

Concurrently with the progress of tenancy legislation, a small group of liberals organized the Southern Policy Committee, which by the spring of 1935 evolved into an active force for reform of the region's rural life. The movement was conceived by a Virginian, Francis Pickens Miller, executive secretary of the Foreign Policy Association, a pro-League of Nations and low tariff organization. In November, 1934, Miller suggested to President Frank P. Graham of

33   Washington *Post*, April 21, 1935; New York *Times*, May 20, 1935, p. 36.
34   New York *Times*, April 17, 1935, p. 1.

the University of North Carolina and editor Jonathan Daniels of the Raleigh *News and Observer* the formation of a network of local study groups of leading citizens to recommend policies to deal with national and regional problems. Miller thought the South was an appropriate place to experiment with the idea. At Daniels' home on December 17, Miller explained his plan to a meeting of North Carolina journalists and Chapel Hill academicians who then organized a local "public policy committee" to advocate federal programs for "sound economic and political development in the South." The movement spread rapidly; by spring policy committees had been established in Atlanta, Dallas, Nashville, New Orleans, Raleigh, Louisville, and Lynchburg, Virginia. Many of these concentrated on southern agricultural problems. Meanwhile, Miller had arranged a regional conference of local committees for April in Atlanta.[35]

Miller thought the value of the meeting would depend on the issues discussed. To Daniels he suggested an agenda which hinted at his own view of New Deal programs. His first topics, the social effects of crop control and the impact on the South of declining cotton exports, revealed his sympathy with two groups of AAA's critics: those who condemned its inequities for the landless and the exporters who wanted crop restrictions eased in an effort to expand production and recapture world markets. Miller also made clear that he regarded the Atlanta conference as a gathering of activists who would not merely discuss these matters but also make specific recommendations to Congress. Concerning one measure to advocate, he told Daniels, "I am sure that as far as agrarian reform is concerned, the Bankhead Bill is the right line to take. . . . The problem then becomes one of [encouraging] public opinion favorable to such

35 Jonathan Daniels to Frank P. Graham, November 12 and 19, 1934, "Purposes and Procedure of Southern Policy Groups," November 16, 1934, "Memorandum Adopted at a Meeting of the Southern Policy Committee in Atlanta," April 30, 1935, Francis P. Miller to Graham, February 12, 1935, Miller to Daniels, January 12, 1935, all in Frank P. Graham Papers, Southern Historical Collection, University of North Carolina; Francis P. Miller to Howard Odum [after December 17, 1934], in Jonathan Daniels Papers, Southern Historical Collection, University of North Carolina, Chapel Hill; Herman Clarence Nixon to Charles S. Johnson, March 30, 1935, in Commission on Interracial Cooperation Papers, Atlanta University; hereinafter cited as CIC Papers.

legislation. This is one reason why I attach importance to our Atlanta conference."[36]

If Miller was interested in the bill, its promoters were also aware of the policy movement and worked to gain its support. While his staff contacted most of the leadership, Alexander discussed the measure with H. C. Nixon, then organizing the New Orleans committee. Nixon was also informed of the legislation's progress by Bankhead, and by the spring of 1935 was describing the bill as a practical plan to move millions toward independence. The policy movement also attracted interest from the Agriculture Department. Paul A. Porter, Chester Davis' executive assistant in the AAA, recommended the Atlanta meeting to Brooks Hays, the Democratic national committeeman from Arkansas. Although his agency was sensitive to attacks for its social and economic inequities, Porter was confident that this conference would analyze rural problems objectively and thought Hays could contribute an informed estimate of the Arkansas tenancy situation. Hays, shortly to become prominent in the movement, agreed to attend.[37]

The conference met April 25–28 and formed a permanent organization, the Southern Policy Committee. H. C. Nixon and Brooks Hays were chosen chairman and vice-chairman, respectively, and Francis P. Miller became executive secretary. Among several resolutions adopted was a "statement of agrarian policy" which called for a revitalized rural life centered on small farm own-

36   Miller to Daniels, January 12, 1935, Miller to Graham, February 12, 1935, in Graham Papers; Miller to Daniels, March 25, 1935, in Daniels Papers. The policy movement momentarily united advocates of land reform with major cotton exporters, several of whom participated in the conference. Afterwards some of the leadership's statements suggested that self-sufficient small farm ownership would not only alleviate poverty, but also increase the efficiency of cotton planting by removing tenants from it. In turn this might allow profitable production of low-priced cotton, without AAA restrictions, for the world market. See "Objectives of the Southern Policy Committee," (undated memorandum in Daniels Papers).
37   Alexander to Tannenbaum, February 18, 1935, in Tannenbaum Papers; John H. Bankhead to Nixon, April 12, 1935, and "Notes on Farm Tenancy and the Bankhead Bill," undated, in Herman Clarence Nixon Papers, in possession of the Nixon family, Nashville; Paul A. Porter to Brooks Hays, April 12 and 17, 1935, in "Records of the Agricultural Stabilization and Conservation Service," Record Group 145, National Archives.

ership and unreservedly endorsed the Bankhead bill. Aware that the legislation had just been recommitted, the SPC recommended that in case it failed to become law its program should be effected insofar as possible through other means. This reflected the conference's agrarian predilections and probably also showed the influence of Will Alexander, who attended and must have pressed the case for the bill. The conference also commended FERA's rural rehabilitation.[38]

Some of those at the conference contacted senators in behalf of the Bankhead bill. Clarence Poe and other North Carolinians wired Josiah Bailey that by hindering the measure he had "struck a serious blow to our economic structure . . . and [jeopardized the] greatest opportunity for revitalizing the South's rural life, its greatest interest." Ten days after the conference the Nashville policy group notified Cotton Ed Smith that they were "shocked" by his negativism toward the bill, which they called "the most constructive measure yet proposed for the benefit of the South," without which the region faced "increasing poverty."[39]

Miller, Nixon, and Hays intended to use the SPC to mobilize opinion and exert pressure for the bill. Miller explained to Daniels that the conference had developed such "unanimity" for the legislation that he was confident no one attending would object to action in its behalf. Hays regarded as "highly significant that the Atlanta conference developed some differences of opinion upon every subject except the Bankhead-Jones Bill," and added that "the complete

---

38 *Southern Policy* (N.p.: Southern Policy Committee, 1935), 16, copy in National Policy Committee Papers, Library of Congress; "Minutes of the Southern Policy Committee—Atlanta, Georgia, April 28, 1935," in Daniels Papers. The Jeffersonian tone of the meeting was enhanced by the presence of four of the "Nashville Agrarians," whose anti-industrial southern ruralist manifesto had appeared in 1930. See John Crowe Ransom *et. al.*, *I'll Take My Stand: The South and the Agrarian Tradition* (New York: Harper and Brothers, 1930). One of them was the Southern Policy Committee's new chairman, Herman Clarence Nixon, the only Agrarian who wrote in 1930 on the South's economic condition and had been consistently concerned with it since. As an SPC leader until 1938, Nixon contributed more than anyone else to its continuing small-farm outlook.

39 Clarence Poe, W. T. Couch, Hugh MacRae and B. F. Brown to Josiah Bailey, April 27, 1935, Donald Davidson, Frank Owsley, Lyle Lanier, Robert Worke, Eugene Woodruff, Brainerd Cheney and James Waller to Ellison D. Smith, May 7, 1935, in Tannenbaum Papers.

unanimity with which this bill was received leads me to believe that the South has a real stake in it." Thus the SPC leaders became advocates of the measure in time to work for its return to the Senate floor.[40]

Immediately after the recommitment, a concerted effort to bring the bill back for quick passage began. Tannenbaum was convinced that "the bill was really returned to the Committee by a group of liberals rather than the reactionaries." But he thought the votes of these senators could be won back because, as he told Alexander, "most of them are friends of Tugwell's and Tugwell definitely told me that he could take care of them."[41] In addition, Tannenbaum and Alexander sought ways to change the minds of the six members of the Agriculture and Forestry Committee who had voted for the recommitment. Assessing the bill's chances, Tannenbaum was sure that with the change of a half dozen votes it could be reported and passed easily.[42]

Alexander made some plans to influence recalcitrant senators through intermediaries. For example, Negro college presidents and "friends of Negroes in New England" would be asked to contact senators from that region. Senator Gore would be approached through President William B. Bizzell of the University of Oklahoma, and Peabody would try to persuade Bernard Baruch to use his great influence in South Carolina to pressure Cotton Ed Smith. Along with these efforts, Tannenbaum tried to quiet some of the criticism from outside Congress. He wrote that he planned to go to New York "to see Roger Baldwin . . . and see if he can't pull his dogs off the bill here in Washington," since in his opinion Baldwin and the American Civil Liberties Union were "as much responsible for recommitting the bill as any one . . . group."[43]

Tannenbaum and Alexander concluded that the two southerners most responsible for the legislation's lack of progress were Josiah

40 Francis P. Miller to Daniels, May 20, 1935, in Daniels Papers; Hays to Dale Miller, August 9, 1935, in National Policy Committee Papers.
41 Tannenbaum to Alexander, April 25, 1935, in Tannenbaum Papers.
42 Tannenbaum to Alexander, April 24, 1935, Tannenbaum to Poe, April 24, 1935, *ibid.*
43 Alexander to Embree and Johnson, May 6, 1935, in CIC Papers; Tannenbaum to Alexander, April 25, 1935, in Tannenbaum Papers.

Bailey and Cotton Ed Smith. Tannenbaum doubted that Smith could be influenced. But realistic plans were made to "build a fire under Bailey," who had led the attack against the bill on the Senate floor, by approaching him through influential North Carolinians. Tannenbaum was acquainted with Josephus Daniels (then ambassador to Mexico) and planned to contact him during his scheduled return to the United States. He hoped to persuade the elder Daniels to use his Raleigh *News and Observer* to pressure Bailey.[44] But Jonathan Daniels had already editorially attacked the senator's position, suggesting that "unless he [Bailey] has a plan which will serve as well [as the Bankhead bill] to cut the growing numbers of the landless and . . . hopeless on the land . . . he ought to move carefully in striking at a bill which thoughtful men . . . have designed to give every American on the land an American chance."[45]

Bailey was not immediately convinced. In reply to Daniels he restated his position from the Senate debate. He also justified his actions by asserting that since Roosevelt had not uttered a single public word for the bill, it could not be considered an administration measure. Moreover, he pointed out that the secretary of the treasury had recently issued a general warning against increasing government obligations, as Bailey contended the billion-dollar bond issue would.[46]

At Tannenbaum's request, another powerful North Carolinian, Clarence Poe, imparted to Bailey a conservative agriculturalist's view of the solution to tenancy problems. Poe stressed that the bond issue would not be mere spending, but a recoverable investment to help the landless. He also commended the bill because he understood it would benefit deserving tenants who were good credit risks, and was therefore superior to FERA rehabilitation with its aid to farm relief cases. He further declared that all the agricultural leaders he knew preferred a credit policy like that of the Bankhead measure. Finally, Poe emphasized that whereas the new program would raise

---

44 Tannenbaum to Poe, April 24, 1935, Tannenbaum to Alexander, April 25, 1935, in Tannenbaum Papers; Alexander to Embree and Johnson, May 6, 1935, in CIC Papers.
45 Raleigh *News and Observer*, April 24, 1935.
46 Bailey to Daniels, April 25, 1935, in Daniels Papers.

the status of tenants, it would not increase the number of farmers or their production of major commodities. [47]

Bailey may have been swayed by Poe, but the decisive persuasion must have come from Josephus Daniels. On May 25 Alexander reported that the ambassador had seen Bailey in Washington and had extracted from him a promise to vote for the measure's final passage. [48] Bailey not only kept his word, but also remained completely silent in debate after the bill returned to the floor, in contrast to his earlier open attacks. Thus the hostility of one leading opponent was neutralized.

During the first week in May, Alexander arrived in Washington to assume his duties with the Resettlement Administration. Dividing his time between that work and lobbying for the bill, he found the measure's supporters optimistic. Tugwell told him there was a "fair chance" of passage. Bankhead reported that Senator Robinson saw the legislation as a possible political credit for himself in case his enemy Huey Long attacked him in Arkansas. Accordingly, as soon as the bill reemerged from committee Robinson would assure it a place on the crowded Senate calendar. This would almost guarantee Senate approval, but because such large measures as social security, utility, banking and tax legislation, and the Wagner labor proposal were also on the agenda, it might not be possible to send the bill to the House promptly enough for action before adjournment. However, Alexander had heard confidentially that the president would use his influence for House passage. [49]

Although the outlook seemed promising, there were still questions about the administration of the tenancy program. At the time Roosevelt was understood to prefer placing it under the Department of Agriculture, as in the earliest versions of the bill, rather than under a special corporation. And it should be recalled that Tugwell also did not favor an independent corporation, but hoped to coordi-

---

47 Poe to Bailey, May 1, 1935, Poe to Smith, May 1, 1935, in Tannenbaum Papers.
48 Alexander to Embree and Johnson, May 27, 1935, in CIC Papers.
49 Alexander to Embree and Johnson, May 6, 1935, *ibid.*; New York *Times*, April 17, 1935, p. 1. The crowded agenda made a legislative logjam likely, even before Roosevelt launched the Second Hundred Days in the summer of 1935.

nate the Bankhead bill with the RA. There is evidence that by about the summer of 1935 Tugwell had secured Roosevelt's consent to RA control of tenant purchase lending. Resolving these matters would surely consume much time if the bill were considered by the House.[50]

On May 5, 1935, the Agriculture and Forestry Committee returned the bill. The only substantive change was a limitation on the rate of issuance of the $1 billion of bonds to not more than $300 million in the first three years. Bankhead said this restriction had been accepted in order to win the support of several senators who wanted the corporation to move in its first years with "deliberation and care" under the oversight of Congress.[51] Due to the crowded legislative calendar, debate did not resume until June 21. The discussion was characterized by repetition of old arguments, the silence of Josiah Bailey and the vociferous attacks of Huey Long.

A few changes were made during the debate. One important broadening amendment allowed the corporation to lease land to tenants for as long as five years before they began purchasing it. This was expected to permit supervision and technical assistance for impoverished tenants who lacked the experience and managerial ability to purchase and operate a small farm. A more restrictive amendment removed the corporation's authority to make emergency subsistence grants to needy clients; however, the RA already had such authority. Robinson, Bankhead, and Norris also turned back an attempt by opponents of the bill to permit a client to mortgage his newly acquired land.[52]

On June 24 the Senate passed the bill by a vote of 45 to 32. Among the southerners only Byrd, Glass, Gore, Smith, Walter F. George of Georgia, and Long voted "nay."[53] The Senate had ap-

---

50 Alexander to Embree and Johnson, May 6, 1935, in CIC Papers; Tugwell to Roosevelt, November 21, 1935, in Official File 1568, Franklin D. Roosevelt Library. For Tugwell's views and Bankhead's apparent consent to them, see Rexford G. Tugwell Diary (Typescript in Rexford G. Tugwell Papers, Franklin D. Roosevelt Library), May 7, 1935.

51 *Congressional Record*, 74th Cong., 1st Sess., 9846.

52 *Ibid.*, 9934, 9943–45.

53 *Ibid.*, 9960. Senate Republicans, except for Norris, Thomas D. Schall of Minnesota, and Lynn Frazier of North Dakota, were solidly opposed. According to "Reminiscences

proved a broad and flexible land purchase plan which, if administered as its original framers intended, could have provided its clients, through the corporation's contractual procedures, adequate supervision as well as credit. Although the program was not expected to reach every tenant, and probably would have excluded the poorest ones, it did propose to lend $1 billion over several years and its efforts conceivably could have had significant impact upon rural poverty. Moreover, the program was complementary to the RA, and if Tugwell had his way would be attached to it, thus creating in 1935 an agency similar to the Farm Security Administration of 1937. Indeed, the 1935 bill was superior to the 1937 Bankhead-Jones Act, in that it would have permitted the government to take the initiative in buying, dividing, and selling land to tenants, rather than merely extending credit to them as the latter legislation provided.

The Senate's passage of tenancy legislation was not received with great enthusiasm in the South. A New York *Times* correspondent reported from Memphis that there were few endorsements or condemnations of the bill; in fact there was little concern on the part of those who would normally be interested. Not even landowners, whom the reporter thought would be willing to sell surplus land for an adequate price, were aroused. The general opinion seemed to be that existing credit facilities were adequate for energetic tenants wanting land, and nothing further was required. The *Times'* observer characterized the reaction in the Delta region as one of "marked indifference."[54]

---

of Will W. Alexander," 594, Bankhead was "amazed" at George's vote. George reportedly was reluctant to see landlords lose good tenants they had worked some time to get.

54 New York *Times*, June 30, 1935, Sec. E, p. 6.

Tenant children, Caroline County, Virginia, 1941

Tenant family transportation

Sharecroppers' shacks near West Memphis, Arkansas, 1935

Family near Greensboro, Alabama, 1941

Farm Security Administration clients, Coffee County, Alabama, 1939

Sharecropper families evicted from a plantation near Parkin, Arkansas,
1936, for membership in the Southern Tenant Farmers' Union

Farm Security Administration client family, Greene County, Georgia, 1941

Cabin of sharecropper family to be resettled on the FSA's Transylvania Project, East Carroll Parish, Louisiana, 1939

Resettlement Administration client family on Ladies' Island, South Carolina, 1936

PHOTOGRAPH BY ARTHUR ROTHSTEIN

Sharecropper's wife, Pulaski County, Arkansas, 1935

Senator John Hollis Bankhead
of Alabama in 1932

Rexford G. Tugwell, head of the
Resettlement Administration

PHOTOGRAPH BY ARTHUR ROTHSTEIN

Will W. Alexander as assistant administrator of the
Resettlement Administration in 1935

CHAPTER VII

"The Delay Drives One Almost to Despair"

THE SENATE passed the Bankhead bill, the legislative expression of the rehabilitative approach to poverty, on June 24, 1935, and sent it to the House. There, on June 26, it was assigned to the Agriculture Committee, chaired by Marvin Jones of Amarillo, Texas. It never came to the House floor, but languished in committee until Congress adjourned on August 26.

The summer of 1935, known as the Second Hundred Days, was the period of the New Deal's most intensive legislative drive since the crisis-packed weeks of early 1933. During the first half of 1935 Congress maintained a slow pace, passing only one major act, the relief appropriation. By early June adjournment was expected, but Roosevelt, angered by the Supreme Court's Schechter decision of May 27, suddenly insisted upon a new legislative program. The administration's demands included the Wagner labor proposal, social security, the 1935 "soak the rich" tax bill, a major banking measure, and legislation to break up public utility holding companies. Since passage of these would require maximum legislative effort, it is not surprising that the tenancy bill, never formally identified with the administration, did not attain a high priority in the House. Those who delayed its Senate passage had effectively killed it, because the House agenda during the Second Hundred Days made action before adjournment unlikely, especially since open White House support was lacking.

Among the measure's other disadvantages was lack of favorable publicity in the House. Francis P. Miller thought that "while adequate education was going on among the Senators, little or nothing was done among the Congressmen. The result was that even the best Congressmen know very little about the bill and are unprepared to give it their enthusiastic support." Will Alexander recalled that many southern representatives were indifferent to legislation which would benefit only the uninfluential and nonvoting poor among their constituents. Similarly, Brooks Hays found little concern among the eight southerners on the Agriculture Committee and sought ways to influence them through their districts.[1] Finally, the chairman, Marvin Jones, did not work energetically for the bill. A possible explanation for his lack of ardor is that he doubted his committee could approach unanimity for it. Since he usually regarded strong committee backing as necessary before reporting any controversial proposal with hope of passage, he may have thought the cause already lost for 1935.[2] But Jones also hinted that he considered the Bankhead bill unsatisfactory. Since it would retain its current status when Congress returned in January, 1936, Jones hoped that "on the basis of this bill a practical measure may be enacted during the next session," and reassured Alexander that action would be taken then.[3]

Alexander was especially disappointed with the lack of progress because of his conviction that the Resettlement Administration and

1 Francis P. Miller to Herman Clarence Nixon, July 19, 1935, Brooks Hays to Dale Miller, August 9, 1935, both in National Policy Committee Papers, Library of Congress, hereinafter cited as NPC Papers; "Reminiscences of Will W. Alexander" (Typescript, 1952, in Oral History Collection, Columbia University), 594–95.

2 This interpretation of Jones's motives is from Sidney Baldwin, *Poverty and Politics: The Rise and Decline of the Farm Security Administration* (Chapel Hill: University of North Carolina Press, 1968), 153. One might also argue that Jones had nothing to lose by pushing the bill to the House floor with whatever committee majority he could muster, particularly since there are indications that the president was willing to lend his support (though perhaps not publicly) to passage.

3 New York *Times*, September 1, 1935, Sec. 3, p. 7; Will Alexander to M. C. Holmes, September 18, 1935, in Commission on Interracial Cooperation Papers, Atlanta University, hereinafter cited as CIC Papers.

the Bankhead program should be closely related, if not administered together. He wrote that the RA's task was the "rehabilitation of a million one hundred thousand farm families who are now on relief." The agency was already helping 350,000 families and increasing its coverage as rapidly as possible. "Part of the plan," Alexander continued, "is that ultimately a great many of these people may be assisted toward the ownership of their land." He envisioned that "the work of the Resettlement Administration may become the foundation on which to build a long-time program of rehabilitation for the landless rural population of this country." But to make that possible Congress would have to enact the Bankhead bill or a similar measure. Anticipating a well-coordinated rehabilitative program combining the features of the RA and the Bankhead principles, Alexander was frustrated by the inactivity in the House. He concluded that the extent to which Congress would go in tenancy legislation would depend upon the country's general mood when the next session began.[4]

Southern Policy Committee leadership also became increasingly pessimistic in the fall of 1935. Francis P. Miller informed H. C. Nixon that reliable Washington opinion held that Roosevelt wanted the 1936 session of Congress to be short and would not favor new programs with large expenditures. Furthermore, since the South (due to the assassination of Huey Long) was considered safe for the New Deal in the coming election, there was no pressure to extend "additional sops" to the region. Miller's confidential information was that these circumstances made the chance for the passage of the Bankhead measure "very small indeed," and that likelihood was further reduced "by the fact that Tugwell does not like the present bill because it sets up an independent corporation. He would prefer to have the [tenant purchase] plan [made] an integral part of his resettlement program." Miller had heard that Tugwell "would rather see the bill fail than have it go through in its present form." He concluded that "in view of Tugwell's influence with the President it is more than likely that the latter's attitude toward the bill will be re-

4 Alexander to Holmes, September 18, 1935, in CIC Papers.

served, to say the least." The main hope for tenancy legislation, Miller thought, was for the SPC to organize a sustained effort, like that which midwesterners had developed for the parity legislation of 1933. He anticipated a two- or three-year campaign to enact the Bankhead proposal.[5]

Tugwell was in fact greatly concerned about the administration of tenant purchase lending. On November 21, having heard that Roosevelt has asked Wallace, William I. Meyers, and Treasury Secretary Henry Morganthau to suggest effective tenancy policies, and apprehending that the credit program might not be coordinated in any way with the RA, Tugwell wrote to the president:

> I had supposed you were aware that all that [rehabilitative] work was being done by the Resettlement Administration. We are taking care of about 200,000 tenant families now . . . and I have been working actively with members of Congress on the Bankhead-Jones bill. I haven't talked with you about this lately but I had supposed you knew what we were doing. You told me some time ago to begin tenant resettlement this year on a small scale and said that duing this [1936 Congressional] session you would help with permanent legislation. You told both Bankhead and Jones that you expected me to administer it. I only write this to find out whether things have changed. . . . I am deep in the tenant business by now and if I am to pull out I should like to make it as easy as possible.

Roosevelt replied that he was quite aware of the RA's work, and while not specifically mentioning RA administration of the Bankhead program, he did indicate that he had asked Wallace, Myers, and Morganthau to confer with Tugwell on the problem. Preparing to depart for Warm Springs, he saw no need to revise the tenancy legislation "as we have until the first of the year to work out something with Bankhead and Jones."[6]

Actually, in the fall of 1935, Roosevelt was neither so "reserved" about the Bankhead bill as Miller pessimistically supposed, nor as unaware of antipoverty work as Tugwell thought. On the contrary, he had finally determined to throw his full weight behind the ten-

5 Francis P. Miller to Nixon, November 30, 1935, in NPC Papers.
6 Rexford G. Tugwell to Franklin D. Roosevelt, November 21, 1935, and Roosevelt to Tugwell, November 25, 1935, in Official File 1568, Franklin D. Roosevelt Library, Hyde Park, N.Y.

ancy measure, although he wanted it significantly modified. Among other things, he agreed with Tugwell at least to the extent of not wanting an independent corporation to administer the new program. On December 4, at Warm Springs, the president indicated publicly for the first time his support for the legislation. A delegation of Georgia farmers, Roosevelt's "neighbors," saw him at the Little White House and then informed reporters, undoubtedly at his suggestion, that he favored the measure.[7]

During his stay in Georgia, Roosevelt also discussed the bill with George Foster Peabody, who immediately wired Alexander in Atlanta and urged him to come to Warm Springs. Alexander arrived on the fifth and, after a hint to Roosevelt from Peabody, was invited to lunch with the president. In an unhurried private discussion Alexander "found him thoroughly committed to a program in line with the Bankhead Bill and determined to put the thing through in the coming session," although with "certain very definite amendments" by the House. After the conference Alexander was optimistic. He wrote Embree, "I had never before been quite certain of the President's attitude. I now have no doubt as to his whole-hearted support, and I firmly believe that we will get a bill which will enable us to begin on the big program which is contemplated by the Bankhead Bill. It is the hope of the President that the beginning may be somewhat less conspicuous than had been anticipated, but once we get a start, although it may not be on as grand a scale as we had contemplated, I shall feel that we have attained our major goal." On the sixth Alexander left Warm Springs for Alabama to confer with Bankhead about the modifications Roosevelt wanted.[8]

7 New York *Times*, December 5, 1935, p. 1. H. C. Nixon, then visiting George Foster Peabody at Warm Springs, also heard indirectly of Roosevelt's opinions. Nixon to Francis P. Miller, December 6, 1935, in NPC Papers.

8 Alexander to Edwin R. Embree, December 5 or 6, 1935, in CIC Papers. The letter bears both dates. This paragraph assumes that December 6 is correct. At this meeting Alexander gave Roosevelt a copy of the just-published *Collapse of Cotton Tenancy*. The president remarked that he had heard of the book and appreciated the work behind it, which, he thought, had increased general awareness of the tenancy problem and had given him the necessary public support to enable him to back the Bankhead measure. All available evidence indicates that this conference was the first private meeting between Roosevelt and Alexander, even though other secondary works (*e.g.*, Baldwin, *Poverty and Politics*, 131) place the initial meeting almost one year earlier.

Although Roosevelt was strongly interested in tenancy legislation, his commitment was qualified. He told another visitor, Chattanooga newpaper editor George Fort Milton, that he wanted the measure revised. Milton found him "thoroughly reluctant to establish a new Federal unit." The president said that the bill would have to be "switched around" to eliminate the independent corporation. Influenced by Tugwell and William I. Myers, he thought tenant purchase lending should be conducted by either the FCA or the RA. Concerning spending, Roosevelt "didn't think that too big a bite could be taken in the matter right off the jump." Milton reported that the president estimated that 2 million tenants needed aid in acquiring land, but not more than 75 percent of them could be economically cared for. Therefore he envisioned a ten-year program in which the government would buy and resell 150,000 farms per year, ultimately serving 1.5 million cases. Milton concluded that Roosevelt, while not opposed to the Bankhead program, was "rather definitely uninterested in it unless both form and tempo . . . were changed" as he suggested.[9] Thus the president wanted to narrow the legislation's coverage by slowing its implementation and reducing its spending.

As 1936 began and Congress convened, the president pressed vigorously for his version of the legislation. On January 4, the day after his State of the Union address, he met with Alexander and others to review the desired changes in the bill. Then on January 6 a larger group, including Alexander, Bankhead, Jones, Wallace, Myers, and others conferred with Roosevelt at the White House. According to Alexander, "the President laid down the law to them in no uncertain terms and asked for amendments to which all agreed." The changes, to which Bankhead probably consented with reluctance, included elimination of the independent corporation, administration of the program by an agency of the Department of Agriculture, and replacement of the $1 billion bond issue with gradual financing of government land purchases by direct appropriations.

9 George Fort Milton to Nixon, December 6, 1935, in Herman Clarence Nixon Papers, in the possession of the Nixon family, Nashville.

Concerning actual passage, "Jones agreed to proceed at once to put it through the House, the President insisting that he didn't want it left to the end of the session."[10]

Unfortunately, these promising efforts for passage were abruptly terminated. As the White House conference broke up, the Supreme Court was announcing its decision in *U.S.* v. *Butler,* which declared the AAA processing tax unconstitutional and overthrew the principal New Deal farm program. Because of this judgment, it was clear that the Bankhead bill could not progress until the Agriculture Department and administration forces in Congress could write and enact a substitute for the AAA. Alexander wrote Edwin Embree, "You can imagine the confusion which we have been in since that time [the announcement of the decision] but I still hope that we can salvage the bill from the wreck." But Alexander still retained his optimism. He told Tannenbaum that Roosevelt had asserted that as soon as general farm legislation was enacted the tenancy measure "must be put through next," and that Wallace and Tugwell had lawyers preparing it for House passage "when the first opening appears." Moreover, Jones had again promised action, and Brooks Hays and H. C. Nixon were lobbying vigorously.[11]

Other friends of the bill were more discouraged. M. L. Wilson informed one North Carolina supporter that there was much uncertainty about the measure's future, and even if it were enacted its appropriations would be "on a rather modest scale" because, he thought, current administration policy was to "hold fast to the going things this year, and not initiate anything new . . . which would involve additional expenditures."[12]

Even Bankhead seemed apathetic about his namesake's progress.

10   Alexander to Embree, January 13, 1936, in Julius Rosenwald Fund Papers, Fisk University; John H. Bankhead to L. C. Gray, December 14, 1936, in "Records of the Office of the Secretary of Agriculture," Record Group 16, National Archives. Tugwell seems not to have been present on January 6, although he may have been on the fourth.
11   Alexander to Embree, January 13, 1936, in Rosenwald Fund Papers; Alexander to Tannenbaum [*ca.* February, 1936] and February 27, 1936, in Frank Tannenbaum Papers, Columbia University. Tannenbaum, then on the faculty of Columbia University, had not worked actively for the bill since May, 1935.
12   M. L. Wilson to Hugh MacRae, January 29 and February 12, 1936, in RG 16, NA.

Hearing of this, Tannenbaum wrote the senator to encourage a renewal of his efforts. In clear Jeffersonian terms he told him that "American democracy cannot survive the conversion of our farm population into a property-less and homeless race of migrants," a likely outcome unless current trends were reversed. Expressing confidence that Bankhead would not allow legislation so closely associated with his name to die, he told the senator that "passage of this bill makes you the great statesman of our day in helping preserve the stability of our rural life, upon which our entire institutional system depends." He further advised Bankhead not to be unduly concerned about recent alterations in the measure, since the most important thing was to enact it, establish the principle of opposition to tenancy and begin working to reduce landlessness. The letter was flattering in tone, but conveyed Tannenbaum's feeling that the bill would fail unless someone took decisive action.[13]

The White House continued its efforts. During February Alexander received repeated assurances that the president wanted the tenancy bill taken up by the House as soon as a new general farm program was enacted. On February 28, Congress passed the Soil Conservation and Domestic Allotment Act, clearing the way for other matters. By spring Roosevelt began to press the House Agriculture Committee to report the Bankhead measure.[14]

One factor that may have added urgency to the administration's desire for legislation was an outbreak of violence against the Southern Tenant Farmers' Union in eastern Arkansas in the early months of 1936. The occasion for this was the union's plan for a strike of cotton day laborers in the spring. Since the strike vote was taken three months before the peak of the farm labor season, planters and their local allies had time to try to forestall the action with antiunion violence and evictions of STFU members from the land.[15] Roosevelt

13 "Reminiscences of Will W. Alexander," 597; Tannenbaum to Bankhead, February 28, 1936, in Tannenbaum Papers.
14 Alexander to Tannenbaum, February 27, 1936, and April 22, 1936, in Tannenbaum Papers; transcript of report by Will Alexander to the board of the Commission on Interracial Cooperation, April 16, 1936, in CIC Papers.
15 Donald H. Grubbs, *Cry from the Cotton: The Southern Tenant Farmers' Union and the New Deal* (Chapel Hill: University of North Carolina Press, 1971), 100–106.

received considerable pressure to intervene in this situation. Both Norman Thomas and Gardner Jackson, the STFU's Washington spokesman, pressed him to order federal investigation of the disorders, and he was sufficiently influenced by these critics to have Tugwell quietly look into the matter.[16] Then on March 6 the president introduced the subject in a cabinet meeting. Perhaps to avoid possible embarrassment of Senator Robinson, he rejected a suggestion by Labor Secretary Frances Perkins that federal strike mediators be sent to Arkansas. But he did direct Tugwell to see the majority leader and suggest that he persuade Arkansas governor J. Marion Futrell to take stronger measures to discourage violence and appoint a state tenancy commission to recommend ways to improve the sharecroppers' condition. On March 10 Tugwell reported that Robinson had accepted the idea and had begun to pressure Futrell. A state commission was subsequently appointed. This cautious attempt to ease the turmoil illustrates that the administration found the tenancy problem extremely troublesome, yet impossible to ignore.[17] This predicament must have added to the desire to produce some tangible legislative benefits for the landless.

On April 16, 1936, Alexander reported to the board of the interracial commission that the bill was still in committee because "Mr. Jones is very hard to reach. He is one of the most powerful men in Congress—and as politicians go he wants something for whatever he does.... Unfortunately, we haven't found anything we can swap with Mr. Jones." This assessment contrasted to Jones's continual assurances to Alexander and Roosevelt since the previous January that he would bring the legislation to the floor, and indicated that for Alexander, at least, Jones's promises were wearing thin. Another

16 Gardner Jackson to Roosevelt, January 21, 1936, and to Marvin McIntyre, March 20, 1936, in Official File 4207, Franklin D. Roosevelt Library; Norman Thomas to Roosevelt, February 28, 1936, and Roosevelt to Tugwell, memorandum, March 2, 1936, in Official File 1650, Franklin D. Roosevelt Library.

17 Grubbs, *Cry from the Cotton*, 99; Tugwell to Roosevelt, memorandum, March 10, 1936, in Official File 1650, Franklin D. Roosevelt Library. A generally accepted interpretation is that the STFU was an embarrassment to the administration because of the New Deal's need to keep on good terms with powerful cotton belt senators such as Robinson. See, for example, Baldwin, *Poverty and Politics*, 80–81.

reason for the lack of progress was the recalcitrance of several other southern committee members, including E. M. Owen of Georgia, Richard M. Kleberg of Texas, and Harold Cooley of North Carolina. Nevertheless, Alexander still saw a chance for passage because the measure had Roosevelt's "whole support."[18]

The president's influence and the patient work of Alexander and other supporters nearly brought success in April, 1936. On the twenty-second Alexander informed Tannenbaum that "we have finally worn down the members of the Committee," and after the "most realistic check," he predicted that all Democratic members, an independent, and one or two Republicans would vote to report the bill on the next day. The anticipated action, he said, was "due in large measure to pressure from the President." With Roosevelt's strong commitment and a nearly unanimous committee vote, Alexander expected the bill to develop a powerful momentum toward passage.[19]

On April 23, to Alexander's dismay, something went wrong and "the Committee decided to take a little more time." To Embree he confided "the delay drives one almost to despair." Francis P. Miller, who had watched the committee closely, determined that favorable action had been prevented by Harold Cooley and three other Democrats. Accordingly he asked Jonathan Daniels to try to "educate" Cooley. Daniels wrote to the congressman, but was informed that "it does not appear . . . that legislation will be enacted at this session of Congress."[20]

At about this time Roosevelt reached the same conclusion. Writing to Bankhead and Robinson shortly after May 8, he assumed that the session would produce no tenancy act, but expressed hope for action by the next Congress.[21] Although Congress did not adjourn

18   Report by Will Alexander to the board of the Commission on Interracial Cooperation, April 16, 1936, in CIC Papers.
19   Alexander to Tannenbaum, April 22, 1936, in Tannenbaum Papers.
20   Alexander to Embree, April 28, 1936, in Rosenwald Fund Papers; Francis P. Miller to Jonathan Daniels, April 29, 1936, and Harold Cooley to Daniels, May 1, 1936, in Jonathan Daniels Papers, Southern Historical Collection, University of North Carolina, Chapel Hill.
21   Roosevelt to Bankhead and Joseph T. Robinson, undated memorandum [after May 8, 1936], in Official File 1650, Franklin D. Roosevelt Library.

for another six weeks, Roosevelt had not given up the measure prematurely. Time was indeed limited and congressional leaders were planning for quick adjournment for the national political conventions.[22] Congress recessed June 9 through 15 for the Republican convention and then adjourned on June 21, just before the Democrats met. Therefore the session was virtually finished at the time Roosevelt abandoned hope for the bill. Even had the House passed the legislation, it would have differed substantially from that approved by the Senate in June, 1935, and the necessary conference probably would have been lengthy. With conventions nearing and the session ending. Roosevelt reluctantly decided to defer the Bankhead bill again, until 1937.

Although some were concerned that the failure of the Bankhead bill could expose the Democratic party to charges that it was indifferent to the poor, tenancy did not become a major public issue in the 1936 election campaign. Except for an innocuous statement that "we recognize the gravity of the evils of farm tenancy," the party's platform was silent on landlessness and chronic poverty, while stressing New Deal accomplishments in raising commodity prices, reducing farm indebtedness, and instigating other programs benefiting landowners. Roosevelt mentioned tenancy only twice in the campaign. On September 21 he released to the press letters to Bankhead and Jones requesting them to outline new legislation for 1937. Then, at Omaha on October 10 he pledged to propose measures in January to promote "the ultimate objective of every farm family owning its own land." Except for his indirect hint from Warm Springs in December, 1935, these statements were Roosevelt's first public endorsement of the Bankhead bill. But they also failed to indicate whether the president then had any ideas beyond the simplistic notion that farm purchase credit was the final answer to landlessness and poverty.[23]

22 New York *Times*, May 2, 1936, p. 1.
23 [Lister Hill] to James A. Farley, June 4, 1936, in RG 16, NA; New York *Times*, June 26, 1936, pp. 1, 13, and October 11, 1936, p. 1; Roosevelt to Marvin Jones and to Bankhead, September 21, 1936, in Official File 1650, Franklin D. Roosevelt Library. Baldwin, *Poverty and Politics*, 165, attributes the tenancy statement to Marvin Jones.

Behind the scenes of the 1936 election campaign there were important developments in administration poverty policy. In the RA Tugwell and Alexander continued to coordinate land classification, retirement of submarginal acres and relocation of their residents, and rural rehabilitation. To this they hoped to add farm purchase lending, and as early as the fall of 1935 Tugwell apparently had Roosevelt's tentative approval of RA administration of the Bankhead program. But by November, 1936, Tugwell was concerned that this comprehensive rehabilitative program might be dismantled. Writing to the president, he deplored Roosevelt's apparent "disposition not to understand why the Resettlement Administration was put together as it was" and his "easy assumption that it can be broken apart again." Tugwell emphasized that all RA functions were interrelated and "if the land [classification] program were . . . separated from the rehabilitation and resettlement work, we should lose all we gained in putting them together." Moreover, passage of the Bankhead program without tying it to the RA would not better the condition of the poor because, standing by itself, it contemplated "simple ownership without the protection of real security [or] the supervision which is essential." Furthermore, if the RA could not administer tenant purchase loans it would remain incomplete, left with its submarginal land and resettlement programs, "both of which should be joined together and to the tenant operations."[24]

The occasion for Tugwell's concerns was that in the fall of 1936 he desired to transfer his agency intact to the Department of Agriculture. The RA was then vulnerable to criticism for several reasons: the similarity to relief of its subsistence grants, its challenges to the rural South's status quo, the fact that its authority was derived only from executive order and not from federal law, its administrative expenses which many thought excessive, and the reputation of Tugwell himself as a controversial braintruster.[25] In addition, the RA was financed by relief funds, an uncertain source, and Tugwell prob-

24 Tugwell to Roosevelt [*ca.* November, 1936], in President's Secretary's File. Agriculture: Tugwell, 1936, Franklin D. Roosevelt Library.
25 Baldwin, *Poverty and Politics,* 119–123.

ably hoped that as part of the Agriculture Department it would have better access to regular appropriations. Accordingly, he suggested to Roosevelt that the Bankhead bill, which then contemplated a land purchase credit corporation within the department, be amended to allow the president to assign to the corporation the assets and functions of any agency, such as the RA, set up under the 1935 relief reorganization. This would assure that the RA and the Bankhead program would be combined within the department. The president was reportedly sympathetic to the general idea of transfer.[26]

Wallace and other agriculture officials were reluctant to accept the change. They may have feared that Tugwell, heading a vigorous program within their jurisdiction, might antagonize planter elements and revive the intradepartmental dissensions of 1935. Furthermore, although Wallace had previously admitted to the press that he thought most of the RA belonged in the department, he wanted a free hand in choosing which functions should be taken over. (He particularly disliked Tugwell's suburban development projects.) The secretary's attitude evidently accounted for the apprehension Tugwell expressed to Roosevelt that the RA might be broken up.[27]

Tugwell, however, had made known his intention to leave government service, in part because he expected his resignation to strengthen the RA by facilitating its transfer to the department. As a further effort to win Wallace over, Tugwell and RA officials persuaded him to tour agency projects from Arkansas to Florida. The trip, beginning November 17, had the desired effect. Shocked by the poverty he saw and impressed by the RA's activities, Wallace began speaking frequently on the value of the rehabilitative process.[28]

On November 18, 1936, Tugwell resigned. As he left the admin-

---

26 Tugwell to Roosevelt [*ca.* November, 1936], in President's Secretary's File, Agriculture: Tugwell, 1936, Franklin D. Roosevelt Library; New York *Times*, November 14, 1936, p. 3.

27 Baldwin, *Poverty and Politics*, 121–22; New York *Times*, November 14, 1936, p. 3.

28 Baldwin, *Poverty and Politics*, 121–22; Donald Holley, *Uncle Sam's Farmers: The New Deal Communities in the Lower Mississippi Valley* (Urbana: University of Illinois Press, 1975), 98–99; New York *Times*, January 13, 1937, p. 13.

istration he was instrumental in selecting his successor; Alexander, who had genuine feeling for the South's poor but who was not handicapped by controversiality, became administrator. On December 31, 1936, Roosevelt, by executive order, made the entire Resettlement Administration part of the Department of Agriculture.[29]

Another of the administration's efforts to encourage tenancy legislation for 1937 was the creation of a presidential tenancy commission in the fall of 1936. As early as June, 1936, as it became apparent that the Bankhead bill would not be passed that year, Roosevelt contemplated a major government report as the basis for an act by the next Congress. On October 13, during the election campaign, Morris L. Cooke of the Rural Electrification Administration wrote the president suggesting preparation of a report to help Congress keep tenancy legislation consistent with administration thinking. Cooke said he was not speaking merely for himself, but for others, whom he did not name, but probably including Tugwell.[30]

The president referred Cooke's letter to Wallace and Tugwell, who both endorsed the suggestion. To enhance the report's prestige, they advised appointment of a sponsoring commission of prominent persons sympathetic to the landless. They proposed a list of members with L. C. Gray of the Bureau of Agricultural Economics as director. Roosevelt accepted this idea and appointed the commission on November 16, designating Wallace as nominal chairman and Gray as technical advisor. Directing them to report by February 1, the president specified that they should outline a land tenure system which would provide security and opportunity for the landless masses. At the same time he also strongly endorsed as a goal "the traditional American ideal of owner operated farms." The commission met on December 16–17 and formed a technical committee to prepare the report. It consisted of Gray, Alexander, Charles S. Johnson, Bureau of Agricultural Economics chief A. G. Black, economists E. G.

29   Baldwin, *Poverty and Politics*, 122; New York *Times*, January 1, 1937, p. 18.
30   Roosevelt to Edward G. Lowry, June 8, 1936, in President's Personal File 3593, Franklin D. Roosevelt Library; Morris L. Cooke to Roosevelt, October 13, 1936, in RG 16, NA; "Reminiscences of Will W. Alexander," 393–94; interview with James G. Maddox, July 10, 1970.

Nourse and John D. Black, Lowry Nelson of the Extension Service, and M. W. Thatcher of the Farmers' Union.[31]

Although the presidential tenancy commission conducted formal hearings in several parts of the country during January, 1937, the technical committee independently drafted a report early that month.[32] The statement, released February 16, proposed a comprehensive federal rehabilitative program under one jurisdiction within the Agriculture Department, building on the RA. It envisioned government purchase and resale of farms on twenty-year minimum contracts, undertaken only after supervisory lease periods of at least five years. The agency should also lease land from owners and sublet it to tenants under its guidance. Selection of clients would give preference to those already farming the acquired lands. The report advocated the family farm as the major type of holding, but also suggested experimentation in aiding cooperative groups to buy or lease acreages. Congressional appropriations would support all this initially, but broader financing (presumably a bond issue by the agency) might be attempted later.

The commission favored extension of rehabilitative credit, technical guidance, and debt adjustment loans to about 1.3 million families, including a large fraction of the 1.8 million southern tenants then financed only by lien merchants. The report expected that the ablest of these clients could be built up to the point of purchasing farms. Considering the plight of destitute wage laborers, it proposed government camps for migrants and rehabilitation credit for those who could be established as tenants. Finally, the commission endorsed the submarginal land and resettlement work of the RA.[33] This report was not only designed to promote congressional action, but was also the blueprint for the Farm Security Administration.

In the interval between the Seventy-fourth and Seventy-fifth

31 Henry Wallace and Tugwell to Roosevelt, November 5, 1936, and typescript agenda of tenancy commission meeting, December 16–17, 1936, in RG 16, NA; Roosevelt to Wallace and members-designate of the tenancy commission, November 16, 1936, in Official File 1650, Franklin D. Roosevelt Library.

32 Gray to commission members, December 22, 1936, in RG 16, NA.

33 U.S. National Resources Committee, *Farm Tenancy: Report of the President's Committee* (Washington: Government Printing Office, 1937), 11–20.

Congresses, from June, 1936, to February, 1937, the administration
had secured a place for the RA within the Agriculture Department
and had finally clarified the RA's relationship to the proposed Bankhead program. And with the report of the presidential commission,
the Tugwell-Alexander design for a comprehensive antipoverty effort had become New Deal policy.

Another development of the latter part of 1936 was the
emergence of a distinct radical antagonism to the Bankhead bill, in-
cipient since its introduction. As early as November, 1935, some
radicals began thinking of alternatives to the measure. One Socialist
and active STFU sympathizer, William Amberson of the University
of Tennessee medical college in Memphis, participated in outlining
a substitute measure for consideration by the union, and apparently
by his party as well. The preliminary draft proposed that a national
land authority, through power of eminent domain, appraise and purchase all arable landholdings in excess of 160 acres, and divide and
lease (but not sell) them to the landless. Farms of any size owned
and operated by cooperative associations of working farmers would
continue as units, while the new agency established other such
cooperatives.[34] Amberson had a low opinion of the Bankhead measure, which he described to Gardner Jackson as "just another bit of
administration hypocrisy," and hoped that "various left wing groups
interested in the agricultural problem could agree upon some radical
alternative." But he recognized that Congress would never seriously
consider such a bill unless its origins were concealed and its "radical
implications" soft-pedaled. This created a dilemma for him, however. "I want to see the S.P. get publicity," he told the Socialist
party's national secretary, Clarence Senior, adding that he foresaw a
"long-range effect of strengthening the Socialist sentiment" if Congress rejected a "recognized Socialist proposal." But on the other
hand, having observed conditions in eastern Arkansas, he knew that

34   William Amberson to Clarence Senior, November 15, 1935, with draft pages of a bill, in
     William R. Amberson Papers, Southern Historical Collection, University of North
     Carolina; "A New Homestead Law," undated typescript outline [*ca.* December, 1935],
     in Southern Tenant Farmers' Union Papers, Southern Historical Collection, University
     of North Carolina, Chapel Hill, hereinafter cited as STFU Papers.

the "pressing need of these people cries out for some immediate alleviation," which might necessitate acceptance of some less sweeping legislation.[35]

The land nationalization proposal was "adopted in principle" by the STFU's convention in Little Rock in January, 1936. But it was soon dropped, after Gardner Jackson advised the union leadership that "pressure for such a completely revolutionary bill at [this] time... is bad tactics" and that "we ought to unite our forces in hammering for adequate amendments to the Bankhead-Jones ... legislation."[36]

As early as February 21, 1936, representatives of the STFU had opposed the Bankhead bill in conferences with Tugwell, Alexander, and Brooks Hays.[37] But the union's first broad counterproposal came in the fall of 1936 in response to the report of the Arkansas state tenancy commission. The state commission, it will be recalled, had been appointed by Governor Futrell, prompted by Senator Robinson, who in turn had acted upon a White House suggestion conveyed by Tugwell. It consisted of businessmen, editors, planters, educators, lawyers, and, to avoid adverse publicity for barring union spokesmen who appeared at its session, representatives of the STFU. These members met at Hot Springs on September 21 and issued a statement which stressed the value of individual farm ownership and favored a program essentially like the 1935 Bankhead bill. The commission also called for government-supervised production credit to replace the "furnish" system, federal loans for family subsistence goods, standardized written contracts between landlord and tenant, and improved state health and educational services for the landless.[38]

Even before the state commission published its report, the STFU prepared its response. Anticipating that the Hot Springs con-

35 Amberson to Jackson, December 31, 1935, and to Senior, November 15, 1935, in Amberson Papers.

36 "A New Homestead Law," with endorsement statement of STFU convention, January 3–5, 1936, and Jackson to H. L. Mitchell, January 15, 1936, in STFU Papers.

37 Howard Kester to H. L. Mitchell, February 21, 1936, in STFU Papers.

38 Arkansas Farm Tenancy Commission, *Findings and Recommendations* (Hot Springs, Arkansas, November 24, 1936), copy in RG 16, NA; Grubbs, *Cry from the Cotton,*

ference would endorse the Bankhead bill, the union concentrated its
criticism on the measure, which it called "nothing more than a flank
attack on the problem of tenancy." The critics assumed that because
of limited funds and other factors, the Bankhead program would be a
highly selective process which would assist some tenants to landownership, but neglect a "vast residium [*sic*]" of those unable to meet
its standards, who really constituted the "heart of the problem." In
short, the union believed nothing would be solved by making a few
men home owners; rather, tenancy had to be abolished completely.[39]

The STFU questioned whether Bankhead-style land redistribution would even benefit those who qualified to purchase farms. Plantation interests which held the best lands in the Delta regions with
which the union was most familiar were expected to be reluctant to
part with them. Besides, the statement asserted, there was no real
chance that family-sized farms could compete in cotton production
with increasingly mechanized plantations. Nor could small owners
attain adequate living standards if limited to subsistence farming,
growing only small amounts of cotton for incidental cash. The statement continued that there had been a half-century trend toward
concentration of landownership. This was a natural development because "the large plantation has an economic justification which we
neglect at our peril." Its advantages included efficiency of operation
and greater productivity than small farms, features worth preserving. "The fundamental readjustment" that the STFU believed
necessary was in the "character of the ownership of the large farm."

120–21. According to Edward J. Meeman to Wilson, December 1, 1936, in RG 16, NA,
the state commission's report was written by C. T. Carpenter, a lawyer from Marked
Tree, Arkansas, who had once represented the STFU but was no longer connected with
it.

39 "STFU Recommendations to the Governor's Commission on Farm Tenancy in Arkansas" (Typescript in Amberson Papers). This statement was a supplement to one already
presented at the commission's meeting, and which was more general in criticizing the
Bankhead bill. See "A Statement Concerning Farm Tenancy Submitted to the Governor's Commission on Farm Tenancy by the Executive Council Southern Tenant Farmers' Union," August 15, 1936, typescript in Socialist Party of America Papers, Duke
University, Durham, N.C.

A new type of farm organization was needed and it *"must perforce* be a communal or village farm economy."[40]

Specifically, the STFU recommended collective ownership of large acreages by tenants. Individuals would retain their own houses and garden plots, probably grouped in rural villages, but field crops would be grown cooperatively without division of land. This system could preserve the advantages of the large plantation by hiring experts to supervise crops, providing cooperative ownership of machinery, group marketing and purchasing (perhaps through cooperative stores) and efficient division of farm labor. Although critical of the Bankhead proposal to purchase land from private owners, and of the government's land acquisitions for its community projects (particularly the Works Progress Administration's Dyess Colony in eastern Arkansas), the statement made no suggestion about how land for collectively owned farms should be obtained.[41]

The National Committee on Rural Social Planning, the Washington voice of the STFU, headed by Gardner Jackson, also issued a statement, on November 12, 1936. It fully endorsed the union's position and added other criticisms of the Bankhead measure. Because of the trend toward large mechanized holdings, the committee stated, a rigid policy of promoting small farms "would at best . . . anchor millions of our rural people to a subsistence or a near subsistence level" by providing them acreages too small for economical operation.[42]

The committee acknowledged that the final version of the 1935 bill had offered several possibilities for the landless: credit for long-term purchase, five-year leases of land from the proposed corporation, and encouragement of cooperatives. But it regarded these alternatives as inadequate because the major emphasis of the legisla-

---

40 "STFU Recommendations to the Governor's Commission on Farm Tenancy in Arkansas" (Typescript in Amberson Papers).

41 *Ibid.*

42 Unsigned letter to Tugwell and Wallace from National Committee on Rural Social Planning, November 12, 1936, in RG 16, NA. The probable author was Gardner Jackson.

tion had been on ownership. Lease provisions were neither detailed nor renewable and might not protect tenant rights. Furthermore, the requirement that farms sold be capable of supporting a "decent standard of living" did nothing to define that standard. Having pointed out these flaws in the measure (and ignored any possibility that they might have been substantially overcome by enlightened administration), the statement then leaped to a conclusion about its intent by declaring that "there can be no doubt that the main purpose of the Act was to set up an American peasantry." [43]

Finally, the committee thought that if the Bankhead bill were enacted in 1937 it should be amended to assure that individual farms provide an adequate living, safeguard against alienation of land to speculators, and specifically ban racial discrimination in the program. Moreover, banks, insurance companies, and landlords should be prevented from dumping their least valuable acreages on a government agency which in turn would unload them on tenant purchasers. [44]

At the presidential tenancy commission's hearing in Dallas on January 4, 1937, officials of the STFU stressed that southwestern tenants and small farm owners were already being rapidly displaced by the consolidation of landholdings and the introduction of tractors pulling four-row equipment. Surplus day laborers swelled the relief rolls, while many others were employed only part time. Wages in West Texas cotton fields ranged downward from fifteen cents per hour, even for semiskilled machinery operators. Citing these conditions, union official Fred Mathews asserted, "It will not be sufficient... to set the working farm population on small tracts of land, trusting blindly that they will be able, in the cultivation of a commercial crop, to withstand the competition of the large-scale, machine-equipped landowner." He too saw the alternative as cooperative farming, with collective ownership of machinery for the remaining family-sized farmers. [45]

43 *Ibid.*
44 *Ibid.*
45 "Memorandum submitted by Fred Mathews of the Texas Southern Tenant Farmers' Union to the President's Special Committee on Farm Tenancy, meeting at Dallas, Texas, January 4, 1937," in STFU Papers.

Howard Kester, another STFU spokesman, made similar points at the commission's hearing in Montgomery, Alabama, on January 6. Dismissing the Bankhead bill as a "return to the post bellum philosophy of '40 acres and a mule,'" he condemned "the idea of approaching so gigantic and critical a problem with so antiquated an instrument," adding that family-sized farms would be practical only in southern hill sections, not in Delta or plains areas. Kester also emphasized that in addition to the expected mechanization, the soil exhaustion of older cotton regions and the shift of cotton growing westward would speed the dislocation of the landless in the Southeast. Kester thought the government should purchase and lease land to tenants, lend for livestock, equipment and dwellings, and provide "socially enlightened supervision." He also called for federal encouragement of unionization and collective bargaining by tenants.[46]

Despite the positions of several of its leaders and sympathizers, the STFU was not unanimously committed to collective landownership. Although it claimed that a substantial number of its members preferred cooperative farming of large tracts, it admitted to the presidential commission that most of them desired to own small farms. Earlier, the National Committee on Rural Social Planning had also noted this sharecropper opinion and had maintained that the New Deal should help improve their understanding of the benefits of a cooperative system. "Until the government and other organizations undertake an educational campaign to dispel the romantic notions that still prevail concerning the advantages of rugged individualism on the farm, such desires will continue to prevail," the committee declared. But at the Dallas hearing, even J. R. Butler, president of the STFU and a Socialist, advocated Bankhead-style land sales to tenants, although he insisted that small owners had to be assisted to own machinery cooperatively. In its official recommendations at Dallas and in the statement Kester read at Montgomery, the STFU stopped short of specifically proposing collective landownership, suggesting instead widespread long-term government land leasing to

46 "Statement given before the President's Commission on Farm Tenancy at Montgomery, Alabama, January 6, 1937, by Howard Kester, Member Executive Council Southern Tenant Farmers' Union," *ibid.*

tenant groups and individuals. But even though STFU statements were not consistent and sometimes did not go far beyond RA plans, cooperative farming was the proposal advocated most prominently in the union's name.[47]

These radical critics did hit the mark by showing that simple credit for buying farms was no panacea for tenancy, not to mention other poverty conditions. However, many of their criticisms had already been anticipated by the RA and the inner group of the Bankhead bill's supporters. That farm purchase lending would be selective and leave most unaffected had long been recognized and was still being emphasized. For example, H. C. Nixon told the presidential tenancy commission in Montgomery that the bill's credit would reach "hardly five per cent" of the South's landless, while still stressing the "extreme importance" of aiding that group.[48] In the RA Tugwell and Alexander, with their vision of a coordinated program for the landless, saw rural rehabilitation and subsistence grants as ways of reaching those without immediate prospects of ownership while assisting the most capable toward possession of homes. Likewise, the idea that credit for the poor had to be combined with supervision of their farming had been present since the FERA originated rural rehabilitation. Furthermore, advocates of the Bankhead program intended to safeguard clients from land speculators by leaving title to their farms with the government during a long amortization period.

As for obtaining adequate lands for clients, Tugwell favored a redistribution program only if carefully coordinated with the RA's retirement of submarginal lands, assuring that tenants received only those acres suitable for cultivation. The 1935 bill also had provided that farms sold be of sufficient size and fertility and properly equipped to provide a "decent standard of living," although admittedly that

47 *Ibid.*; "Statement of the Southern Tenant Farmers' Union, presented to the President's Special Committee on Farm Tenancy, Meeting at Dallas, Texas, January 4, 1937," in STFU Papers; unsigned letter to Tugwell and Wallace from National Committee on Rural Social Planning, November 12, 1936, in RG 16, NA; Dallas *Morning News,* January 5, 1937.
48 Draft of Southern Policy Committee Recommendations, December 14, 1936, in NPC Papers.

would have to be defined by administrators. Moreover, the 1935 version of the bill authorized five-year leases of land prior to sale, a feature that could have been generally applied by the RA to provide a period of supervision for most prospective purchasers. Another section permitted government encouragement of cooperatives. Finally, concerning prohibition of racial discrimination, the architects of the legislation had determined in 1935 to rely on equitable administration (an enhanced possibility with Alexander heading the RA) rather than burden the measure with an explosive issue.

There was also an expectation that the Bankhead program, once enacted, could be improved in time. Paul Appleby wrote that deeper understanding of tenancy problems "would be brought out... in administrative operations growing out of enactment of the Bankhead-Jones Farm Tenant Bill," while at the same time there would occur an "actual improvement in the status of some tens of thousands of persons," and "the whole thing could be achieved without becoming necessarily a center of controversy."[49]

Outside of government, some members of the agrarian-minded Southern Policy Committee were aware of the complexities of southern rural problems and were willing to advocate significant changes in southern agriculture, going considerably beyond the RA program and the proposals of radical critics. In a statement prepared for the Montgomery hearing, for example, Charles S. Johnson suggested that any government program should broadly distinguish between the Southeast, where exhausted land and high production costs had reduced the profitability of cotton growing, and the Delta and Southwest regions, well suited to mechanization and capable of expanding production. Long-range policies, he thought, should gradually phase out southeastern cotton farming and guide the area's people into other agricultural pursuits.[50]

Johnson and H. C. Nixon were flexible in considering a desir-

---

49 Paul Appleby to Lee R. Hays, February 24, 1936, in RG 16, NA.
50 Draft of Southern Policy Committee Recommendations, December 14, 1936, in NPC Papers. SPC recommendations were drawn up individually by Johnson, H. C. Nixon, Arthur Raper, and Rupert B. Vance, but submitted at Montgomery by Nixon.

able land tenure system. While preferring the goal of small ownership, they also favored federal land leasing for a trial period for
those thought capable of farm ownership and as a permanent program for those who were not. Johnson also wanted federal financial
assistance for group purchase of large acreages for operation on a
"profit sharing basis." Concerning other measures for the landless,
the spokesmen urged government production credit for those
served only by lien merchants and proposed federal ownership and
operation of some lands as a "yardstick" of equitable standards for
tenants and farm laborers. Johnson advocated inclusion of farm
workers in social security and enactment of a minimum wage for
them.[51] The latter proposal was particularly advanced since Congress was still a year and a half from passing the Fair Labor Standards Act.

There still remained the essential question, raised by the critics
on the left, of the adequacy of the small farm in a mechanized cotton belt. The pertinence of the issue is suggested by subsequent
experience in the tenant purchase program of the Farm Security
Administration, in which many units were provided which ultimately proved too small for economical operation.[52]

Gardner Jackson and the STFU maintained that small ownership was uneconomical and the alternative "must perforce" be a
village or communal system. However, a concept emerging within
the administration by the end of 1936 was that small farmers could
cooperate without resorting to collective land ownership. The
permissive language of the 1935 Bankhead bill might have allowed
government encouragement of cooperative buying, marketing, or
acquisition of machinery. That idea, apparently not frequently
stated in 1936, did appear in the report of the President's Commission of Farm Tenancy of February, 1937, in Secretary Wallace's
testimony on February 18, 1937, before the House Agriculture
Committee in support of the Bankhead measure, and in the South-

51 *Ibid.*
52 Edward C. Banfield, "Ten Years of the Farm Tenant Purchase Program," *Journal of
Farm Economics,* XXXI (1949), 469, 483; interview with James G. Maddox.

ern Policy Committee's statements at Montgomery in January, 1937.[53]

The recognition that cooperative ventures were not precluded by a tenancy program which emphasized the goal of individual ownership grew in succeeding years and found a prominent place in the policy of the Farm Security Administration. In 1940, for example, T. J. Woofter, an FSA economic advisor, wrote:

A middle ground between large-scale and family-sized farms lies in the development of family-sized units which will be bound together with cooperative devices. I do not mean to imply that it is desirable to collectivize our farms. Some large scale cooperatives might help to test the idea. . . . [Although] the pride of ownership is deeply ingrained in American farmers—cooperative ownership of bulls and boars, heavy machinery, community facilities for storing[,] first processing, purchasing, and selling can bring to the family-sized farm many of the advantages of large-scale operations without loss of individual initiative.[54]

This was virtually a restatement of Wallace's testimony of February, 1937.

Whatever the merit of these ideas, belief in small ownership as the goal of rehabilitative efforts was widespread in Congress and the administration. Alexander thought no other policy could be successfully promoted; indeed he wrote in the spring of 1937 that the favorable effect on public opinion was one justification for including land purchase credit in the RA's pattern of assistance for the landless. Moreover, some of the advocacy of small farm ownership may not have been based merely on traditional values. In 1939 Woofter, referring to his tenancy research of 1936, considered the place of small scale "live at home" farming in the midst of commercial agriculture and rejected the assumption that it would lower living standards. His investigations revealed that, while the cash income of landlords

53 National Resources Committee, *Farm Tenancy,* 13; *Farm Tenancy, Hearings Before the Committee on Agriculture,* House of Representatives, 75th Cong., 1st Sess., 221–24; draft of Southern Policy Committee Recommendations, December 14, 1936, in NPC Papers.

54 Thomas Jackson Woofter, Jr., *Rural Planning for More Workers* (Washington: Farm Security Administration, mimeographed, 1940), 6; interview with Robert W. Hudgens, July 8 and 9, 1970.

grew proportionately with their acreage in staple crops, the real income and living standard of sharecroppers, so low to begin with, increased almost directly with their production for home use. Presumably these findings could have applied to the impoverished tenant who became an owner.[55]

If small ownership was an incomplete answer to rural poverty, neither was there any assurance that collective land ownership would fulfill the expectations of advocates like Gardner Jackson. The RA was already operating or developing eight major cooperative plantations in the STFU's own area, the lower Mississippi Valley. Acquiring both uncleared and improved land, it created communities for resettling displaced farmers. Most of these projects fit a family farm pattern, leasing thirty- or forty-acre units to residents who could expect eventually to purchase the land. Stores, gins, and community centers were owned cooperatively. But at least two resettlement projects, Lake Dick, near Pine Bluff, Arkansas, and Terrebonne, near Thibodaux, Louisiana, approximated the system STFU spokesmen proposed. In those places the RA sponsored, and loaned money to, client associations which leased large government-acquired tracts for ninety-nine years and held their land, homes, and crop-processing facilities in common. Resident members worked for wages and dividends from any association profits.[56]

But even with government credit and backing, New Deal communities were costly failures as business enterprises. In Arkansas, Louisiana, and Mississippi the RA and its successor, the Farm Security Administration, invested more than $14.3 million in 26 community projects of all kinds by 1943, losing about $2.2 million. Lake Dick and Terrebonne were among the most financially unsuccessful projects. While the RA-FSA made serious management mistakes in its cooperatives, it was also evident that these communities required

---

55 "Reminiscences of Will W. Alexander," 414; Alexander to Roosevelt, April 27, 1937, in Official File 1650, Franklin D. Roosevelt Library; Woofter, *Rural Planning for More Workers,* 7–8. See also Thomas Jackson Woofter, Jr., *Landlord and Tenant on the Cotton Plantation,* Works Progress Administration Research Monographs, V (Washington: Works Progress Administration, 1936), 183, for a suggestion that the South might experience parallel development of both big commercial agriculture and small farming.
56 Holley, *Uncle Sam's Farmers,* 107, 156–63, 275.

a thorough transformation of their residents' individualistic values. Apparently many of them did not develop a cooperative outlook, and the projects were disappointing as social experiments.[57]

In 1938 the New Deal began one other cooperative program to improve poor farmers' land tenure in the lower Mississippi Valley. Following proposals by T. Roy Reid, its regional administrator, the FSA assisted 827 of its standard rehabilitation borrowers to form seventeen land-leasing associations. With FSA guidance and a large operating loan, each of these groups leased the plantation on which its members lived, on a five- or ten-year agreement, paying the owner cash rent in advance. The association then acted as a landlord, subletting small acreages to each member family, usually on a crop-sharing basis. It also hired an expert farm manager and provided tractors, major equipment, and land for feed crops and pasture. If the plantation had such facilities as a commissary or a gin, the association operated them cooperatively. Each participating family still had a standard rehabilitation loan and FSA supervision.[58]

The FSA eventually aided fifty-two land-leasing associations, mostly in Arkansas and Louisiana. Although they did not own or operate land collectively, these associations had real potential for changing farming patterns in the Delta. Moreover, they could assist some of the very poorest sharecroppers, providing them effective rehabilitative services in whole plantation groups, as the FSA's regular program often could not. Although about ten of the associations were financial failures, the others operated profitably, at least in the long run, and gave their members incomes and living standards comparable to those of FSA's regular rehabilitation borrowers.[59]

But the land-leasing associations were a short-lived experiment. Congress was not pleased with this cooperative innovation. In July,

57 *Ibid.*, 166–69, 274–75.
58 *Ibid.*, 113–14; Olaf F. Larson, *Ten Years of Rural Rehabilitation in the United States* (Washington: Bureau of Agricultural Economics, mimeographed, 1947), 218–20; James G. Maddox, "The Farm Security Administration" (Ph.D. dissertation, Harvard University, 1950), 223–24, 234–36.
59 Maddox, "Farm Security Administration," 244–45, 247; Larson, *Ten Years of Rural Rehabilitation*, 220–21. By 1943 land-leasing associations included more than 2,000 families on 136,000 acres.

1943, it prohibited the establishment of new associations and required existing ones to disband. The program was then liquidated within two years.[60]

All of the controversy over the merits of small holdings, cooperative farming, collective landownership, and the value of rehabilitative programs erupted as 1936 ended. These matters would be resolved, insofar as federal policy was concerned, in the first half of 1937 as Congress passed the Bankhead-Jones Act.

---

60 Maddox, "Farm Security Administration," 241; Larson, *Ten Years of Rural Rehabilitation*, 220. Land-leasing associations had been recommended in the 1937 presidential tenancy commission report, but were not mentioned in the Bankhead-Jones Farm Tenancy Act of 1937.

CHAPTER VIII

The Bankhead-Jones Act and the Farm Security Administration

IN HIS State of the Union message on January 6, 1937, President Roosevelt urged the new Congress to reduce the "prevalence of an un-American type of tenant farming." He recognized that not every poor rural family could benefit from a farm purchase loan but he still suggested such credit as the heart of new legislation. Bankhead and Jones, having consulted the administration, introduced identical bills.[1]

In important respects the new measure was much more limited than the 1935 version. It proposed a farm homes corporation within the Department of Agriculture. As contemplated in 1935, the FHC's fundamental power would be its initiative to buy, improve, and resell farms to tenants on liberal credit terms. But it would have no bond-issuing power and would depend for ten years upon annual appropriations of $50 million. Under a new provision, committees of local farmers, agents of the FHC, would approve all land acquired and select "desirable" borrowers. Alexander objected to this feature, foreseeing abuses, favoritism, and concentration on the risk-worthiness of applicants rather than their need. But he gave way at Jones's insistence. The new bill also did not clearly provide aid to

---

1 New York *Times*, January 6, 1937, p. 2, January 7, 1937, p. 2, January 9, 1937, p. 4.

new small owners in establishing cooperative associations for processing, marketing, buying, or ownership of machinery.[2]

Likewise the measure fell short of several important recommendations of the presidential tenancy commission. As developed by the House Agriculture Committee, it did not adopt the commission's proposal to safeguard purchasers from speculators by leaving title to their lands with the government for twenty years. The bill mentioned no program for migratory laborers, and ignored the commission's recommendations for subsistence loans or grants to 420,000 of the most destitute rural families. It also did not specifically sanction the RA's rural rehabilitation or provide for its submarginal land and farmer resettlement program.[3]

As in 1935 and 1936, serious opposition developed in Congress, especially within the House Agriculture Committee. This became evident in the committee's hearings in January and February. The thinking on rural poverty of some witnesses and members of the committee extended no further than the idea of price parity. For example, Hampton Fulmer of South Carolina lectured one witness that the tenants' and sharecroppers' greatest need was "better prices to reach the cause [of their] downfall" and that they "would be better off if they could receive a fair price for their commodities." Likewise Ed O'Neal of the American Farm Bureau Federation advised the committee to "remember that a fair price system and parity of income... will do more to prevent the loss of farm homes through foreclosure than any other one factor." Harold Cooley of North Carolina put it even more simplistically. Because of poor prices, he said, "the owners of the land are dropping into the tenant class" and "if you will make [farming] profitable the tenancy question will take care of itself."[4]

These views, attributing the obvious decline of security on the

---

2   *Ibid.*, January 9, 1937, p. 4; *Farm Tenancy, Hearings Before the Committee on Agriculture,* House of Representatives, 75th Cong., 1st Sess., 221–22, hereinafter cited as Farm Tenancy Hearings; "Reminiscences of Will W. Alexander" (Typescript, 1952, in Oral History Collection, Columbia University), 601.

3   New York *Times,* January 4, 1937, p. 14, January 9, 1937, p. 4; Farm Tenancy Hearings, 216, 218, 221–23.

4   Farm Tenancy Hearings, 208, 216, 232.

land merely to price conditions, completely overlooked landlessness as a basic historic condition of southern poverty. By their remarks Fulmer, O'Neal, and Cooley illustrated how powerful and influential southerners, supposedly well informed about farm matters, often had slight understanding of the plight of their region's most impoverished people, and probably little concern as well. Administration spokesmen, as in 1935, saw the Bankhead program as complementary to their parity policies and readily agreed that better prices were an essential precondition for antipoverty efforts. But they found it necessary to remind southern congressmen, as Wallace told Cooley, that "we must not forget that farm prosperity in itself... will not take care of the tenant's problem. You could have a very prosperous agriculture during the next twenty years and with it a very great increase in tenancy." [5]

Another major issue was the type of tenant to be aided toward ownership. Several Extension Service spokesmen thought the FHC's primary concern should be "those at the top of the tenant pile," while the RA tried to develop the credit-worthiness of others. They would have assisted only applicants with experience and managerial ability, who had acquired, debt-free, enough household goods, workstock, and equipment to operate a "one-horse farm." Some of them admitted that such beneficiaries would be cash and share tenants, not impoverished sharecroppers. Administration officials responded that farm purchase help should not be limited to any particular stratum of the landless. M. L. Wilson envisioned "a program which reaches down through the whole of the tenancy population," not merely assisting the "cream at the top." Jones also pointed out that the only stated requirement was that borrowers be "worthy and ambitious," not necessarily owners of equipment or other assets. [6]

Throughout the hearings administration officials and members of the presidential commission called for a multiple attack on tenancy. Will Alexander, especially, stressed the need to deal with the poor

5   *Ibid.*, 233.
6   *Ibid.*, 14–15, 20–21, 28, 56.

on several levels, including those who could be assisted to home ownership, as well as the landless needing rehabilitation loans. The latter he described as "under the group provided for in this bill," and reminded the committee that "while you cannot finance them in land-ownership, something has got to be done immediately for them." Concerning their condition, he said: "This New Deal, through its activity, has drawn out of the dark a lot of information as to poverty and need that has been going on in this country for a long time. Much of it was not caused by the depression. Many of these people have lived in poverty all their lives. Now, they are expecting something and we ought to do something for them . . . . These people have had nothing."[7] Among New Dealers, Alexander had the clearest understanding of the chronic nature of the rural South's poverty.

M. W. Thatcher of the Farmer's Union, a member of the technical committee which prepared the tenancy commission's report, outlined the minimum needs of the destitute for 1937. His estimate included $60 million to continue standard rehabilitation loans to 300,000 clients and $84 million to extend such credit to 210,000 families then receiving RA subsistence grants. Another half million "marginal" families, mostly midwestern, who could not qualify for Farm Credit Administration assistance, needed emergency aid totaling $200 million to keep off relief, while $15 million would provide hundred-dollar subsistence grants for 150,000 cases. Including emergency feed loans and drought relief, Thatcher proposed spending at least $404 million in the coming year. A farm purchase program would be additional.[8]

Funding farm purchase lending was indeed a major concern. Since Roosevelt was convinced that the program should develop gradually and desired small initial expenditures, the bill proposed only $50 million for the first year, an amount which was expected to provide no more than one loan in each of the nation's counties. Consequently, when asked whether the legislation would significantly

7 *Ibid.*, 102.
8 *Ibid.*, 300–303.

improve the situation within ten years, Alexander was forced to admit, "Not unless you do a great deal more than is attempted . . . by this bill."[9]

Fully aware of its inadequacy, Alexander and other administration figures still favored the measure as part of an overall attack on poverty. Slightly later, in April, Alexander told Wallace and the president that only a combination of rehabilitation credit, submarginal land retirement and resettlement, and a farm purchase program could raise the living standards of the "lowest third" of the rural population. Furthermore, he stressed, "it is important to secure this *pattern* of assistance now, through legislation, even though adequate money for the work is not immediately available." What actually was at stake in 1937 was authorization for government initiative in purchase, improvement, and resale of land to tenants as one part of the "pattern of assistance" the RA desired.[10]

Several committee members assailed provisions for such government initiative and client supervision. John R. Mitchell of Tennessee thought tenants should receive direct loans (of only $500 or $1,000) to acquire farms. When Alexander responded that government selection was necessary to assure that clients received worthwhile property, and that supervision would protect federal investment in the land, Mitchell retorted, "I do not think that the government . . . should be dictating how [the farmer] is to do everything. . . . This country was developed and made great [because] our granddaddies built it up with individual initiative."[11]

Others even attacked the idea of helping low-income farmers obtain tools and supplies. Fulmer, a former lien merchant, condemned a proposal to extend credit for "furnishings, equipment, implements and machinery, supplies, facilities, and livestock." Alexander explained that this would provide mules, plows, simple tools,

9 *Ibid.*, 100–101.
10 Will Alexander to Henry Wallace, undated memorandum in "Records of the Office of the Secretary of Agriculture," Record Group 16, National Archives; identical memorandum, [Alexander] to Franklin D. Roosevelt, April 27, 1937, in Official File 1650, Franklin D. Roosevelt Library, Hyde Park, N.Y.; interview with James G. Maddox, July 10, 1970.
11 Farm Tenancy Hearings, 87–88.

and even food, and that "facilities" might refer to a cabin or a well. But Fulmer stretched the wording to an extreme and professed to foresee an extravagant government furnishing tractors, threshing machines, barns, and cotton gins to indigent clients.[12]

Still more opposition stemmed from hostility to the RA. For example, Harold Cooley demanded of Alexander whether the real purpose of the bill was the continuation of the agency. Alexander soft-pedaled the possibility that farm purchase lending could be conducted by the RA. But it seemed clear that the bill would not prevent the combination of RA activities with the Bankhead program in a comprehensive agency as recommended by the presidential commission.[13]

While most testimony concerned the form and size of the farm purchase program, Gardner Jackson, speaking for the National Committee on Rural Social Planning, again questioned its concept. Contending that concentration on small ownership was misguided, he reiterated that the government should lend to organizations of sharecroppers for group purchase of large tracts. Envisioning an important role for the Southern Tenant Farmers' Union in establishing a new system, he had already stressed to Wallace that its leadership could organize the cooperatives to which the government could lend money or lease land. Jackson also favored expansion of the RA's community projects, but with liberalized client selection standards.[14]

Although such critics as Jackson challenged the bill's assumptions about small farming, its administration friends not only regarded home ownership goals as the capstone of the rehabilitative foundation built by the RA, but they also knew those aims were eminently acceptable to Congress and the public. L. C. Gray advised the committee that the ideal of landholding was "strongly entrenched in

12 *Ibid.*, 85–86.
13 *Ibid.*, 114–15. See Sidney Baldwin, *Poverty and Politics: The Rise and Decline of the Farm Security Administration* (Chapel Hill: University of North Carolina Press, 1968), 123–25, 155–56, 190–91, on the RA's need, as an institution, for specific legislative sanction. This need was not adequately met by the Bankhead-Jones Act.
14 Farm Tenancy Hearings, 179, 181–82, 186, 193–96; National Committee on Rural Social Planning to Wallace and Rexford G. Tugwell, November 12, 1936, in RG 16, NA.

the consciousness of our rural people. That consciousness is unusually strong. It is a psychological factor that we cannot afford to disregard in any broad program we may develop." And Alexander told Wallace and the president that even minimum land purchase credit reaching relatively few families would be valuable because "the experience gained and the effect on public opinion would fully justify it."[15]

In the last important testimony of the hearing Secretary Wallace endorsed the small farm ownership program. He acknowledged its limitations but hoped Congress would overcome them by providing aid for cooperative buying, processing, marketing, and joint ownership of machinery and breeding stock by farm purchasers. As a recent convert to a broad rehabilitative poverty policy, Wallace also affirmed the Tugwellian view of the tenancy commission that farm purchase credit, rehabilitation loans, and submarginal land and resettlement programs should all be conducted by one agency.[16]

After the hearings, in March and April, a sharp struggle occurred in the House Agriculture Committee over the central issue of government initiative in land acquisition. On March 30 Roosevelt conferred with Bankhead, Wallace, and Alexander, and then with Jones and other committee members. He reportedly insisted on the principle of government purchase and resale, but agreed to accept cuts in the spending for that purpose. So long as the ultimate aim was the elimination of tenancy, the size of the first appropriation made little difference, he said in a press conference the same day, adding that the program "would be spread very, very thin. Practically speaking, it would be on an experimental basis... because, obviously, if you did it for all the tenant farmers it would run into the billions."[17]

On April 1, despite the president's accommodations, the committee struck the $50 million appropriation for government land

15 Farm Tenancy Hearings, 60; Alexander to Wallace, undated memorandum in RG 16, NA; [Alexander] to Roosevelt, April 27, 1937, in Official File 1650, Franklin D. Roosevelt Library.

16 Farm Tenancy Hearings, 216, 218, 221–22, 270–71.

17 Baldwin, *Poverty and Politics*, 181–82; New York *Times*, March 31, 1937, p. 11, April 1, 1937, pp. 1, 40, April 6, 1937, p. 22; Roosevelt Press Conferences, IX, 226–28 in Franklin D. Roosevelt Library.

purchases. Administration efforts to change several votes and reverse the decision failed. Jones commented that the action was final and "takes the government out of the picture as a land purchaser." To hasten the bill to the House floor and then to the Senate where government purchasing might be restored, the administration agreed to accept direct lending to tenants who would select and buy their own farms, with preference to those who could make down payments and who owned livestock, and providing the government could prevent alienation of the land pending complete amortization. On April 15 the committee reported the bill. The measure now authorized rehabilitation and submarginal land programs.[18]

As in 1935, the general congressional situation delayed the bill in 1937. The great court reform controversy consumed the spring and summer and undermined New Deal influence in Congress. Equally serious was Roosevelt's strongest economy drive since early 1933. He desired to balance the budget, defer new taxes, and postpone new programs. On May 15, as the president called for congressional action on court reform, on a general relief appropriation, and on tenancy, the press reported that probably no more than $10 million could be expected for farm purchase loans in the first year. Bankhead was so dissatisfied with this latest reduction that he informed the president he was dropping action for the bill unless he received word that the White House was still seriously interested in it. Only Roosevelt's personal assurances persuaded the senator to accept the change.[19]

As the House Agriculture Committee cut essential features from the bill, its administration friends saw it as hopelessly unsatisfactory and sought to salvage what they could for the immediate future. To Wallace and Roosevelt, Alexander outlined a minimum program for assisting the "lowest third" of American farm families during fiscal 1938. It included $75 million to continue rehabilitation credit for

18 New York *Times*, April 1, 1937, pp. 1, 40, April 7, 1937, p. 10, April 15, 1937, p. 13.
19 *Ibid.*, April 21, 1937, p. 1, April 22, 1937, p. 22, May 15, 1937, p. 1, June 5, 1937, pp. 1, 2; John H. Bankhead to Roosevelt, June 3, 1937, in Official File 1650, Franklin D. Roosevelt Library.

about 300,000 clients taken on since 1935 and extend it to 30,000–50,000 more "who sorely need it." Alexander thought submarginal land retirement and resettlement should have $10 million. Acquiescing in the economy drive, he proposed only $10 million for farm purchase loans. Finally, he insisted that whatever the amount appropriated, adequate supervision had to be provided or the money would be largely wasted.[20]

The House Agriculture Committee reconsidered the bill and reported it again on June 18. This final version provided $10 million for direct farm purchase loans in the first year and allowed an increase to no more than $50 million per year by fiscal 1940. It gave preference to borrowers who had some equipment and livestock or who could make small down payments. It also authorized the submarginal land program and rehabilitation loans, although the latter were to be funded from the annual relief appropriations. The measure sought to curtail the RA's cooperative farm projects by permitting only the completion and operation of those already started. The House passed the bill on June 29.[21]

In the meantime Alexander had had a substitute measure prepared in the Agriculture Department for Bankhead to introduce in the Senate. It would have restored the corporation's initiative in purchase and resale of land, allowed trial leases for potential farm buyers, and helped borrowers obtain livestock and equipment. The Senate approved this substitute on July 3. But unyielding members of the House Agriculture Committee prevailed in the conference, and on July 16 the act was sent to the president without the Senate changes. Roosevelt signed it on July 22.[22]

To Frank Tannenbaum, Alexander recalled the modest antipov-

20 Milo Perkins to Wallace [filed May 2, 1937], Alexander to Wallace, [filed May 3, 1937], in RG 16, NA; [Alexander] to Roosevelt, April 27, 1937, in Official File 1650, Franklin D. Roosevelt Library.
21 Baldwin, *Poverty and Politics*, 183–84; New York *Times*, June 18, 1937, p. 33, June 30, 1937, p. 7. For the act, see U.S. *Statutes at Large*, L, 522–33.
22 Mark Oppenheimer to Alexander, memorandum, May 27, 1937, in RG 16, NA; New York *Times*, June 29, 1937, p. 1, July 3, 1937, p. 4, July 24, 1937, p. 4; Baldwin, *Poverty and Politics*, 185–87.

erty proposals they had considered with Edwin Embree and Charles
S. Johnson in Atlanta in the fall of 1934 and concluded "in this legislation we have gone a long way." Conceding that the farm purchase
credit features were "not all I would want," he still thought the measure "a good beginning." But among themselves, New Dealers in
the Agriculture Department were acutely aware of the act's
deficiencies. On several occasions just after passage Alexander, Paul
Appleby, M. L. Wilson, and surplus commodities administrator
Milo Perkins conferred. For a brief time they even considered asking Roosevelt to veto the bill and insist on one more in line with the
report of his tenancy commission. But, compelled to acknowledge
the unsatisfactory bill as "something of a beginning in organic law,"
they commended it to the president.[23]

These pragmatists were determined to accept the best measure
Congress would pass and were convinced that the Bankhead-Jones
Act represented the maximum at that time. They anticipated that its
objectives, methods, and appropriations could be expanded later.
M. L. Wilson hoped that in time Congress could be persuaded to
improve the law and sought to implant that idea with its enactment.
As he drafted a bill-signing statement for Roosevelt, he particularly
stressed the need to allow the government to purchase farms and
enter into supervised trial leases with clients to select those most
capable of ownership.[24]

There were occasional thoughts in the administration of seeking
improvements in the new act. Two weeks after he signed the bill,
the president requested Wallace to begin a study of possible
amendments by the next Congress. The following January Wallace
replied that the congressional situation seemed too unfavorable for
any action. But as the New Deal's fortunes in Congress waned during
the next two years, changes in the law, once put off, were continually postponed. As late as December, 1939, C. B. Baldwin, assistant
administrator of the Farm Security Administration, wanted to estab-

---

23 Alexander to Frank Tannenbaum, July 15, 1937, in Frank Tannenbaum Papers, Col-
     umbia University; Paul Appleby to Wallace, memorandum, July 19, 1937, M. L. Wil-
     son to Daniel W. Bell, July 19, 1937, in RG 16, NA.
24 Wilson to Bell, July 19, 1937, Wilson to Roosevelt, July 10 [19], 1937, in RG 16, NA.

lish government land purchase initiative, but doubted the advisability of asking Congress for an amendment.[25]

The Bankhead-Jones Act was the culmination of efforts begun by Alexander and his associates in 1934. It was founded on the assumption that some of the poor could be rehabilitated by supervision and credit for the acquisition of small farms. Most of its proponents never saw it as a complete answer to rural poverty, and in fact it allowed far less sweeping action than the permissive and loosely drawn 1935 measure. It was also inadequately funded, partly because of Roosevelt's periodic economy efforts. The long campaign to enact the bill illustrated that regardless of the reformers' patient and persistent work for legislation to uplift the poor, congressional resistance remained strong. Therefore they had to accept a less far-reaching measure than they desired, and one far short of the solutions advanced by radical critics of the New Deal. But they were also confident that they had, at last, a foundation upon which to build.

The land purchase program was promptly attached to the RA, which was renamed the Farm Security Administration (FSA). The new agency retained the RA's centralized organization. Its line of authority ran from Alexander, who continued as administrator, to twelve regional offices. Four of these covered the South: Regions IV (the Virginias, North Carolina, Kentucky, and Tennessee), V (South Carolina, Georgia, Florida, and Alabama), VI (Arkansas, Louisiana, and Mississippi), and VIII (most of Texas and Oklahoma). Regional directors responsible for the entire FSA program in their areas, overseeing state, district, and county offices, and giving final approval to all loans. This centralization was intended to insulate the agency's operations from local pressures. For the same purpose the FSA did not work through the Extension Service or, except as required by the Bankhead-Jones Act to approve farm purchase applications, delegate authority to committees of local farmers.[26]

Most of the FSA's programs affected the South, and indeed many

25 Roosevelt to Wallace, August 6, 1937, Wallace to Roosevelt, January 13, 1938, C. B. Baldwin to W. A. Jump, December 7, 1939, in RG 16, NA.

26 James G. Maddox, "The Farm Security Administration" (Ph.D. dissertation, Harvard University, 1950), 120–22; interview with Robert W. Hudgens, July 8 and 9, 1970.

were concentrated there. Besides lending for farm buying and re-habilitation, the agency retired submarginal land, administered the resettlement communities inherited from the RA, and operated camps for migratory farm workers. By 1944 it had provided 200,000 emergency subsistence grants, of twenty to thirty dollars each, to relieve destitute southern families not qualified for rehabilitation loans. But rural rehabilitation was by far its largest undertaking, fol-lowed by farm purchase lending. These were the main efforts in the FSA's attack on southern poverty.[27] To evaluate their effectiveness it is necessary to determine how many people the programs served, to what extent they reached the poorest farmers, and how they applied credit and supervision.

Between 1938 and 1946 the FSA assisted 44,300 tenants to buy land. Since the law required apportionment of loans according to each state's farm population and prevalence of tenancy, about seven-tenths of these borrowers were in the South. Farm purchase lending was never supported by large appropriations. Even the law's maximum authorization of $50 million per year would reach rela-tively few farmers. Indeed, the program's banner year was fiscal 1941, with 8,695 loans. By that time the FSA had been able to assist only about one of every twenty-two southern applicants. FSA leaders freely admitted that this modest effort would do little to reduce land-lessness. But they saw it as a demonstration, a "public study" of supervised credit as a remedy for tenancy. Paul V. Maris, head of tenant purchase operations, described the objective as "providing a pattern . . . in keeping the highway from tenancy to ownership open and reasonably passable."[28]

27   Baldwin, *Poverty and Politics*, Chap. 7; *Farm Security Administration, Hearings Before the Select Committee of the House Committee on Agriculture, to Investigate the Activi-ties of the Farm Security Administration*, House of Representatives, 78th Cong., 1st Sess., Part 3, p. 992, hereinafter cited as Cooley Committee Hearings; Maddox, "Farm Security Administration," 84–85, 135–38. From July, 1935, to June, 1946, the RA-FSA spent $1,955,000,000, of which 59 percent was for rural rehabilitation loans or grants, with another 17 percent for supervisory expenses mostly connected with that program. Thirteen percent was loaned for farm purchases, while 9 percent was spent for reset-tlement projects and 2 percent for migratory labor camps.
28   Maddox, "Farm Security Administration," 422, 424; Baldwin, *Poverty and Politics*, 196–99; Paul V. Maris, "How May the Conditions of Tenant Farmers and Share Crop-

The FSA reached its greatest number of clients with its standard rural rehabilitation loan. From July, 1935, to September, 1943, the RA-FSA advanced this credit to 399,000 southern families, about three-fifths of the standard clients in the nation. Borrowers were about 9 percent of all farm operators in Region IV and about 15 to 16 percent in the rest of the South. But standard loans never reached the majority of low income farmers. For example, in 1940 the Region V administrator estimated that in the Southeast rural rehabilitation had served only about 35 or 40 percent of those who needed it.[29]

Farm purchase borrowers were clearly in the upper stratum of landless farmers. Although the law specified that purchasers should be unable to borrow from any other source, its preference for those with some equipment, livestock, and down payment money effectively set eligibility just below the bank credit level. Furthermore, Maris was committed to lending to good risks who showed management potential. County client selection committees adhered to this policy; in 1938 Maris commended them for choosing "persons of substance who compare well with any group of farmers." This selectivity excluded virtually all farm laborers and most sharecroppers. During the FSA years more than a fifth of southern farm purchase borrowers were former cash tenants, 60 percent share tenants, and only 17 percent sharecroppers.[30]

pers Be Improved" (speech to American Country Life Association, Lexington, Kentucky, November 4, 1938), and "The First Year Under the Bankhead-Jones Farm Tenant Act" (undated typescript), both in Agricultural History Office, Economic Research Service, U.S. Department of Agriculture; U.S. Farm Security Administration, *Report of the Administrator of the Farm Security Administration, 1941* (Washington: Government Printing Office, 1941), 17.

29   Olaf F. Larson, *Ten Years of Rural Rehabilitation in the United States* (Washington: Bureau of Agricultural Economics, mimeographed, 1947), 354; *Interstate Migration, Hearings Before the Select Committee to Investigate the Interstate Migration of Destitute Citizens*, House of Representatives, 76th Cong., 3rd Sess., Pt. 2, p. 719, hereinafter cited as Tolan Committee Hearings.

30   U.S. *Statutes at Large*, L. 522–33; U.S. Farm Security Administration, Administrative Instruction 137, January 22, 1938, in "Records of the Farmers Home Administration," Record Group 96, National Archives; Maddox, "Farm Security Administration," 458; Edward C. Banfield, "Ten Years of the Farm Tenant Purchase Program," *Journal of Farm Economics*, XXXI (1949), 477; Maris, "First Year Under the Bankhead-Jones Farm Tenant Act"; interview with Robert W. Hudgens.

The standard rehabilitation borrowers accepted in the South in the prewar years were unquestionably needy. A composite measure by the Bureau of Agricultural Economics of their cash incomes, value of general assets, possession of animals and implements, and net financial worths ranked them as the poorest in the program, with those in the Deep South and Southwest significantly lower than those in the upper and border states. Nevertheless, most standard borrowers had some assets and were usually not at the very lowest levels of destitution. This was increasingly true under the FSA after 1937, when client selection moved above the relief or near-relief standard of 1935–1936 and tended steadily toward less impoverished farmers.[31]

Nearly all southern rehabilitants accepted during 1936–1939 had at least some foothold on the land; less than one in twenty was a wage laborer. About 42 percent were tenants above the sharecropper level, while close to a third were full or part owners of farms. Region VI, the lower Mississippi Valley, selected the largest proportion of sharecroppers, 23 percent. Most of the borrowers had little off-farm work and were heavily dependent on their meager cash crop sales. Almost half the 1936–1939 families had total cash incomes of less than $250 during the year before receiving loans, and 17 percent were under $125. Such incomes provided very little for family support. Four out of ten of the families accepted during 1938–1939 spent less than $100 annually for general living needs.[32]

The rehabilitants' poverty was also evident in their lack of capital assets. Those who owned land usually had small, infertile, eroded, or otherwise marginal farms with inferior houses and buildings. Likewise, practically all borrowers ranked low in working capital, Forty-two percent of those coming into the program during 1936–1939 had equipment and livestock valued under $125, while another

31 Larson, *Ten Years of Rural Rehabilitation*, 86–87, 106–07, 126. Beginning in late 1939, Larson directed this exhaustive BAE study of rural rehabilitation for the FSA. Sampling 39,295 standard borrowers, about one-fifth of those accepted in each region between 1936 and 1939, the study analyzed their characteristics when accepted and attempted to measure their progress.

32 *Ibid.*, 104–107, 361–62, 368.

21 percent were under $250. Most did not have adequate draft animals, or cattle other than scrub stock. Still another measure of the rehabilitants' deficiency of capital was their low net financial worth, their assets less liabilities. Excluding any equities in real estate, more than two-fifths of the 1936–1939 families came into the program with a net worth of less than $250.[33]

The southern Negro was an important part of the FSA's constituency of poor farmers. In the late 1930s 4.5 million blacks—38 percent of the nation's total—worked in southern agriculture.[34] Alexander, whose long efforts to improve race relations were well known, was unusually sensitive to their needs, as were several regional administrators. No New Deal agency worked more conscientiously than the FSA to eliminate racial discrimination. Yet the selection of both farm purchase and rehabilitation borrowers was plagued with grassroots inequities.

The number of farm purchase loans made to blacks fell far short of their percentage of landless farmers. In the eight states with 30,000 or more black tenants, Negroes received only a fifth of the loans for 1938–1939, even though they comprised 51 percent of all tenants. Nor did this proportion improve; the figures remained nearly the same in 1945, the FSA's last year. Among the reasons for this failure to reach blacks was their low application rate, especially at first, caused partly by their lack of information about the program. A much more fundamental problem was that the selectivity of farm purchase lending was weighted against landless blacks. Since they were concentrated in the ranks of sharecroppers and wage laborers they usually did not have the equipment or down payment money preferred for such credit. Finally, the county selection committees established under the Bankhead-Jones Act were often unresponsive to national nondiscrimination policies.[35]

33 *Ibid.*, 117–19, 375, 380, 383.
34 U.S. Farm Security Administration, *The Southern Negro on the Farm* (Washington: Farm Security Administration, 1940), title page.
35 Baldwin, *Poverty and Politics*, 196–97; Maddox, "Farm Security Administration," 430; George S. Mitchell to Charles S. Johnson, July 27, 1938, and September 20, 1938, Mitchell to Alexander, October 8, 1938, in RG 96, NA. In FSA's four southern regions

In March, 1938, Region IV administrator George S. Mitchell told his state directors that his office would set a ratio of loans to whites and blacks for each tenant purchase county. This would be based on the Negroes' percentage of tenant farmers in the county and their proportion of the applications. State directors would have to justify to the regional office any significant deviations from census ratios.[36]

Mitchell found this policy hard to enforce when loan committees had their own statutory power. In June, 1938, he admitted to Alexander that "it is proving difficult to get my views about the proper proportion of loans to Negroes ... across in the field." The number of black applications had been "quite low," and Mitchell suspected that his "pressure to get through as high a proportion as these County Committees would pass has ... brought us to the verge of resentment ... in some cases." But he was willing to risk friction with the committees "to get it securely established that the Regional Office wishes [them] to resist ... a pervasive but unavoidable pressure in the heavy Negro counties toward benefiting white people first." Later, in the fall, Mitchell reported that although Negro applications were up, he still could apply no effective leverage to some committees "which do not care to certify [borrowers] in close accord with these ratios."[37]

Racial discrimination also distorted the selection of rehabilitation borrowers. County supervisors probably tended to conform to local racial attitudes, and often assumed that whites were better credit risks than blacks. Moreover, in some areas landlord disapproval, well understood even if unspoken, may have discouraged many Negro applicants. Nevertheless, blacks were 22 percent of the South's rehabilitants. This was in line with their 23 percent of all

blacks were 35 percent of all tenant farmers but received 23 percent of the loans for 1938–1939. U.S. Farm Security Administration, *Report of the Administrator of the Farm Security Administration, 1939* (Washington: Government Printing Office, 1939), 15.

36   "Policy for TP Loans as Between Races" (Typescript), Mitchell to L. H. Haltom, March 25, 1938, Mitchell to Alexander, October 8, 1938, in RG 96, NA.

37   Mitchell to Alexander, June 3, 1938 and October 8, 1938, in RG 96, NA. By the second year of the program black applications had risen from 19 to 26 percent of the total. Farm Security Administration, *Southern Negro on the Farm*, 2.

farm operators, but it was far short of their proportion of low income farmers. For example, in Region V, where blacks comprised about three-fourths of the farmers with incomes under $500, they received a little less than a third of the loans. Summarizing the problem for the regional administrator, Alexander candidly observed that "it certainly looks as if our program is not reaching enough of the low income colored farmers." The blacks who were accepted, however, were poorer than the white rehabilitants, reflecting the concentration of Negroes at the bottom of the economic ladder. Black borrowers chosen through 1939 averaged lower than the whites in net worth ($414 compared to $762), as well as in net income for the year prior to acceptance ($208 compared to $326). But despite their greater poverty, the blacks received average loans and supplements of $606, while the whites received $659.[38]

The heart of the FSA's aid to all clients in both its main programs was supervised credit. As Robert W. Hudgens later summarized it, any attempt to raise masses of people from poverty required an injection of capital directly to the poor. This could only be done through loans, and the only safe way to lend to people who could offer no security was to supervise them. Thus, the FSA's policy, in both tenant purchase and rural rehabilitation operations, was to make only sound loans which the agency anticipated the client could repay *under its direction.*[39]

The FSA offered the most liberal land purchase credit available, lending at 3 percent annual interest on 40-year mortgages. The Bankhead-Jones Act permitted credit only for efficient farm units, as determined by the county committees. These were defined as acreages on which one family could produce enough income to meet expenses, support an acceptable level of living, and repay the loan.

38 Baldwin, *Poverty and Politics,* 200–201; Larson, *Ten Years of Rural Rehabilitation,* 103; Alexander to E. S. Morgan, September 28, 1939, in RG 96, NA; U.S. Farm Security Administration, Rural Rehabilitation Division, "Racial Aspects of Rural Rehabilitation Family Progress" (Program Analysis Report No. 15, December 6, 1940, copy in USDA History Office), 4,7,8. According to the latter source, in Kentucky, Tennessee, North Carolina, Virginia, and Louisiana, loans to blacks averaged slightly higher than those to whites.
39 Interview with Robert W. Hudgens.

The size of such farms varied throughout the country, but as of June, 1943, the average southern purchase was 122 acres. In the Southeast 40 or 50 acres was considered the minimum. The cost of farms also varied, but in 1938 the FSA set a national loan ceiling of $12,000. The agency estimated that productive farms could be obtained in the South for well under that limit. The average southern loan, as of June, 1940, was $4,950, or $786 below the national average. Responsive to local opinion, agency officials and county committees kept credit to a modest level to avoid raising the borrower's living standard above his neighbors'.[40]

In 1938, as the FSA began financing farm purchasers, Paul Maris declared, "We do not want it said five or ten years hence that the borrowers never had a chance because the farms sold were not economic units." In the 1930s FSA loans were probably adequate for establishing the diversified family farms the agency promoted in the cotton and tobacco belts. But by the 1940s forces were accelerating in southern agriculture which undermined the position of small low income farmers. The 1940s were years of rising land values, capital needs, and mechanization. Increasingly, economic units were defined not only by adequate acreage, but also by sufficient capital and technology. But the expansion of these needs was not so obvious in the prewar period as later, and the FSA continued to finance borrowers with modest loans which could cover land and buildings, but not machinery. By the postwar period there was growing doubt that many of the farms were economic units. In 1949 one critic, economist Edward Banfield, concluded that based on the cash income potential of the farms sold, the program "probably could not be justified in the South."[41]

---

40   U.S. Farm Security Administration, Administrative Instruction 137, January 22, 1938, in RG 96, NA; Cooley Committee Hearings, Pt. 3, p. 1017; Tolan Committee Hearings, Pt. 2, p. 718; Farm Security Administration, *Report of the Administrator, 1941*, pp. 31–32; Banfield, "Ten Years of the Farm Tenant Purchase Program," 470–72, 475.
41   Maris, "First Year Under the Bankhead-Jones Farm Tenant Act"; Banfield, "Ten Years of the Farm Tenant Purchase Program," 476, 482–84; interview with James G. Maddox; Maddox, "Farm Security Administration," 424, 434. According to Maddox, the 1937–1946 average purchase loan in the South was about $5,400, compared to $8,100 in the Midwest.

Actually, the FSA could not have increased the size of farm purchase credit very much in the 1940s because Congress severely restricted its lending ability. Amendments to the Appropriations Acts of 1941 through 1945, sponsored by Malcolm Tarver of Georgia, limited loans to the average value of farms of thirty acres or more in each county. Tarver thought borrowers should not exceed their neighbors in property values and maintained that the FSA should make smaller loans and spread them more widely. But average southern farms were not always adequate units. For example, all but two Alabama counties had average values under $3,000. The FSA estimated that farms under that limit would produce incomes allowing less than $400 for living expenses. Barred by law from lending for inadequate farms, and unable to shift funds between states, the FSA often could not finance borrowers within the limits. In 1942–1943 it was forced to withdraw or curtail the program in 840 of its 1,888 counties.[42] Thus, even farm purchase lending, supposedly enjoying more congressional support than any other FSA activity, was crippled by legislative restrictions.

Between 1936 and 1944 the RA-FSA advanced $163 million in initial standard rehabilitation loans in the South. Since most clients needed long-term assistance to raise their living standards permanently, the agency extended another $208 million in annual supplements. Although the South received 47 percent of all rehabilitation credit in the nation, this did not match its 56 percent of all borrowers. Consequently, southern loans were smaller than those elsewhere. During 1936–1940 first loans averaged $427 in the nation and $288 in the South, while supplemental advances were $190 and $141, respectively.[43]

Rehabilitation credit was intended for two broad purposes: capital improvements (acquisition of draft animals, domestic livestock, implements, and major house and building repairs) and "non-recoverable" expenses (current farm operations and family neces-

42 Banfield, "Ten Years of the Farm Tenant Purchase Program," 474–75; Cooley Committee Hearings, Pt. 3, pp. 1012, 1014.
43 Larson, *Ten Years of Rural Rehabilitation*, 162–64, 387–390.

sities). Since capital credit would build up the farmer's productivity, it would be the more rehabilitative in the long run. But as Olaf Larson of the Bureau of Agricultural Economics found in his exhaustive survey of rural rehabilitation, "borrowers in Southern regions, having less resources at the time of acceptance than those elsewhere, were... not only made the smallest initial, supplemental, and total loans, but in addition, received a larger proportion of their loans for nonrecoverable rather than capital goods." On the other hand, James G. Maddox, head of the rural rehabilitation division, later wrote that it was necessary to lend most heavily to southern tenants for current farm and family expenses because the FSA was replacing their traditional furnish merchant credit. Providing these farmers with more capital goods, Maddox thought, was tied to reforming their pattern of small cash cropping and would require many supplemental loans over a period of years.[44] Thus, whereas rehabilitation lending in the South helped meet clients' immediate farming needs, it probably did not reach its full potential in raising their economic level permanently.

The FSA supervised all farm purchase and standard rehabilitation borrowers through a farm and home plan which the county director wrote, or assisted the clients to write, after reviewing their resources and needs. The plan, a signed agreement between the borrower and the FSA, was a condition of the loan. It covered current cropping operations (emphasizing diversification and soil conservation) and outlined equipment requirements for the next few years. It also served as a family budget. All plans required families to plant gardens and called for maximum home food preservation. In the cotton belt they nearly always included keeping cows, hogs, and poultry, and growing feed crops.[45]

---

44   *Ibid.*, 172–73; Maddox, "Farm Security Administration," 182. Larson indicates that except in Region V, the largest part of southern original loans was for capital goods (ranging from 37 percent in Region V to 61 percent in Region IV, compared to a national average of 50 percent). But in combined farm operating and family expenses the South was above the national loan average of 33 percent (ranging from 33 percent in Region IV to 52 percent in Region V).

45   Maddox, "Farm Security Administration," 188; Larson, "Ten Years of Rural Rehabilitation," 138–39.

The county FSA director was responsible for all supervision. He usually had a staff of one or two assistants (often including a Negro assigned to the black clients) and a woman home management associate to work with housewives. To assure implementation of the farm and home plans, staff members visited borrowers on their farms to check progress and offer advice. The county director could also exercise financial control over rehabilitation borrowers by depositing their loans in joint bank accounts requiring his signature for use of the money. This device was used most frequently in the South, where many tenants had always been dependent on landlords' advances and were unaccustomed to handling cash for themselves.[46]

FSA leaders saw supervision as an educational process. In September, 1937. Robert Hudgens urged a conference of southern administrators to develop the program's teaching role, which he considered as vital as its lending. "These families of ours," he stressed, "are to be educated out of their conditions through supervision, and not merely credited out of it through a loan." Similarly, George S. Mitchell thought the rehabilitants' greatest need was "teaching... in the form of frequent visits to poorer men's farms by sympathetic people who have learned the science and practice of good farming."[47]

But supervision tied to credit and enforceable through signed farm and home plans and joint bank accounts was also paternalistic. Hudgens observed that southern tenants and croppers had never learned to differentiate between credit and direction by landlords and lien merchants, and saw no need for the FSA to make the distinction. Because of the clients' heritage of deprivation and their lack of education, skills, and managerial ability, he thought it "unlikely that there will be a time during the next two generations when there

46 Larson, *Ten Years of Rural Rehabilitation*, 132, 135, 146; Maddox, "Farm Security Administration," 195–96. Home management supervisors often served more than one county.

47 Robert W. Hudgens, "Looking Back, Looking Around, and Looking Forward" (speech to Region V and VI FSA administrators, Biloxi, Mississippi, September 14, 1937) and draft of speech for George S. Mitchell, March 22, 1938, both in RG 96, NA.

will not be an urgent need among the low income farmers of the South for . . . supervision close to the source of credit." Most rehabilitants, in his judgment, would require years of gradually decreasing guidance to attain complete independence. In fact, he thought the FSA should maintain its oversight by "allowing all clients who need limited supervision to remain in debt to us." But he saw none of this as incompatible with the education of borrowers, affirming that the program's "ultimate goal . . . is to cure the need for supervision."[48]

The effectiveness of supervision in the field is difficult to evaluate. It is clear, however, that county offices were too understaffed for intensive work with all borrowers. Besides conducting all other local FSA activities, the county director and his small staff might have responsibility for several hundred standard rehabilitation borrowers. Consequently, home visits might be infrequent and clients' farm and home plans might not be updated each year. Moreover, supervisory contact declined still further as FSA suffered personnel cuts after 1942.[49]

Rehabilitation director Maddox later wrote that most supervisors were able to give more careful planning and direction to farm buyers than to standard rehabilitants. Although evidence of borrowers' responses to supervision is quite scarce, the farm purchasers, as the least impoverished and generally most capable of the FSA's clients, were probably most able to benefit from it. A BAE survey in 1946 indicated that most southern farm purchasers had been receptive to technical guidance. Four-fifths of them said they had changed their farming as a result of FSA advice, mentioning most frequently improved cultivation methods, increased planting of cover crops, and more emphasis on stock raising. Similarly, their wives reported improvements in home management practices.[50]

Supervisors also gave technical advice to standard rehabilitants. But in dealing with the poorer farmers it was especially important to

48   Hudgens, "Looking Back, Looking Around, and Looking Forward," in RG 96, NA.
49   Larson, *Ten Years of Rural Rehabilitation,* 140, 147–48.
50   Maddox, "Farm Security Administration," 80, 99; Banfield, "Ten Years of the Farm Tenant Purchase Program," 481–82.

establish personal relationships with them which were conducive to their rehabilitation. Apparently the greatest difficulty, and necessity, in working with poor farmers was to gain their trust, involve them in their own planning, inspire them toward self-help, and encourage their personal independence. This relationship became harder to achieve with those farther down the economic ladder. The very poorest people might be unresponsive to advice because of ignorance or a discouraged and mistrustful outlook. One supervisor in a special intensive program for the FSA's most destitute clients complained of uncooperative families who conveyed "a feeling that I am not wanted. They just sit and stare out the window... and... never pay any attention to anything that I say. All I can get out of them is usually a yes or no." But a more perceptive director in the same program observed that "it takes time to win the confidence of some families and convince them you are sincere in your desire to help—they've been exploited and gypped by so many people, it's no wonder they are suspicious."[51]

There were failures in this leading and teaching role. In at least some cases rehabilitants resented their supervision enough to leave the program at the earliest opportunity. Evidently one of the greatest problems of rural rehabilitation was the inability of many technically competent supervisors to develop an empathetic relationship with their clients.[52] Yet the progress of rehabilitants was real enough to suggest an overall success of supervision. Just how many county directors had the sensitivity, tact, and patience to guide low income farmers' growth in personal competence is impossible to know.

In conducting rural rehabilitation the RA-FSA discovered the need to give many clients a foundation of security before supervised credit could work. For example, a standard loan might be a disservice to a farmer with an already heavy debt load. Therefore, having acquired the debt adjustment service from the Farm Credit Admin-

---

51 Maddox, "Farm Security Administration," 183–84, 336; Rachel Rowe Swiger and Olaf F. Larson, *Climbing Toward Security* (Washington: Bureau of Agricultural Economics, 1944), 4, 7, 18, 26.
52 Larson, *Ten Years of Rural Rehabilitation*, 135, 139, 149.

istration in August, 1935, the RA-FSA arranged debt refinancing or reductions for about 47,000 borrowers and 23,000 other farmers of all income levels in the South by June, 1941.[53]

The FSA also sought to strengthen clients' security on the land by encouraging written leases, an effort which had far-reaching potential to change southern tenancy. In 1937, soon after taking charge of the RA, Alexander determined to promote multiple-year leases to keep clients on the same farms for the duration of their loans. By 1938 FSA required satisfactory written leases before lending to tenants. It also encouraged landlords to adopt its model lease, which gave tenants from three to five years' occupancy, allowed them garden and pasture acreage, set minimum housing and sanitation standards, and compensated them for any permanent improvements they made. Although few landlords accepted these terms fully, many granted at least some written agreement, which helped stabilize many clients. In 1940 the Region V administrator reported to a congressional committee that although half the South's tenants still moved every year, less than a fourth of his rehabilitation families had moved in 1939. By 1944 the percentage of southern borrowers with at least a two-year lease ranged from twenty-six in Region IV to forty-eight in Region V. There are indications, however, that the FSA was least successful in improving tenure for the clients accepted before 1937, who were generally its poorest.[54]

Since 1936 the RA and FSA had maintained that cooperation could overcome the economic handicaps of small farmers compared

53 Maddox, "Farm Security Administration," 213–221; Farm Security Administration, *Report of the Administrator, 1941*, p. 42. Estimates of the average amount of debt reduction vary widely. Larson, *Ten Years of Rural Rehabilitation*, 258, indicates a range of from $101 to $267 per case in four southern regions. The 1941 FSA administrator's report shows average reductions ranging from $174 (Alabama) to $1,656 (Florida). But these figures include some large group cases. Moreover, the sources do not clearly show original indebtedness per family. Finally, Maddox has noted the tendency of the program to give much attention to relatively high-income farmers, especially those with real estate debts. Many of these may have been non-clients.
54 Maddox, "Farm Security Administration," 225–232; Alexander to Edwin R. Embree, June 29, 1937, in Julius Rosenwald Fund Papers, Fisk University; Tolan Committee Hearings, Pt. 2, pp. 705, 711–17; Alexander to Morgan, September 28, 1939, in RG 96, NA.

to big mechanized commercial producers. Accordingly, the agency organized cooperative associations among its borrowers, sometimes by making loans to start the groups or by lending to clients to enable them to join. Often loans were not required and the FSA merely provided supervision. Most of these groups were for occasional bulk purchase of supplies, feed, or fertilizer, or for marketing produce, but a few were for crop storage or processing. By June, 1941, the FSA directly financed only 40 associations in the South, serving about 80,000 members. Although the agency greatly expanded the program between 1941 and 1943, eventually organizing 2,064 cooperatives in the nation, probably relatively few southern rehabilitants were affected. Nevertheless, cooperatives could provide significant services for low income farmers. A fertilizer-purchasing association, for example, lessened dependence on furnish merchants. A cooperative facility for storing cotton seed enabled farmers to avoid selling it to a gin at the peak of the season when it netted very little. Selling later at a better price could directly affect family living standards since small farmers' wives customarily spent cotton seed money for home improvements. Likewise, the 185 veterinary service groups sponsored in the Deep South and the statewide workstock insurance associations organized in Arkansas, Louisiana, and Mississippi could protect tenants from the economic disaster of losing their work animals.[55]

The FSA's most widespread promotion of cooperation was its organization of small unincorporated associations of neighbors for the purpose of acquiring and using machinery or breeding stock. These "group services" usually had no more than ten or twenty members, not all of whom were necessarily FSA borrowers. The agency financed these groups either by lending to the participants for joint ownership of equipment or a purebred sire, or by lending to one "master borrower" who agreed to provide services to others on a small fee basis. By June, 1943, the South had 8,237 group services.

55 Maddox, "Farm Security Administration," 261–62, 275–79, 281–86; Larson, *Ten Years of Rural Rehabilitation,* 209–210, 219; Farm Security Administration, *Report of the Administrator, 1941,* pp. 52–53; interview with Robert W. Hudgens.

These were spread quite unevenly, however, with about half in the upper South and border states.[56]

Congress severely restricted the FSA's cooperative efforts in the 1943–1944 Appropriations Act, which prohibited loans to associations or participants. Although the FSA could still offer management advice, the congressional action, along with wartime reductions in supervisory personnel, greatly reduced the agency's staff to assist cooperatives. Hard-hit by this loss of support, many small purchasing and marketing groups failed. Group services were not affected by the lending restrictions, but in the general deemphasis on cooperatives relatively few new ones were established after 1943.[57]

Of all FSA cooperatives the health care associations had the greatest impact on the South. The agency had not originally intended to enter this innovative field, but it soon discovered that borrowers with debilitating diseases or suffering from malnutrition were unable to farm effectively or repay loans. For example, an inquiry into the reasons for dropping 155 clients in Butler County, Alabama, in 1937 revealed that besides their endemic hookworm infection, four-fifths of them had other health conditions requiring a physician's treatment. Moreover, most southern rehabilitants could not afford medical care even for acute ailments. A survey of 43,000 Texas and Oklahoma clients reported 16,000 serious illnesses in 1939–1940, of which less than half had received a doctor's attention. With little exaggeration the FSA's chief medical consultant later declared that "the loan program was in jeopardy until some feasible plan for getting medical aid to ... borrowers could be found."[58]

56 Larson, *Ten Years of Rural Rehabilitation*, 200–205, 412; Maddox, "Farm Security Administration," 263–64, 270–72.

57 Maddox, "Farm Security Administration," 267–274, 292–95. Maddox indicates that most group services were financially successful enough to repay FSA loans, and about 84 percent of those established in the South were still functioning by mid-1946. The Deep South regions, V and VI, however, had the highest failure rates, about 28 and 24 percent, respectively, by 1946.

58 Interview with Robert W. Hudgens; report on Butler County, Alabama, October 10–15, 1938, in RG 96, NA; Larson, *Ten Years of Rural Rehabilitation*, 102; R. C. Williams, "The Medical Care Program for Farm Security Administration Borrowers," digest of paper presented to American Public Health Association [1939], copy in Wisconsin State Historical Society.

The FSA's health care associations were prepayment groups, usually organized countywide for clients who chose to participate. The agency loaned or granted families their membership fees, typically fifteen to thirty dollars per year. It then assisted the groups to negotiate contracts with county medical associations, under which the doctors treated members, charging the cooperatives uniform reduced rates. Started as a limited experiment under the RA in 1936, this program grew rapidly between 1938 and 1942. It reached its peak in the latter year with 512 southern groups (about two-thirds of those in the nation) serving about 81,000 families. The number of groups and participants fell off rapidly, however, with wartime reductions in the FSA's program and shortages of doctors in rural areas. As Maddox later pointed out, the program reached only a minority of FSA clients and did not begin to cope with the chronic health deficiencies of all the rural poor. But it gave thousands their first regular health care and the agency justifiably counted it a success. [59]

The effectiveness of rural rehabilitation in uplifting its borrowers should be evaluated by several standards. First, although data is imprecise, it is clear that southern rehabilitants increased their incomes in the 1930s. An FSA report on active borrowers in the 1939 crop year listed average net incomes ranging from $180 in Alabama to $654 in Kentucky and noted the clients' improvement (from $155 and $533, respectively) since their first loans, one to five years earlier. Average incomes of southern borrowers also advanced during the war years when rising crop prices facilitated their progress and when many of the earlier, more impoverished clients were no longer in the program. Nevertheless, many still remained at a relatively low level. In 1943 total cash receipts from crop and livestock sales averaged only a little over $600 in Regions V and VI, $889 in Region IV, and $1,131 in Region VIII. Rehabilitants in other regions averaged between $1,729 and $3,375. There are few estimates of what consti-

---

59 Maddox, "Farm Security Administration," 306–310, 313–18, 325–26; Larson, *Ten Years of Rural Rehabilitation*, 231, 235–37, 241–44, 415–16; Williams, "Medical Care Program."

tuted the "poverty line" in farm income in the 1930s or 1940s, but in 1939 Maddox suggested $705 yearly (including home-produced food) as necessary to support the minimum physical and cultural needs of a southern family of five.[60]

Borrowers amply supplemented their cash incomes by the live-at-home farming the FSA stressed so heavily in the South. The agency's voluminous statistics on increases in family gardening, ownership of livestock and poultry, and food preservation indicate the success of its efforts. Improved diets, along with the FSA's promotion of health care associations and its efforts to raise housing and sanitation standards, could upgrade poor families' living standards substantially.[61]

At least to some extent the FSA was able to rehabilitate its clients *as farmers*, strengthening their security on the land and building up their working capital. Of the sharecroppers and laborers accepted as rehabilitants from 1936 through 1939 who remained active borrowers, about 83 percent of the former and 89 percent of the latter became share tenants. In addition many obtained better leases. This movement up the tenure ladder indicates some success in the agency's efforts to help its farmers acquire workstock and equipment. Nationally, clients accepted between 1936 and 1938 increased the median value of their animals and implements from $311, at the time of acceptance, to $536. But because southern borrowers received less capital credit than others, their gains were below the national aver-

---

60   C. B. Baldwin to Henry Wallace, July 13, 1940 (FSA administrator's report on rehabilitation progress), in Lowell Mellett Papers, Franklin D. Roosevelt Library; Larson, *Ten Years of Rural Rehabilitation*, 309, 317–18; James G. Maddox, "Suggestions for a National Program of Rural Rehabilitation and Relief," *Journal of Farm Economics*, XXI (1939), 888–89. It is difficult to estimate clients' progress in income and net worth. Each year after 1939 the FSA made progress studies of current borrowers. These indicated an upward trend, but they averaged borrowers accepted in each of the program's preceding years, who had had varying periods in which to progress. Because of the FSA's trend toward choosing clients from higher income levels, borrowers selected in different years might have very different starting points from which to measure improvement. Finally, as Maddox, "Farm Security Administration," 384–85, points out, the active borrower group constantly changed as new borrowers were added and others were dropped. In short, there are no measurements of year-to-year progress of groups of clients who all came on the program at the same time.

61   Maddox, "Farm Security Administration," 387–88; Larson, *Ten Years of Rural Rehabilitation*, 313, 421–22.

age. In 1943 the value of their working capital remained the lowest in the program, ranging from $818 in Region VI to $1,892 in Region VIII, compared to a national clients' average of $2,074.[62]

But the permanence of the borrowers' progress was bound up with the question of whether they could remain in farming at all in a rapidly changing agricultural economy. The growth of mechanization and technology was clearly reducing opportunities for poor farmers. With increased use of tractors, the number of farm operators in eight cotton states had decreased almost 12 percent in the 1930s and would drop another 4.7 percent by 1945. FSA leaders were fully cognizant of this trend. Appearing before the Temporary National Economic Committee in May, 1939, Alexander quoted estimates that agricultural production required 1.6 million fewer workers than it had ten years earlier. These trends affected rehabilitants. Maddox later estimated that a large proportion of the clients taken on in the 1930s left agriculture in the 1940s. Some of the more capable, at least, secured war employment. It may be true that the FSA's most important contribution to its clients was its process of improving their general competence and independence, whether they continued as farmers or not.[63]

Despite the FSA's services to its clients, it was always clear that rural rehabilitation never came close to reaching all low income farmers. In fact it became steadily more selective. This trend, discernible even in the FERA's rehabilitation program, accelerated under the FSA around 1938.

Throughout the country during the prewar years the FSA accepted new borrowers from progressively higher net income groups. This trend was less marked in the Deep South regions, V and VI, than elsewhere; in 1940 those areas still had the highest proportion of borrowers with net incomes under $300 per year (65 and 47 percent, respectively). But the rise was still significant; in the four-state

62 Larson, *Ten Years of Rural Rehabilitation*, 313, 319–20, 421.
63 Arthur F. Raper, *Machines in the Cotton Fields* (Atlanta: Southern Regional Council, 1946), 9; statement of Will Alexander to Temporary National Economic Committee, Hearings on Savings and Investment, May 24, 1939, copy in USDA History Office; interviews with James G. Maddox and Robert W. Hudgens.

southeastern region new clients' net incomes before acceptance averaged $207 in 1935 and $324 in 1940. Similarly, FSA selected clients with higher net worths. Surveying the Southeast, Alexander pointed out that Alabama clients in 1936 and 1937 had an average net worth, when accepted, of $106, but for those taken on in 1938 the figure was $405. During the same period the average "before acceptance" net worth in South Carolina rose from $80 to $490. In fact, the administrator found only two Georgia counties and six in South Carolina in which 1938 borrowers were selected from a lower economic level than the 1937 group. Disturbed by this trend, Alexander saw "reasonable ground for the fear that our program is not serving those very low income farm groups for . . . whom it was instituted."[64]

In his analysis of rural rehabilitation Olaf Larson found that the rise in incomes and assets of new rehabilitants resulted not from raising the upper eligibility limits, but from simply accepting fewer destitute clients. He noted a "striking decrease" between 1936 and 1939 in new borrowers with incomes under $125.[65] Furthermore, because many of the earliest, and poorest, rehabilitants seemed to make little progress, the agency dropped many of them in the late 1930s to an unsupervised inactive status. By 1940 it was estimated that close to half the nation's original rehabilitants of 1935 were inactive.[66]

Still another part of the selectivity trend was the choice of borrowers operating larger land units. Between 1935 and 1940 the average acreage farmed by new rehabilitants in Region VI expanded moderately, from 37 to 42 acres. At the other extreme (for the South), the increase in Region VIII was from 70 to 150 acres. Moreover, there were indications that newer rehabilitants were more likely than earlier clients to be located on good land.[67]

---

64 U.S. Farm Security Administration, Rural Rehabilitation Division, "Trend in Family Selection for the Rural Rehabilitation Program, 1935–40" (Program Analysis Report No. 17, October 20, 1941, copy in USDA History Office), 2,3; Alexander to Morgan, September 28, 1939, in RG 96, NA.
65 Larson, *Ten Years of Rural Rehabilitation*, 113, 125.
66 Maddox, "Farm Security Administration," 151–52; Farm Security Administration, "Trend in Family Selection," 13.
67 Farm Security Administration, "Trend in Family Selection," 6, 8–9, 13.

Finally, the newer borrowers received larger loans, with the greatest increases occurring between 1936 and 1937. Average first loans in Region IV, for instance, went from $164 to $396 in that period, while those in Regions V and VI advanced from $180 to $336 and from $130 to $324, respectively. The size of loans in the latter two regions continued to move steadily upward, reaching the $400–$450 range by 1939. Clearly, the FSA was shifting from lending small amounts to very low income farmers toward extending larger loans to a less needy group. In 1941 an agency report recalled that one purpose of rehabilitation had been to help poor farmers build up their capital equipment, but observed that the trend in acceptances had not encouraged this. "Even with the introduction of this 'new kind of credit,'" the study concluded, "the fewer the resources that the farmer has . . . the more difficult it is for him to secure the additional capital he needs."[68]

The reasons for this upward trend were probably inherent in rural rehabilitation. Conducting a program of credit, not relief, the FSA intended to make only sound loans that would be repaid. Therefore it had to aid those with at least some assets and debt-paying potential. In making loans the county supervisors felt pressure to produce program "results" and client "progress" in the form of increased net worths and good repayment records. It was difficult to achieve such results with the most destitute clients. Borrowers with somewhat higher economic standing were better prospects, and would also require less supervision. With limited funds and heavy caseloads, the local directors developed strong leanings toward conventional banking practices. As Hudgens recalled, they had a "craving for respectability" in lending which national and regional officials found hard to counteract.[69]

Committed to "digging deeper" in an effort to reach the most destitute and dependent, Alexander, Hudgens, and other top FSA officials resisted the trend. As early as September, 1937, Hudgens urged a conference of southern administrators to consider "the large

68 *Ibid.*, 8; Larson, *Ten Years of Rural Rehabilitation*, 393.
69 Larson, *Ten Years of Rural Rehabilitation*, 6, 125, 181; Farm Security Administration, "Trend in Family Selection," 8; interviews with James G. Maddox and Robert W. Hudgens.

number of so-called 'sub-standard clients,'" bypassed by the regular program. Asserting that "there is an answer for this group and sooner or later we will find it," he foresaw "some plan . . . to lift them by the educational value of our supervision to the level of standard clients." In another speech in February, 1938, he advocated aiding hundreds of thousands of the poorest farm families "for whom we have been dodging responsibility by saying they can not be rehabilitated." [70]

At Alexander's direction FSA administrators considered ways of digging deeper in regional meetings in April, 1938, and in a national conference in May. By July the agency had outlined a limited experimental program, which it started in the field before the end of the year. This effort, known as the Non-Commercial Farm (NCF) project, was the FSA's only program aimed exclusively at clients at the very lowest level. [71]

The FSA conducted this experiment in ten counties throughout the nation. Within small areas of each county it accepted all families who could not qualify as regular rehabilitants, setting no eligibility standards except physical and mental ability to carry out a simple farm and home plan. To allow intensive supervision the agency slashed the usual caseload, assigning a farm director and a home management specialist to each fifty families. Supervisors were carefully chosen, given wide discretion to make loans and grants, and encouraged to use "constructive imagination" in guiding clients. As Maddox later described it, the program was less a controlled experiment than an "open invitation" to selected field personnel to try new approaches. In practice it adapted standard rehabilitation techniques to very poor clients. [72]

70 Baldwin, *Poverty and Politics*, 218–19; Robert W. Hudgens, "Looking Back, Looking Around, and Looking Forward," and "Deficiencies in Southern Agriculture as Revealed in the Home and Home Life of the People," speech to Home Economics Section, Association of Southern Agricultural Workers, Atlanta, February 2, 1938, in RG 96, NA.

71 Alexander to Mitchell, April 29, 1938, Mitchell to W. C. LaRue, undated, memorandum by Earl Mayhew, undated, and A. C. Tate to Frank J. Brechenser, November 4, 1939, in RG 96, NA.

72 Swiger and Larson, *Climbing Toward Security*, iii, 6; Maddox, "Farm Security Administration," 334–35.

Two cotton belt counties, both in Georgia, were selected for the project. These were Laurens and Oglethorpe, both submarginal land areas. Most of the sixty-six families accepted in Laurens were white, while the majority of the fifty Oglethorpe families were black. Nearly all were sharecroppers struggling to work inadequate land units. Their farms averaged 54 acres in Laurens and 119 in Oglethorpe, although in the latter county the land was so poor that only 23 percent of it was cultivable.[73]

The year before the project began the Laurens families had average gross incomes of $174, while those in Oglethorpe made $99. The average net worths of these families were $75 and $142, respectively. The clients possessed almost no equipment or livestock. For example, only twelve of the Laurens families had cows, none owned horses or mules, almost a third had no hogs, and most lacked even adequate flocks of chickens.[74]

Project families inhabited the usual dilapidated tenant houses of the cotton belt. None had electricity, few had screens, and most were without privies. They drew water from springs or open, unprotected wells. They also lacked the most elementary household furnishings, such as beds, mattresses, adequate stoves, dishes, or cooking utensils. Fertilizer sacks were commonly used as bedding. The total possessions of one Laurens farmer, described as representative, were valued at $20 and "consist[ed] of 1 cultivator ($4), 6 hens, 3 very poor beds, 1 chair, 1 table, 1 very small stove, 3 sheets, 6 quilts, 6 plates, 2 cups, 2 saucers, 3 knives and 6 forks." He also had "absolutely no food on hand, not even a bushel of potatoes." Indeed,

73 Swiger and Larson, *Climbing Toward Security*, 41, 43; Rachel Rowe Swiger and Conrad Taeuber, *Ill Fed, Ill Clothed, Ill Housed—Five Hundred Families in Need of Help* (Washington: Bureau of Agricultural Economics and Farm Security Administration, 1942), 6–7, 33–34.

74 Swiger and Larson, *Climbing Toward Security*, 61–62; "Progress Report of the Non-Commercial Project," Laurens County, June, 1941, and "Annual Report, Non-Commercial Group, Oglethorpe County," [1940] in Department of Rural Sociology Survey Records, Department of Manuscripts and University Archives, Cornell University, hereinafter cited as Rural Survey Records; Conrad Taeuber and Rachel Rowe, *Five Hundred Families Rehabilitate Themselves* (Washington: Bureau of Agricultural Economics and Farm Security Administration, 1941), 3; Swiger and Taeuber, *Ill Fed, Ill Clothed, Ill Housed*, 35, 38–39. The latter source gives income figures of $143 in Laurens and $105 in Oglethorpe.

the living level of these families was so low that Hudgens, no stranger to the poverty of the Southeast, recalled that his "heart sank" when he first visited some of them.[75]

Most of the families suffered from malnutrition. Concentrating exclusively on cash cropping to repay furnish bills, they grew very few vegetables. Some went without fresh meat, having sold their hogs to settle accounts. Since nearly all the families lacked cows, they rarely had milk; two-thirds of those in Laurens drank none during 1938. Even when landlords permitted gardens most food preservation was impossible for lack of ice boxes, pressure cookers, and canning jars. Besides, acute hunger led to immediate consumption of any available food. The mother of a family of thirteen which had eaten most of the meat from four hogs slaughtered just two weeks before remarked, "We was so hungry we just couldn't seem to get enough."[76]

Initial medical examinations of 565 family members revealed appalling health conditions. Some clients were chronically sick due to poor diets: 121 children had rickets, more than 40 persons were anemic, and 14 had pellagra. Others suffered from neglect of relatively simple conditions: about three quarters had defective teeth, half had diseased tonsils, 21 of the men had hernias, and nearly all the wives needed surgical repairs following childbirth. In Laurens lack of sanitary privies resulted in a hookworm infection rate of about 25 percent. Other serious ailments included high blood pressure (for 13 percent in Oglethorpe), tuberculosis, and scattered cases of malaria and syphilis.[77]

To meet these families' immediate security needs the FSA made grants for treatment of their most serious health problems. It also tried to arrange debt adjustments, and asked landlords to sign written leases, reduce rents, repair houses, and improve sanitation

75 Swiger and Taeuber, *Ill Fed, Ill Clothed, Ill Housed*, 7, 10–13, 48–49; interview with Robert W. Hudgens.
76 Swiger and Taeuber, *Ill Fed, Ill Clothed, Ill Housed*, 2–3, 14–16, 54–56; Swiger and Larson, *Climbing Toward Security*, 8–9.
77 Swiger and Taeuber, *Ill Fed, Ill Clothed, Ill Housed*, 52–53; Alexander to Fellow Workers, August 8, 1939, in RG 96, NA.

facilities. Lease negotiations with skeptical landlords were especially difficult at first.[78]

Farm and home plans in the NCF program might set very modest goals, especially at first, on the assumption that simple accomplishments would raise discouraged clients' morale. These objectives might include producing a recommended amount of milk and vegetables during the first year, or providing each family member one change of clothes suitable for school, church, or community participation. Plans might call for at least one bed for each two persons, new mattresses and sheets, stoves adequate for baking, pressure cookers and jars for canning, or enough dishes to serve a meal. Supervisors made outright grants to supply mules, subsistence livestock, and basic equipment, while gradually extending credit for operating expenses and farm implements. They stressed the need for small advances since clients had very little ability to pay, or even comprehend large debts. Total grants during 1939–1942 averaged $593 per family in Oglethorpe and $311 in Laurens, while loans averaged $1,110 and $929, respectively.[79]

The NCF program improved the lives of its clients. From 1938 to 1942 their average total cash incomes increased from $174 to $368 in Laurens and from $99 to $272 in Oglethorpe. By the end of 1940 the average net worth of the Laurens clients had increased from $75 to $332 and that of the Oglethorpe families had risen from $142 to $162. But the rehabilitants' most significant progress was in their security, health, and living conditions. By 1941, for example nearly all the clients in both counties could obtain five-year written leases from increasingly cooperative landlords, and all were renting their land for a fixed amount of cotton or cash instead of sharecropping. Housing and sanitation had been upgraded with screens, privies,

78 Tate to Brechenser, November 4, 1939, in RG 96, NA; interview with Robert W. Hudgens; Taeuber and Rowe, *Five Hundred Families Rehabilitate Themselves*, 10; Swiger and Larson, *Climbing Toward Security*, 8, 10.

79 Swiger and Larson, *Climbing Toward Security*, 8–9, 13–17, 59–60; "Progress Report of the Non-Commercial Project," Laurens County, June, 1941, "Annual Report, Non-Commercial Group, Oglethorpe County" [1940], and "Semi-Annual Report, Non-Commercial Group... Oglethorpe County" [July, 1941], all in Rural Survey Records; interview with Robert W. Hudgens.

and new wells with pumps. In both counties all project families were members of FSA medical and dental care associations. All owned workstock and cows (often two per family), as well as hogs and poultry. They also had diversified their farming with feed crops, grew much of their own food, and might preserve as many as three or four hundred quarts of their produce per year.[80]

The NCF experiment was curtailed after 1942 by wartime reductions in the FSA's program. But it had demonstrated the feasibility of uplifting some of the poorest southern country folk, even if it did not make them completely self-supporting. To aid such people, however, the FSA would have to be willing to use grants extensively to create minimum living conditions before extending credit. It would also have to provide much remedial medical care and go to great lengths to arrange secure land tenure. Large county supervisory staffs would be necessary. Even then, the agency would have to expect only very gradual progress and accept relatively poor loan repayment rates. All of this would necessitate a high cost program sure to invite congressional attack.[81]

Despite the FSA's desire to reach more people at the level of the Laurens and Oglethorpe clients, the selection of new rehabilitants ran steadily in the other direction. Alexander always deplored this and persisted in trying to set the FSA on a course of digging deeper. Even in June, 1940, while in the process of resigning as administrator, he scheduled still another round of national, regional, and district conferences to concentrate on means of aiding poorer

80 Taeuber and Rowe, *Five Hundred Families Rehabilitate Themselves*, 3–5, 10, 15; "Progress Report of the Non-Commercial Project," Laurens County, June, 1941, "Annual Report, Non-Commercial Group, Oglethorpe County" [1940], and "Semi-Annual Report, Non-Commercial Group . . . Oglethorpe County [July, 1941], all in Rural Survey Records; Swiger and Larson, *Climbing Toward Security*, 28–36, 61–62. The latter source indicates average net worths in 1942 of $173 in Laurens and $46 in Oglethorpe. This decline from 1940 probably reflected continued lending but decreased grants to clients, resulting in their debt liability rising faster than their assets. This condition might have proved temporary if clients' rising incomes increased their debt-paying ability.

81 Maddox, "Farm Security Administration," 336–37; Swiger and Larson, *Climbing Toward Security*, 40; interview with James G. Maddox.

families.[82] It was probably at these meetings that the FSA adopted a policy of supplementing standard borrowers' loans with grants. The FSA had previously made small grants to regular rehabilitants for specific purposes, such as improving home sanitation facilities or joining a health association. The NCF program had used a loan-grant combination to aid its clients. But by the fall of 1939 the agency's southeastern region was using grants to "balance farm and home plans," that is, to supply the minimum needs outlined for the borrower's family if these could not be fully covered by his loan and expected income. This practice was adopted as national policy in 1940–1941, and was a deliberate attempt to dig deeper by making it easier to write farm and home plans for poorer families. It was short lived, however, because of wartime changes in the FSA's objectives and because Congress virtually eliminated all grant funds within two years. Maddox later concluded that the technique had only a limited impact.[83]

Circumstances in the early 1940s also made it impossible for Alexander's successor, C. B. Baldwin, to reverse the upward trend in borrower selection. Changing conditions in the general economy altered FSA's own perspective of the role of low income farmers in American agriculture. Secondly, during the war years the agency accepted new responsibilities which took it still farther from a policy of digging deeper. Finally, the FSA came under heavy congressional attack after 1942.

The FSA's emphasis on digging deeper was connected with its concern for keeping the poor in agriculture. Among the agency's chief worries were the forces, particularly mechanization, pushing tenants and croppers out of farming. In a depressed economy they saw no alternative to maintaining low income people on the land even if a majority could not be fully rehabilitated. Region V adminis-

---

82 Larson, *Ten Years of Rural Rehabilitation*, 6, 125; Alexander to Morgan, June 11, 1940, in RG 96, NA.

83 Tate to Brechenser, November 4, 1939, in RG 96, NA; Maddox, "Farm Security Administration," 161–69. Maddox attributes the grant-loan combination idea to Hudgens, who was Region V director until 1939. Interview with James G. Maddox.

trator E. S. Morgan, testifying before John Tolan's House Committee on Interstate Migration in August, 1940, stressed the role of rural rehabilitation in stabilizing low income farmers, lest they become destitute migrants. And as FSA advisor T. J. Woofter summarized the objective in 1939, "Agriculture must be geared to care for the maximum number, even if some of the devices by which this is accomplished are . . . temporary expedients and stop gaps."[84]

By 1942, however, the FSA's perspective was shifting in fundamentally new directions. As the nation entered a period of full employment and expanding off-farm opportunities, many of the FSA's leaders saw less urgency in rehabilitating the poorest clients as farmers. Baldwin, Maddox, and others concluded that it was unsound to hold on the land those whose acreage, capital, equipment, and skills were inadequate for either commercial production or achieving an acceptable living standard. Instead, they thought, the FSA should encourage them to leave their farms for newly available industrial or agricultural labor.[85] In retrospect it may be doubtful that the poorest and least skilled rural people were capable of gaining a permanent foothold in new employment, especially without much transitional supervision. But a change of course seemed advisable and the FSA abandoned its goal of digging deeper and gave up the attempt to rehabilitate most of the poor as farmers. This was most evident in the agency's policies on food production and agricultural labor.

In 1942 the FSA took a major step away from its antipoverty purposes with its decision to concentrate on building up some low income farmers for commercial food production. This new objective was seen as a contribution to the war effort, but, more importantly, as a new war-related activity to attract political support for the agency at a time when New Deal social programs were being deemphasized. It would require channeling most credit to those rehabilitants, and a few new applicants, who had sufficient land, livestock, equipment, and family labor for significant production. Standard

---

84 Maddox, "Farm Security Administration," 77–78; Tolan Committee Hearings, Pt. 2, pp. 698–727; Thomas Jackson Woofter, Jr., *Rural Planning for More Workers* (Washington: Farm Security Administration, mimeographed, 1940), 5.
85 Maddox, "Farm Security Administration," 77–78, 348–49.

loan eligibility requirements were rewritten accordingly. By the end
of the year Region V administrator Morgan planned to put over half
his area's loan funds into the food production efforts of current borrowers while taking on "no appreciable number of new clients."[86]

As another part of its wartime role the FSA cooperated with the
U.S. Employment Service, the Extension Service, and other agencies in the fall of 1942 in supplying migratory workers for large
commercial farmers. The FSA took charge of transporting the workers and establishing minimum housing and wage standards for them.
Hoping to consolidate all farm labor supply responsibilities under
the FSA, Baldwin called a conference of his regional administrators
in November, 1942, to plan a program. There the FSA laid plans to
recruit some of the needed workers from the ranks of low income
farmers, especially those with inadequate acreage in overpopulated
areas, who were increasingly unlikely to qualify for standard loans.
There was some protest at the meeting against converting small farm
operators to laborers. But Maddox stressed the intention to recruit
only those who could not be satisfactorily rehabilitated on the land.
Similarly, Baldwin maintained that the plan offered the best way to
utilize marginal farmers in the war economy. This policy shift was
fundamental, however, since it assumed that, as Region IV director
Howard H. Gordon bluntly put it, "A digging deeper program based
on small loans to small farmers is not feasible."[87]

This proposed labor policy was expected to help accomplish still
another new objective, the reorganization and rationalization of
southern agriculture. As marginal farmers were assisted to move out
of the area, the FSA could lend to selected remaining small operators to enlarge their farms into more economic units by acquiring
vacated acreages. Howard Gordon declared that such consolidation
would solve permanently the agricultural problems of Region IV. As
he described the situation, "In 32 Kentucky counties there are

---

86   *Ibid.*, 151–52, 349; Larson, *Ten Years of Rural Rehabilitation*, 86–87; Proceedings of
     FSA Administrator's Staff Conference, November 25–29, 1942, copy in USDA History
     Office. See Baldwin, *Poverty and Politics*, 327, 330–31, for the FSA's decision to justify
     its activities in terms of the war effort.
87   Baldwin, *Poverty and Politics*, 222–25, 329; Proceedings of FSA Administrator's Staff
     Conference, in USDA History Office.

76,000 families with gross farm sales averaging $61 per year. I would like for someone to tell me what to do about that, other than move the surplus out and provide those remaining with a better chance to make a living." Another regional director saw the new policy as an opportunity "to reach people we never have been able to reach before, to help part of them increase food production at home and to assist others to move out where their labor can count for more in the war effort."[88]

A major reason for the FSA's efforts to relate its program to the war effort was the need for defense against mounting congressional attacks after 1941. These attacks had several sources. Since the RA period the agency had encountered political opposition. In the South many landlords, furnish merchants, and local politicians recognized its potential to change traditional relationships. It might decrease tenants' dependence on landlords and other creditors, awaken poor people to the benefits of the New Deal, and encourage them to look to a source of authority beyond the local level. Some planters feared disruption of their supply of cheap labor. Local bankers and merchants resented the FSA's lending and promotion of cooperatives. Others protested its extension of services to blacks. Responsive to the attitudes of some of their influential constituents, many southern congressmen were antagonistic to the agency. Secondly, the FSA attracted the opposition of the agricultural power structure. The American Farm Bureau Federation and the Extension Service saw it as a rival for influence in the Department of Agriculture and as a possible threat to their prerogatives in the grassroots administration of farm programs. After 1940 the AFBF, increasingly anti-New Dealish, was openly hostile to the FSA. Finally, the years after 1938 were not propitious for the New Deal in Congress. Attacks on the FSA were part of the pattern of reaction against the New Deal by a coalition of Republicans and antiadministration Democrats.[89]

88 Maddox, "Farm Security Administration," 348–49; Proceedings of FSA Administrator's Staff Conference, in USDA History Office.
89 This discussion relies on Baldwin, *Poverty and Politics*, Chap. 9, which examines the anxieties and opposition FSA aroused as a "disturber of the peace" challenging the

After 1941 Congress made piecemeal reductions in the FSA's program. The Tarver amendment restricting farm purchase lending, the ban on aid to cooperatives or their participants, and the mandate to disband all land-leasing associations under the rural rehabilitation program were all major hindrances to the agency's operations. Resettlement community projects also came under increasing attack. Since 1938, appropriation bills had carried general provisions aiming at their liquidation, without setting a deadline. In the summer of 1942 congressional pressure resulted in the Department of Agriculture's budget director ordering the FSA to prepare a timetable for selling project lands to their residents. The agency was also stripped of the wartime farm labor role which it had hoped to expand. Early in 1943 the FSA was placed under the jurisdiction of the War Food Administration (WFA), an agency within the Department of Agriculture charged with increasing food production. In April, 1943, Congress provided for reassigning all farm labor programs within the WFA. Responsive to congressional desires, the WFA's administrator, Chester Davis, transferred FSA's labor activities to the WFA's Office of Labor. The FSA lost even its camps for migratory workers.[90]

Like other relief or social programs, the FSA was attacked in Congress by anti-New Dealers seeking to cut its funds in the name of war economy. In early 1942, after hostile hearings, Senator Harry F. Byrd's Committee on Reduction of Nonessential Federal Expenditures called for its abolition. While this recommendation aroused no action, the FSA lost heavily in 1942 when Congress slashed its appropriation for fiscal 1943 to little more than half the $287 million Roosevelt requested. These reductions were as detrimental to the agency's work as the program restrictions of the 1940s. For example, money for rural rehabilitation, which the president had hoped to expand as part of the FSA's food production objectives, was cut from

---

status quo in southern communities. For the attack on the FSA by the Farm Bureau, see also Grant McConnell, *The Decline of Agrarian Democracy* (Berkeley: University of California Press, 1953), Chaps. 9 and 10.

90 Baldwin, *Poverty and Politics*, 336–38, 377–383; U.S. War Food Administration, *The Annual Report of the Farm Security Administration, 1942–3* (Washington: War Food Administration, 1943), 23–24.

the $187 million for 1941–1942 to $140 million. The 1944 appropriation was even more disastrous. It lowered the agency's total funds from about $175 million to just under $112 million, with rural rehabilitation absorbing the deepest cuts (from $140 million to $80 million). The latter action, along with the program reductions, the FSA's exclusion from farm labor policy, and Baldwin's resignation in the fall of 1943, marked the end of the FSA's effectiveness as an antipoverty agency.[91]

Finally, the opponents of the FSA sought to disband it completely. Such recommendations were made not only by the Byrd committee in 1942, but also by the House Appropriations Committee, which in 1943 advocated transferring the FSA's farm purchase lending to the Farm Credit Administration and its supervisory activities to the Extension Service. But the most persistent efforts against the agency were those of the House special committee, created in March, 1943, to investigate the FSA. Chaired by Harold Cooley of North Carolina, a long-time foe of the RA-FSA who had also obstructed the Bankhead-Jones bills, the committee held prolonged hearings between May, 1943, and May, 1944. Near the conclusion of these Cooley introduced legislation to liquidate the FSA and create a new agency for farm purchase lending. Cooley did not obtain action at first. But in August, 1946, Congress passed his bill to replace the FSA with the Farmers' Home Administration.[92] With the death of the FSA, the administration's most comprehensive attack on rural poverty had become a casualty of the anti-New Deal climate of the 1940s.

91   Baldwin, *Poverty and Politics,* 317, 347–48, 352–361, 383–396.
92   *Ibid.,* 385–87, 401–402.

CHAPTER IX

Economic Problem Number One: The South as a Poor Region

IN THE late 1930s, as the rehabilitative approach to poverty was established in the Resettlement and Farm Security Administrations, an older stream of thought concerning the South's impoverishment flowed with renewed vigor. This was the idea of general economic development of a backward region, actually an outgrowth of the post–Civil War vision of an industrialized "New South."

The New South movement began in the late 1870s as a "homegrown plan of reconstruction," a program of action to industrialize the section and in the process change the agrarian values of its people to accept the new order. Southern businessmen, manufacturers, and publicists hoped to assure their section an American standard of living by adopting the nation's industrial spirit. While they were optimistic about the future, they frankly acknowledged the region's widespread poverty.

By the 1880s, however, the movement evolved into a promotional campaign which mixed fact with hopes and propaganda. It greatly exaggerated the industrialization which had taken place and the prosperity it generated. Increasingly it ignored the fact that the South remained the poorest part of the country. New South spokesmen also tended to overestimate the region's endowment of natural resources and were convinced that abundance of raw materials alone would assure economic development. Thus they often overlooked such deficiencies as the paucity of capital and local investment, acute shortage of managerial and industrial skills among a rural people, and the mass impoverishment that made the South a poor market for manufactured goods.

New South spokesmen were not successful in industrializing most of the section or raising its living standards. But they implanted a powerful regional creed—a pervasive myth—which pictured the South as economically progressive, always on the verge of developing its rich potential and creating general prosperity. By the end of the nineteenth century the idea was widely accepted as fact.[1]

A corollary of the New South idea in the 1930s was that the region's economy was "colonial." Its industries were owned and managed by outside capital. Since the promoters of industrialism assumed that plentiful resources assured economic development, they focused on this condition to explain why the South's backwardness persisted. At first they stressed that the section produced mostly raw materials and semiprocessed goods which were finished in the North. Thus the profits from manufacturing accrued to outsiders and the South paid high prices to buy items made from its own products.

By the late 1930s the concept of the colonial economy expanded as many concluded that national policies hindered the South's industrial progress. The prime example was the railroads' practice, sanctioned by the Interstate Commerce Commission (ICC), of charging higher freight rates in the South and West than in the Northeast, on the grounds that the latter generated more traffic. This made production costs higher in the South and handicapped new industries. Southern governors, among others, saw the freight differential as a major discrimination against the region, and in 1937 they launched a campaign to secure reform through the ICC. Similarly, others also saw efforts to set national minimum wages as a

---

1 This discussion of the New South movement summarizes the perceptive interpretation of Paul M. Gaston's *The New South Creed: A Study in Southern Mythmaking* (New York: Alfred A. Knopf, 1970). See especially 189–91, 219–20.

northern industrialist-inspired attempt to reduce the cost advantages of growing southern competitors.[2]

The New South idea declined during the worst years of the Great Depression, when public confidence in business and industry was at a low ebb. But it revived in the late 1930s as national economic conditions improved. By 1936 there were solid increases in southern manufacturing; the output of textiles, paper and pulp, and tobacco in that year exceeded 1929 levels, and in 1937 food processing reached that point. In contrast, durable goods (of secondary importance in the South) recovered to the same degree only in 1940. By 1939 the South's overall production regained its position of ten years earlier, although wages still lagged by about 10 percent. This progress, moreover, was relatively better than that of the nation as a whole.[3]

This upswing generated southern optimism about depression recovery and permanent prosperity. Early in 1937 the Southern States Industrial Council (formed in 1933 to publicize industrial potential and oppose wage increases under the National Recovery Administration) reviewed the past year and proclaimed that the section had manufactured goods valued at an unprecedented $8 billion. The council thought these increases meant a wider distribution of wealth in the South. Similarly, in January, 1937, the Birmingham *News* noted rising employment and decreasing relief rolls, and in March declared that Deep South enterprises, paced by steel and textiles, had reached predepression production peaks. It quoted with ap-

2 George B. Tindall, "The 'Colonial Economy' and the Growth Psychology: The South in the 1930's," *South Atlantic Quarterly*, LXIV (Autumn, 1965), 465–77. Tindall points out that New Deal attempts to regulate business, from the NRA on, clashed with the "growth psychology" of New South industrialism. He also summarizes recent historical work showing that freight rate differentials, despite the concern they aroused, were a relatively "minor barrier to regional development . . . that gradually would have yielded in any case." In his *The Emergence of the New South, 1913–1945* (Baton Rouge: Louisiana State University Press, 1967), Vol. X of 10 vols., in Wendell Holmes Stephenson and E. Merton Coulter (eds.), *A History of the South*, 600, Tindall notes that the differential (about 39 percent in the Southeast and 75 percent in the Southwest on intraregional traffic) applied to finished products, not generally to bulk commodities, raw materials, or semiprocessed goods, which were the main southern products. Shortages of capital and skilled labor and inadequate markets probably impaired the growth of secondary manufacturing more than did freight rates.
3 Tindall, *Emergence of the New South*, 359–60, 457, 470–71.

proval a cotton mill executive who predicted a new era of industrial expansion in the region. [4]

Meanwhile, critics of the industrial-recovery enthusiasm continued to point out the South's widespread poverty. As early as February, 1936, the Raleigh *News and Observer* editorialized that, although the condition of the poor had probably improved slightly, they were still little better off than ten years before, and such advances as had been made hardly justified "loose talk" about high American living standards. The editor thought the "spectacle of poverty in a rich land" was "shocking and depressing" and admitted that the worst conditions were in the South. Then, picking up a theme later stressed by New Dealers, he noted that raising living standards for the poor could benefit the whole community. [5]

Agrarians also questioned the new optimism. H. C. Nixon wrote that "it seems more or less futile for the Southern champions of 'agrarianism' and their opposing champions of the industrial way of life to argue the issues which divide them, because the South is widely lacking in what either group would impute to it." He emphasized that the tenancy problem remained unsolved, that poor farmers were still in the lowest of income groups, and that there was far too little farming for home use in the region. He concluded that "Southern civilization is at the bottom of the ladder by any statistical or democratic test." [6]

Nixon also condemned the growing factory-hunting movement with its inducements of cheap labor, tax exemptions, and community-subsidized buildings. Early in 1937 he declared that the first such statewide program, Mississippi's "Balance Agriculture with Industry" (BAWI) plan of 1936, was fundamentally unsound because it set no labor standards whatever, and subsidized manufacturers with tax exemptions without requiring them to contribute to public services. Above all, he said, the plan ignored Mississippi's real need, a "balanced and more cooperative agriculture." Similarly,

4 *Ibid.*, 444, 457; Birmingham *News*, January 5 and 24, and March 21, 1937.
5 Raleigh *News and Observer*, February 14, 1936.
6 Herman Clarence Nixon, "The Paradoxical Scene" (Typescript in Herman Clarence Nixon Papers, in possession of the Nixon family, Nashville).

Francis P. Miller saw little benefit in an impending invasion of the South by "pauper industries" seeking subsidy and low-wage costs. And even the industry-minded Birmingham *News* condemned the BAWI plan with the comment that the South needed more than low-wage factories to prosper.[7]

Some New Dealers, notably Aubrey Williams of the National Youth Administration, feared that a return of normal business and industrial conditions would cause people to ignore poverty as they had before the depression. As early as the spring of 1936 he stressed in his speeches that destitution in the rural South was chronic, that most farmers' incomes had never been commensurate with the prices of necessities, and consequently, even in the "prosperous" 1920s the region had the poorest schools, health facilities, and public services.[8]

By the fall of 1937 Williams was even more outspoken. In October he addressed the Southern Tenant Farmers' Union convention in Memphis and congratulated the union for calling public attention to agricultural workers' "manifest needs" which had "existed for a generation with little constructive effort to meet them." Observing that large numbers of poor farmers and rural laborers had "lived from hand to mouth for years before the financial depression," he credited the relief program and the Resettlement Administration with providing their first, although inadequate, assistance. Slightly earlier, in September, Williams had warned a meeting of North Carolina Young Democrats of the danger that the public, as prosperity returned, would become "callous to human need," and "complacent to the chronic poverty of those on the other side of town." He reminded them that a third of the population was still inadequately housed, fed, and clothed, and "despite the prosperity which we have achieved, if we consider... the unemployed and those on relief, there are probably twice as many families receiving

7 Unidentified newspaper clipping, January or February, 1937, and Francis P. Miller to W. T. Couch, March 6, 1937, in Nixon Papers; Birmingham *News*, March 8, 1937.
8 Aubrey Williams, high school commencement address, Oliver Springs, Tennessee, May 7, 1936, in Aubrey Williams Papers, Franklin D. Roosevelt Library, Hyde Park, N.Y.

incomes below $500 now as did in 1929." And yet, he declared, "reactionaries" and "Liberty Leaguers" urged Congress to slow the enactment of social and economic legislation. Williams' views apparently reflected those of the administration in the fall of 1937, at least to the extent that he used the same theme in drafting statements for the president.[9]

An emerging idea in the New Deal, and among its sympathizers, was that raising, or even maintaining, the living standards of the general community depended on improving the incomes of its neediest members. Roosevelt, for example, was consistently concerned with the lack of purchasing power among the poor. He frequently diagnosed the South's greatest problem as the inability of impoverished masses, especially in rural areas, to buy the goods of industry or retail trade, or contribute to the region's health, educational, or other tax-supported services. At Warm Springs in November, 1934, for instance, he remarked to newsmen that first-time observers of the rural South were usually struck by "what looks like poverty, real poverty. . . . The standard of living is absolutely and totally different from what it is in the prosperous areas of the West or . . . North." He continued that "the average farm family in the South only sees, in the way of cash, perhaps a couple of hundred dollars a year and a great many don't see that." As a result, "the taxing power is almost nil. This state cannot raise money for education because there is nothing to tax."[10]

Similarly, in a speech in Atlanta on November 29, 1935, Roosevelt related inability to buy to widespread hunger. He said doctors had told him that great numbers of Americans lived on a "third-class diet." But raising that standard even to a second-class level, not to mention real adequacy, he said, would greatly expand the market for foodstuffs to the general benefit of American agriculture. But all of this was not immediately possible, he concluded, "for

9 Aubrey Williams, address to joint convention of STFU and United Cannery, Agricultural, Packing and Allied Workers of America, Memphis, September 26, 1937, speech to Young Democrats of North Carolina convention, Winston-Salem, September 11, 1937, and draft of Roosevelt's speech for Annual Mobilization for Human Needs, October 18, 1937, *ibid.*

10 Roosevelt Press Conferences, IV, 212–13, in Franklin D. Roosevelt Library.

the very simple reason that the masses of the American people have not got the purchasing power to eat more and better food." [11]

In 1937 Roosevelt continued this emphasis as the administration began a drive for federal minimum wage legislation. In a press conference on June 15, he declared that in several areas of the country living conditions were "far below any decent standard," and "the more we attack the basic problem of getting a better standard of living for the one-third at the bottom, the quicker we will get rid of relief." He continued that "what we are trying to do is build up national income with special reference to increasing the share of the national income of the lowest one-third." [12] The militant Aubrey Williams concurred with Roosevelt. He told the North Carolina Young Democrats' convention that better incomes for the poor would benefit their communities: "Your self interest is a thousand times more tied up with that laborer who is striking for a decent wage . . . that mill hand . . . who is joining a . . . union, than it is with some banker or manufacturer who is the town's so-called first citizen, but who is trying to make these people work for wages which do not permit them to pay their doctor, to buy the amount of groceries they need . . . or to rent the house which they should have." [13]

Some labor leaders saw better living conditions for the rural poor as essential to prevent their becoming low-wage competitors for industrial workers. For example, A. Steve Nance, Georgia textile organizer for the Committee on Industrial Organizations (CIO), remarked to Jonathan Daniels that "the real threat to the American standard of living . . . [comes] from the poor whites of the South. They are terribly poor and terribly productive. They must be given some sort of standards or no other standards in America will survive." [14]

In 1937 the New Deal sought to provide some of the purchasing power it had determined the poor needed by establishing labor standards by federal law. Wage and hour legislation became a major

11 Franklin D. Roosevelt, speech at Atlanta, November 29, 1935, in Roosevelt Speech File, Franklin D. Roosevelt Library.
12 Roosevelt Press Conferences, IX, 436–48, in Franklin D. Roosevelt Library.
13 Aubrey Williams, speech to Young Democrats of North Carolina convention, Winston-Salem, September 11, 1937, in Williams Papers.
14 Jonathan Daniels, *A Southerner Discovers the South* (New York: Macmillan, 1938), 295.

administration objective with the introduction of the Black-Connery bill on May 24, 1937. The measure proposed a national forty-hour week and a forty-cent minimum hourly wage (and outlawed child labor as well) in industries producing for interstate shipment. Agricultural workers were omitted from its coverage. The Senate passed the bill on July 31. Then it was sidetracked in the House Rules Committee until brought to the floor by a discharge petition in December, only to be recommitted.[15]

The wage issue was the collision point between the New Deal and New South industrialism. Southern businessmen and manufacturers saw cheap labor as a competitive advantage in operating existing industries and attracting new ones. They justified low pay scales by several arguments: that living costs were lower in the South than elsewhere, that sectional wage differentials compensated for unfair freight rates which handicapped southern manufacturing, and that higher wages would retard industrialization and thus prolong poverty. These spokesmen usually insisted that any federal wage legislation should provide regional variations as had NRA codes and work relief programs.[16]

The wages and hours proposal aroused determined southern opposition. C. C. Gilbert of the Southern States Industrial Council informed Democratic national chairman James A. Farley that nearly all the 17,000 manufacturers in the organization opposed the bill because it would "cripple the industrial South beyond repair." A Mississippi Democratic national committeeman argued to Roosevelt that even though minimum wages might raise the standard of living, a uniform scale, combined with unfair freight rates, would inordinately discriminate against southern industry. He charged that the proposal was traceable to northern manufacturers desiring to restrict southern competition. Moreover, he contended, the whole matter was vital because of the agricultural situation; with the impending mechanization of cotton picking, industrialization was imperative to absorb the surplus labor and prevent an intolerable unemployment

15 Tindall, *Emergence of the New South*, 533–35.
16 *Ibid.*, 434–44.

problem.[17] Senators and congressmen repeatedly urged the president to accept either a lower minimum wage or a regional differential. And Clarence Poe, editor of the *Progressive Farmer*, suggested, in letters and during a conference with the president, raising southern wages to a national standard only over a period of several years.[18]

Throughout the long congressional battle over the labor proposal, Roosevelt remained firmly committed to raising purchasing power by a minimum wage without regional differentials. When Texas congressman Martin Dies suggested a scheme to permit states to vary the rate to as little as twenty-five or thirty cents per hour, the president shot back that the idea was "unsound," calculated to "destroy the effectiveness of building up a purchasing power in those sections most needing it," and "the weakest, most dangerous proposition he [had] ever heard."[19] In a letter to Senator Hattie Caraway of Arkansas in December, 1937, he reaffirmed: "What we are all interested in is raising the buying power of the average of our working population—giving special attention to the 'lowest third.' By buying power we mean the annual income of the family. . . . I know you realize . . . that the annual income of workers in the South is so low that they have little purchasing power, little to pay in the way of taxes and that therefore, education and sanitation have greatly suffered in the South."[20]

In the spring of 1938 Roosevelt became increasingly militant on the wage issue in the South. At Gainesville, Georgia, on March 23,

---

17 C. C. Gilbert to James A. Farley, July 27, 1937, in Official File 2730, Franklin D. Roosevelt Library; Louis M. Jiggitts to Roosevelt, January 4, 1938, in Official File 2405, Franklin D. Roosevelt Library.

18 George L. Berry to Roosevelt, October 26, 1937, A. L. Bulwinkle to James Roosevelt, November 1, 1937, in Official File 2730, Franklin D. Roosevelt Library; Clarence Poe to Roosevelt, December 23, 1937, and January 10, 1938, and Roosevelt to Marvin McIntyre, memorandum, December 23, 1937, in President's Personal File 2812, Franklin D. Roosevelt Library. The president accepted the idea of gradually increasing southern wages, judging from the final provisions of the Fair Labor Standards Act of 1938.

19 Martin Dies to Roosevelt, January 11, 1938, Roosevelt to McIntyre, memorandum, January 13, 1938, in Official File 2730, Franklin D. Roosevelt Library.

20 Roosevelt to Hattie Caraway, December 20, 1937, in President's Personal File 5456, Franklin D. Roosevelt Library.

he lashed out at those who blocked the bill. "Georgia and the lower South may just as well face facts," he declared. "The purchasing power of... millions... in this whole area is far too low." Appealing to the New South tradition, he suggested the necessity of improving markets before factories could be attracted. "On the present scale of wages and... buying power," he said, "the South cannot... succeed in establishing successful new industries." He closed by accusing recalcitrant business interests and their congressional spokesmen of believing in the "feudal system," if not the "Fascist system."[21]

On May 24, the House, influenced by victories of proadministration southern senators in Democratic primaries, passed the Fair Labor Standards Act. The new law, the last major New Deal legislative success, established a maximum work week of forty-four hours, to be reduced to forty within two years. It set a national minimum wage of forty cents per hour, but provided that pay scales in low-wage industries would reach the national level by 1945. A wage and hour division in the Department of Labor could, and ultimately did, accelerate the rate of increase. Otherwise the measure allowed no regional differential. Most of the rural poor, of course, were unaffected, since the act did not cover agricultural labor.[22]

The opposition of some conservative Democrats to wages and hours legislation, and the more general stalemate of the New Deal program, persuaded the president, in the spring of 1938, to intervene in several Democratic primary elections to ask voters to oust incumbent senators whom he regarded as obstructionists and a possible threat to New Dealers' control of the party in 1940.[23] One of the principal targets of this "purge" was Senator Walter F. George of Georgia. Roosevelt's involvement in the Georgia campaign furnished the occasion for the New Deal's best-known survey of the

21   Franklin D. Roosevelt, speech at Gainesville, Georgia, March 23, 1938, in Roosevelt Speech File, Franklin D. Roosevelt Library. For Aubrey Williams' contributions to this speech, see Williams to Roosevelt, March 21, 1938, in President's Personal File 1820, Franklin D. Roosevelt Library, Williams to Roosevelt, March 24, 1938, and Roosevelt to Williams, March 28, 1938, in Williams Papers.
22   Tindall, *Emergence of the New South*, 535–37.
23   William E. Leuchtenburg, *Franklin D. Roosevelt and the New Deal* (New York: Harper and Row, 1963), 266.

South's impoverishment, the National Emergency Council's *Report on Economic Conditions of the South.*

While the president planned the purge, Clark Foreman, head of the Public Works Administration (PWA) power division, circulated a new proposal: publication of a pamphlet detailing New Deal accomplishments for the South, a story which he thought the press and politicians had neglected. The power division was an unlikely source for such ideas, but Foreman had deep concern for the South's common people. Before 1933 he had been a member of Will Alexander's Commission on Interracial Cooperation staff, and later was Interior Secretary Harold Ickes' advisor on Negro affairs. Foreman later said that Jerome Frank, then counsel for the power division, first suggested the idea to him when they attended a meeting of the Washington branch of the Southern Policy Committee in the spring of 1938. By June, Foreman and Frank had discussed the matter with presidential advisor Tom Corcoran.

Early in June, Roosevelt summoned Foreman to the White House to discuss the possibilities of defeating Senator George. During their conversation Foreman advised that publication of a strong statement of New Deal contributions to the welfare of the southern people would effectively reinforce the administration's political support in the region. Foreman recalled that the president reacted "positively and favorably," but wanted a report which was purely factual and not overtly partisan. Furthermore, it should outline economic problems without proposing solutions, he thought, because "if the people understand the facts they will find their own remedies." Thus, as Foreman later told Jonathan Daniels, "the Economic Report was in fact a part of the President's program to liberalize the Democratic Party." But the New Dealers expected its effectiveness to lie in the contrast it suggested between the region's problems and the recalcitrance of senators like George in helping the administration meet them.

The president suggested that Foreman take the matter up with James Roosevelt and Lowell Mellett, director of the National Emergency Council. Foreman found the younger Roosevelt interested solely in the report's political potential, while Mellett was apprehensive about its possible repercussions. But sometime between June 12 and 18 the president directed Mellett to outline an economic survey and determine whether it should embrace several regions, or just the South. Mellett, now convinced of the usefulness of a report, recommended the latter course. He drafted a letter requesting it, which Roosevelt signed June 22. By then compilation was already underway.[24]

Foreman supervised the project, which was completed in less than a month. His principal assistants were Texans Arthur Goldschmidt (of the PWA power division) and Jack Fischer (information director of the Farm Security Administration), and Clifford Durr, an Alabama Rhodes scholar and counsel for the Reconstruction Finance Corporation. The report relied chiefly on published government data, and was carefully edited to make it factually "unimpeachable."[25]

The sixty-four-page report consisted of fifteen short sections summarizing the South's economic assets and shortcomings. Several of these, dealing with natural resources, provided a New South emphasis on the region's "immense wealth" of raw materials, and by implication, its industrial potential. Largely ignored, however, was the uneven distribution of resources which left large areas deficient. The report described water, land, and forests as ample, but pointed out shocking waste, especially of the latter two. The discussion of population, on the other hand, tended to run counter to the emphasis on plentiful resources by noting that increased mechanization of agriculture caused problems of surplus labor. Here was a hint that

24 This account of the report's origin is drawn from two letters written a decade later: Clark Foreman to Gay Morenus, November 24, 1948, and to Jonathan [Daniels], June 8, 1948, in Southern Conference for Human Welfare Papers, Atlanta University, hereinafter cited as SCHW Papers. An excellent secondary account is Thomas A. Krueger, *And Promises to Keep: The Southern Conference for Human Welfare, 1938–1948* (Nashville: Vanderbilt University Press, 1967), 11–14. For the NEC director's role see Lowell Mellett to Roosevelt, June 21, 1938, and Roosevelt to Mellett, June 22, 1938, in Official File 788, Franklin D. Roosevelt Library.

25 Lucia M. Pitts, "Memorandum for Miss Foster, National Emergency Council," August 4, 1938, in SCHW Papers; Mellett to Roosevelt, August 6, 1938, in Official File 788, Franklin D. Roosevelt Library; interview with Clifford Durr, August 8, 1972.

the land, previously described as the region's "most valuable asset," could not support all those dependent on it.[26]

The report's second message was the chronic poverty of masses of southerners, their low per capita incomes, inadequate tax base, and consequent dearth of public services. It cited figures to disprove the contention that low living costs justified a wide sectional wage differential, and advanced the New Deal argument that only the growth of mass purchasing power could stimulate regional business and industry. Without bluntly saying so, the report was in part a brief for the recently enacted wage legislation. Rounding out its picture of destitution were discussions of substandard education, health, and housing conditions. A section on the ownership and use of land condemned the tenancy system.[27]

Finally, the report stressed the South's "colonial" economy, the extent of outside control of its industry, and its dependence on northern credit. About half the section on industry was devoted to an attack on high freight rates as an unjustifiable barrier which "penalized [the South] for being rural and handicapped... its efforts to industrialize."[28] As George Tindall has observed, the report was a "kind of climax to the literature of the colonial economy," which placed the administration behind southern efforts to reform freight rates and also implied support for a coordinated program of regional development.[29]

As in the case of the 1937 President's Commission on Farm Tenancy, the authors of the report assembled an advisory committee of prominent citizens to endorse their work. This body was not especially representative of all economic interests in the South, perhaps because it was hastily convened. Its largest component was six members of the academic community, including Frank P. Graham, president of the University of North Carolina, its chairman. Five

26 U.S. National Emergency Council, *Report on Economic Conditions of the South* (Washington: Government Printing Office, 1938), 5–12, 17–20, 53–60.
27 *Ibid.*, 21–40, 45–48, 61–64.
28 *Ibid.*, 49–60. The quotation is from p. 60.
29 Tindall, "The 'Colonial Economy' and the Growth Psychology," 472–74.

businessmen were included, but only one was a manufacturer. Three public officials (including Governor Carl Bailey of Arkansas), two newspaper publishers (including Barry Bingham of the Louisville *Courier-Journal*), and one lawyer were present. Among the three labor leaders were Lucy Randolph Mason of the CIO and H. L. Mitchell of the STFU. Two planters rounded out the list. There were few nonacademic professional men, and no clergymen, agriculturalists, or Negroes present.[30]

The advisory committee assembled in Washington on July 5, heard the report, and endorsed it. The members discussed the needs of the South but, in keeping with the purpose of the document, made no formal proposals. H. L. Mitchell submitted an analysis of rural problems for his union, stressing the displacement of tenants by mechanization in the Delta. He recommended that the WPA place the dispossessed on land for live-at-home farming supplemented by public work until industry could absorb them. Most other talk of solutions centered on the need to industrialize the region.[31]

But the real public impact of the advisory meeting resulted from the president's letter to it in which he stated that "the South presents right now the Nation's No. 1 economic problem—the Nation's problem, not merely the South's." This Rooseveltian phrase—one of his most quoted—became current immediately due to the premature release of the report. While the committee ate lunch, a New York *Times* reporter stole a draft of the document, which was pub-

---

30 National Emergency Council, *Economic Conditions of the South*, 3, lists the committee members. For arrangements to assemble the committee, see Mellett to Jonathan Daniels, June 25, 1938, in Jonathan Daniels Papers, Southern Historical Collection, University of North Carolina; Howard Odum to Clark Foreman, June 24, 1938, in SCHW Papers; Frank P. Graham to Mellett, June 28 and 30, 1938, in Frank P. Graham Papers, Southern Historical Collection, University of North Carolina, Chapel Hill. Howard Odum was offered the chairmanship first, but declined it.

31 Foreman to Morenus, November 24, 1948, and to Jonathan [Daniels], June 8, 1948, in SCHW Papers; STFU recommendations to the NEC, July 5, 1938, and [H. L. Mitchell] to J. R. Butler, July 6, 1938, in Southern Tenant Farmers' Union Papers, Southern Historical Collection, University of North Carolina. The STFU recommendations may have reflected WPA thinking, since Mitchell was working on Aubrey Williams' staff in 1938.

lished in summary the next day. Foreman welcomed the advance
publicity.[32]

New Dealers used information from the report in their political
campaigning in the South. In a Memphis speech on August 5, Harry
Hopkins quoted the president's assessment of the region as an economic problem, condemned inequitable freight rates, and announced that the WPA would attempt to enhance the purchasing
power of sharecroppers and farm laborers by employing 200,000 of
them during the slack season in cotton. More importantly,
Roosevelt, then in his "purge" campaign, arranged to release the
report before his two major Georgia speeches on August 11. In the
first of these, at the University of Georgia, he stressed the then-
familiar themes of improvement of southern wages, incomes, and
taxable wealth, and hinted at a forthcoming program of federal aid to
education. And in his second, at Barnesville, Georgia, he referred to
the report as he openly urged voters to defeat Senator George.[33]
Thus the document served the immediate political purpose which
caused its preparation. The remaining question was how southerners would respond to the needs it delineated.

The report pointedly showed that millions of southerners lived in
poverty. It also stressed that increased purchasing power in their
hands could further the South's business and industry. But its major
concentration was on the reasons why the *region* was poor; the report's implication was that the impoverishment of the South's people

32 Roosevelt to committee, July 4, 1938, in Official File 788 and President's Personal File
    5427, Franklin D. Roosevelt Library, and on pp. 1–2 of National Emergency Council,
    Economic Conditions of the South. Mellett drafted the letter, including the phrase,
    "Nation's No. 1 economic problem." For accounts of the conference see Foreman to
    Morenus, November 24, 1948, and to Jonathan [Daniels], June 8, 1948, in SCHW
    Papers. The news story is in New York *Times*, July 6, 1938, p. 1.
33 New York *Times*, August 6, 1938, pp. 1, 4; Mellett to Roosevelt, August 6, 1938, and
    the president's personal copy of the report with his handwritten notation, "To be held
    for release," in Official File 788, Franklin D. Roosevelt Library; Roosevelt to Mellett,
    naval communication, August 9, 1938, in Lowell Mellett Papers, Franklin D. Roosevelt
    Library; Roosevelt speeches at the University of Georgia and at Barnesville, Georgia,
    August 11, 1938, in Roosevelt Speech File, Franklin D. Roosevelt Library. Foreman's
    part in outlining the speech attacking George appears in T[homas] G. C[orcoran] to
    Roosevelt, August 1, 1938, and Foreman to Rudolf Foster, August 5, 1938, in Presi-
    dent's Secretary's File, Franklin D. Roosevelt Library.

was due to thwarted development of the section's great potential. Consequently, the response to the document focused on the broad question of what could be done to stimulate general economic progress, rather than how to uplift destitute individuals.

Some southern industrial spokesmen reacted indignantly to a report which questioned their faith in growth and prosperity. The *Textile Bulletin* made the earliest sweeping condemnation. On July 7, only two days after the advisory committee adjourned, it attacked the group as Roosevelt's "slumming commission," consisting of handpicked members such as Graham and Miss Mason who had "already voted" to single out the South for criticism. The Atlanta *Constitution* attributed the study to New Deal political motives and thought the accuracy of Roosevelt's comments was "open to question." Blaming southern problems mainly on the tariff, freight rates, and similar discriminations against the region, the paper declared that the "No. 1 Economic Problem" statement was "not so much a criticism of the South [as of] . . . short-sighted interests in other sections which have been chiefly responsible for the condition, to the extent that it exists."[34]

More comprehensive criticism of the report came from Fitzgerald Hall, president of the Southern States Industrial Council, who claimed that it held the South up to "ridicule and shame," and was calculated to hinder his organization's efforts to attract capital and industry. He asserted that southern industrial development, which he equated with the region's economy, had "not only been great in recent years but greater than probably in many other supposedly more favored sections." Hall further charged that the report's statistics were misleading generalities which would apply to any part of the country with the same population, degree of urbanization, and diversification of industry. Moreover, the document failed to stress that 29 percent of the southern population consisted of Negroes, who lowered all averages of income and living standards. He also thought the report exaggerated the South's low in-

34 "Roosevelt Appoints a Slumming Commission," *Textile Bulletin*, July 7, 1938, clipping in Graham Papers; Atlanta *Constitution*, July 6 and 27, 1938.

comes and cited an Agriculture Department study which found that nonrelief white families in South Carolina and Georgia villages earned a median $1,309 per year. As a railroad executive Hall admitted the South was justified in seeking reform of freight rates, but denied that the problem was as fundamental as the study suggested. Finally, he noted that in 1937 the WPA spent less money in eleven southern states than in Pennsylvania, which had a population only 38 percent as large, and used that fact to nominate the latter state as "Economic Problem Number One."[35]

Foreman and Mellett, who had decided to answer critical letters, except for "hysterical diatribes," replied to Hall. Regarding his charges of misleading generalities, they asserted that the report's statistics were specific for the region because there *was* no other area with the same population, urbanization, industrialization, and other characteristics as the South. The whole import of the study was that southern conditions were exceptional. Even if statistics were distorted as Hall claimed, no such methods could "erase the poverty, the ill health, the undernourishment, the living conditions and the exploitation evident to the eyes of Southerners and strangers alike." Furthermore, they told Hall, merely stating that 29 percent of the section's population was black could in no way mitigate the fact that a large proportion of its citizens lived under "subhuman conditions" and that this poverty was not limited to Negroes. Challenging Hall's own use of figures, they noted that the median incomes he cited for southern village families applied only to a small group and were not typical of the region's predominantly rural population. As for the comparison of Pennsylvania and the South, they merely pointed out that the latter received far more spending from the AAA, FSA, and other rural-oriented federal agencies than an industrial state which

35 "Comments on the *Report of* [*sic*] *Economic Conditions of the South*," enclosed in Fitzgerald Hall to Mellett, September 7, 1938, Hall to Graham, August 26, 1938, in Graham Papers. Like Hall, some critics of the report attributed conditions it described chiefly to the black population. See George C. Biggers, *The Nation's No. 1 Economic Opportunity* (N.p., n.d.), and *Discussion of Economic Conditions in South Carolina: Annotations and Comments Relating to the Report Prepared for the President of the United States by the National Emergency Council* (Columbia: University of South Carolina Extension Division, n.d.), 31–32, 36, copies in SCHW Papers.

could be expected to need extensive work relief for its unemployed.[36]

In general, the architects of the report characterized its most strident critics as, in Graham's words, "Southern patriots and anti-New Dealers." It was probably true that the most severe attacks came from administration opponents. Barry Bingham thought this was true of many southern journalists, whose hostility to the study disturbed him. On the other hand, Foreman, with some lack of candor, dismissed charges that the report itself had been politically motivated. These came, he said, "almost uniformly... from agents of northern controlled corporations," and only confirmed what the document said about outside control of southern wealth.[37]

Other business and industrial spokesmen accepted the report as a realistic statement of problems. They recognized that it implied a need for general economic development of the region and sensed its relation to the New South tradition.[38] They generally acknowledged the section's poverty, but stressed those parts of the report which described the South as a new field for expansion of industry and retail markets.

One publicist, George C. Biggers, business manager of the Atlanta *Journal*, described the South in a pamphlet and radio speech as the "Nation's No. 1 Economic Opportunity," a phrase rapidly becoming as widespread as Roosevelt's own. "The ... report on the South," Biggers declared, "is for the most part correct and we in the South must admit it." He continued that whereas cities appeared reasonably prosperous, "out in the country things are different." Rural poverty underlay the South's low wage structure, he observed. But he noted the report's emphasis on the region's resources and, as an advertising executive, stressed that the section was a great untapped retail market. He concluded that a few national policies were the chief barriers to the realization of this potential. "Just take

---

36 Arthur Goldschmidt to Graham, September 14, 1938, Mellett to Hall, September 19, 1938, in Graham Papers. Goldschmidt and Foreman drafted Mellett's reply.
37 Graham to Mellett, July 18, 1938, Barry Bingham to Graham, July 23, 1938, *ibid.*; Foreman to George C. Biggers, January 6, 1939, in SCHW Papers.
38 Tindall, "The 'Colonial Economy' and the Growth Psychology," 472–73.

off the differential in freight rates ... [and] lend us some money at lower interest rates," he asserted, "and we'll do the rest."[39]

Similarly, in October, 1938, A. L. M. Wiggins, president of the South Carolina Federation of Commerce, Agriculture, and Industry, told radio listeners that "there can be no denial ... that in economic development, in wealth and in income the South is far behind the rest of the Nation," but at the same time it "offers the greatest opportunity for development, for improvement and for progress of any section of the Nation." With the decline of cotton tenancy, he thought, the South greatly needed agricultural diversification. Equally vital was expanded manufacturing and "development of more highly skilled industries" to supplement textile mills.[40]

Still other businessmen approved the report generally, but objected to some of its emphasis on the "colonial" aspects of northern ownership of industries. John C. Persons, president of the First National Bank of Birmingham and a member of the advisory committee, told the New Orleans Association of Commerce in March, 1939, that the South's great need for industrialization required that it attract as much outside investment as possible. The flow of capital into the region would uplift both manufacturing and farming, he asserted, because "only by building industry can we supply the purchasing power to buy the things our vast agricultural population can produce."[41]

Some national journals agreed with the report's assessment but thought it overlooked some problems or misplaced its emphasis. The *Nation* said Roosevelt's remark that the South was economic problem number one was obvious. However, the plight of the sharecroppers remained the central issue and nothing adequate had been done about it. It also agreed with the "colonial economy" thesis

39 Biggers, *The Nation's No. 1 Economic Opportunity;* George C. Biggers, "The Atlanta *Journal's* Editorial Hour" (Typescript radio discussion, November 4, 1938, in SCHW Papers).

40 A. L. M. Wiggins, "Looking Ahead in South Carolina" (Printed radio speech, October 25, 1938), in SCHW Papers.

41 John C. Persons, "Absentee Ownership and the South, An Answer to Its Critics," speech to Members Council, New Orleans Association of Commerce, March 30, 1939, in SCHW Papers. For a very similar view see New York *Times,* July 7, 1938, p. 28.

that northern corporations' "financial imperialism" caused much of the South's backwardness. The *New Republic* thought the report should have offered solutions, and supplied some of its own. If the causes of regional poverty were unfair tariffs and freight rates, unbalanced agriculture and weak labor unions, the South needed reform of those conditions, as well as federal aid for education and health programs, efforts to promote public acceptance of collective bargaining, a "square deal" for blacks, aid for sharecroppers, and diversified farming.[42]

There were, of course, southerners who welcomed the report. An indication of the interest it aroused, and perhaps some measure of public approval, was its mass circulation, much of which was within the region. Probably more than 500,000 copies were sold or distributed to schools, civic organizations, and individuals before the end of 1938.[43]

Some of the most wholehearted endorsements came from editors friendly to the administration. Mark Ethridge declared in the Louisville *Courier-Journal* that the report showed that "the nation must help untangle the South" with appropriate regional programs. Jonathan Daniels told Mellett he was "amazed at the amount of fact and intelligence" packed into a brief pamphlet. He saw it as a sign of the president's good intentions for the South. At the same time he thought Roosevelt was not resolute enough in calling for federal aid to education in his University of Georgia speech, and he also feared that in southern mill towns recently enacted wage and hour standards would be as unenforceable as prohibition. Still, he told Mellett, the report had been a great service. Furthermore, he wrote: "These Professional Southern Patriots who [resent] the description of the South as Economic Problem No. 1 are the same old Daughters of the Confederacy—though some wear pants—who . . . have [al-

---

42   "No. 1 Economic Problem," *Nation*, July 23, 1938, p. 81, and "Southern Waste Land," *ibid.*, August 20, 1938, p. 169; "The Plight of the South," *New Republic*, August 24, 1938, p. 61.

43   Mellett to Alexander, October 28, 1938, T. Roy Reid to school superintendents in Arkansas, Louisiana, and Mississippi, October 4, 1938, in Mellett Papers.

ways] been a more destructive crop than cotton. They are not talking for thoughtful men and women. . . . We know we are in a hell of a fix . . . and are grateful for [Roosevelt's] help."[44]

There were numerous suggestions that the National Emergency Council (NEC) conduct studies of individual southern states, or even issue reports on other regions. Congressman Lyndon Johnson, for example, was interested in a study of Texas. Mellett rejected such proposals, fearing that a profusion of pamphlets would reduce the impact of the original. But the University of South Carolina published its own state supplement to the main study.[45]

There was also sentiment for continuing the work of the advisory committee. One of its members, J. S. Wannamaker of South Carolina, president of the American Cotton Association, told Graham he hoped the report would encourage the press to direct "pitiless publicity" at southern backwardness as a first step toward improving conditions. But another essential move, he suggested, was to reconvene the committee to recommend to Roosevelt remedies for the region's needs. Merely to drop the matter without offering solutions, he thought, would be a "fatal blunder." Wannamaker also urged this idea upon Mellett and asked Graham to do the same, but apparently aroused no real interest.[46]

Actually, the NEC expected private southern initiative to meet the problems raised by the report. Mellett, who reflected administration thinking, saw the study as a culmination and summary of several years of regional self-examination. "We picked the problem up . . . when it was ripe for picking," he wrote. He thought correction of southern conditions would have to come not from Washington, but as a result of regional pressure. "Our report is lend-

44 Louisville *Courier-Journal*, September 25, 1938, advance copy in Mark Ethridge to Steve Early, September 21, 1938, in Official File 396, Franklin D. Roosevelt Library; Daniels to Mellett, quoted in Mellett to Roosevelt, August 26, 1938, in Daniels Papers.
45 John Fischer to Mellett, August 21, 1938, Mellett to McIntyre, October 21, 1938, in Mellett Papers; *Discussion of Economic Conditions of South Carolina*, copy in SCHW Papers.
46 J. S. Wannamaker to Graham, August 3, 1938, in Graham Papers.

ing itself to this pressure, as well as [to] efforts to do those things within the South that need to be done," Mellett advised.[47]

The first and largest organized response to the report was the Southern Conference for Human Welfare (SCHW), organized in the fall of 1938. This movement actually originated with the efforts of Joe Gelders, a Birmingham labor activist, onetime victim of antiunion violence, and (not widely known) probable Communist, to organize a regional conference on civil liberties. In the spring of 1938 Gelders met Lucy Randolph Mason, who put him in contact with Mrs. Roosevelt. The First Lady suggested that he broaden his idea to include all regional problems, and also arranged for him to see the president sometime in June, 1938. It was probably Roosevelt who first suggested linking the conference and the forthcoming NEC report.[48]

Gelders contacted H. C. Nixon of the Southern Policy Committee, who was receptive to the idea of a new regional organization. They conferred with Josephine Wilkins of the Georgia Citizens' Fact Finding Movement (a reform-minded study group) and later with Clark Foreman. These four envisioned a regional conference which would respond to the NEC report. The planners recruited two Alabama SPC members, U.S. commissioner Louise O. Charlton and postmaster Cooper Green, both of Birmingham, who made arrangements for a meeting in their city. They saw the conference, as Nixon told Brooks Hays, as "frankly intended to foster the progressive movement in the South, with no reactionaries needing to apply," making a "mass appeal" for action on the section's problems.[49]

On September 8, the Southern Conference for Human Welfare, by then formally organized, issued a call for all interested southerners to meet in Birmingham November 20–23 to consider a broad range of issues raised by the report, as well as some others. These

47   Mellett to McIntyre, October 21, 1938, in Mellett Papers.
48   Krueger, *And Promises to Keep*, 3–18, 76–78; Herman Clarence Nixon to Brooks Hays, July 27, 1938, enclosing Nixon to Francis P. Miller, July 27, 1938, in National Policy Committee Papers, Library of Congress, hereinafter cited as NPC Papers.
49   Krueger, *And Promises to Keep*, 17–19; Nixon to Hays, July 27, 1938, and Nixon to Miller, September 16, 1938, in NPC Papers.

included health, education, child labor, race relations, farm tenancy, suffrage reform, and constitutional rights.[50] More than 1,200 delegates attended the conference. They represented a great variety of interests and a high caliber of capability. Among the prominent public figures present were Mrs. Roosevelt and Justice Hugo Black (both of whom addressed the meeting), Senators John H. Bankhead and Lister Hill of Alabama, Senator Claude Pepper of Florida, Aubrey Williams, Robert W. Hudgens, Brooks Hays, and Governor Bibb Graves of Alabama. Numerous clergymen attended, as did labor leaders from the AFL, CIO, and STFU. Industrialists such as Donald Comer and such scholars as Arthur Raper came, along with Mary McLeod Bethune, F. D. Patterson of Tuskegee Institute, Benjamin Mays of Morehouse College, Forrester B. Washington, Charles S. Johnson, and other black leaders. Journalists and publishers were well represented by Ralph McGill, Clarence Poe, W. T. Couch, Virginius Dabney, and Mark Ethridge. Frank Graham was chosen chairman of the conference, and Nixon became the full-time field secretary.[51]

Of all the SCHW's major figures, Nixon emphasized rural poverty most strongly. Chairing a conference panel on landless farmers, he stressed that tenancy was the South's overriding problem because the regional economy was so largely based on agriculture. He reiterated that sharecroppers and farm laborers had the worst living standards of any large group of Americans, and argued that their low earning power depressed industrial wages, retailers' sales, and manufacturers' profits. Prosperity or poverty in agriculture meant the same for the South, Nixon declared.[52]

The SCHW adopted a strong resolution on tenancy, which called for expanding land purchase loans, rehabilitation credit, debt adjustment assistance, group medical plans, and cooperative enter-

50 "Southern Conference for Human Welfare, Plans and Purposes," printed flier [September, 1938], copy in Official File 396, Franklin D. Roosevelt Library.
51 Krueger, *And Promises to Keep*, 21–25; *Report of Proceedings of the Southern Conference for Human Welfare* (N.p., n.d.), copy in Graham Papers.
52 Herman Clarence Nixon, speech for Southern Conference for Human Welfare (Typescript in Nixon Papers).

prises under the FSA. The conference also proposed a government rural legal aid bureau and a program of subsidized low income farm housing. Likewise, it favored state legislation to require written leases, compensation of tenants for farm improvements, minimum housing standards, and arbitration of landlord-tenant disputes.[53]

But this statement, bearing most directly on rural poverty, was only one of those adopted; the full list of resolutions was as varied as the conference membership and agenda. The SCHW took positions on labor (endorsed the Fair Labor Standards Act and the unity of the AFL and the CIO, and opposed all geographical and racial wage differentials and any weakening of the Wagner Act), race relations (favored extension of the vote to all who met educational requirements, federal antilynching laws, abolition of the poll tax, and fair distribution of school funds to both races), and numerous other issues (commended the LaFollette Committee on Civil Liberties, federal aid to education, expansion of social security coverage, public housing programs, prison reform and birth control, condemned the Dies Committee on Un-American Activities, freight rate discrimination, and sales taxes, and urged clemency for the "Scottsboro Boys" in Alabama). It also praised the NEC report.[54] Thus while the conference manifested concern for poverty, the diffusion of its interests prevented it from focusing on that, or any other specific issue.

Two other problems blunted the SCHW's effectiveness in responding to the NEC report. The racially mixed meeting became embroiled in controversy when forced to observe Birmingham's ordinance requiring segregated seating at public gatherings. This, of course, opened it to attacks which partially overshadowed its pronouncements on southern economic conditions.[55] And even more serious, many southern liberals lost confidence in the SCHW when they suspected that Communists were within its ranks. Conference officials later counted only six known party members (and in fact

53 *Report of Proceedings of Southern Conference for Human Welfare*, 14–15.
54 *Ibid.*, 13–21.
55 Krueger, *And Promises to Keep*, 26–27; Lily May Caldwell to McIntyre, November 22, 1938, in President's Personal File 5664, Franklin D. Roosevelt Library; W. T. Couch, "Southerners Inspect the South," *New Republic*, December 14, 1938, pp. 168–69.

only twenty-seven Socialists) among the Birmingham delegates, plus a few more suspects like Gelders. The most careful student of the SCHW has concluded that it was a "popular front" of diverse reformers, never dominated by Communist participants. Nevertheless such accusations damaged the movement as Francis P. Miller, Brooks Hays, and most southern office holders disassociated themselves from it.[56] Thus the SCHW never voiced the united reply to the NEC report that it originally intended.

Before the end of November, 1938, Miller, Barry Bingham, and Mark Ethridge conceived a second conference to respond to the report in a different way. They proposed to follow an old SPC technique of inviting a select group of "representative" southerners to confer and draw up a specific program for congressional consideration. They were convinced that the demand for legislation should originate in the South; it would be unfortunate, they believed, if any such drive came only from the administration.[57]

Accordingly, Miller, who saw the move as an alternative to the SCHW, issued a call to approximately forty southern leaders to meet in Atlanta on January 14–15, 1939. He described the gathering as an outgrowth of the SPC's past efforts, and linked it to the NEC report. He felt the times were critical for the development of national policy for the South, and therefore the purpose of the meeting would be to draft and publicize a concise proposal for legislation to deal with the issues raised by the report. However, Miller contemplated no organization like the SCHW.[58]

Some prominent SCHW participants were invited to the Atlanta conference. H. C. Nixon and several others attended, but Graham regarded it as a duplicate effort and declined to come. The thirty-two

56 Nixon to Graham, January 17, November 20, and December 7, 1939, Claude Pepper to Graham, February 6, 1939, Hays to Graham, November 1, 1939, Graham to Miller, February 15, 1939, Miller to Graham, April 12, 1939, enclosing Howard Kester to Miller, March 19, 1939, all in Graham Papers; Krueger, *And Promises to Keep*, 23, 38–39, 180–81.
57 Miller to Nixon, December 30, 1938, Bingham to Miller, November 28, 1938, in NPC Papers; Ethridge to Graham, November 30, 1938, in Graham Papers.
58 Miller to Nixon, December 30, 1938, and Miller to invited delegates, December 5, 1938, in NPC Papers.

delegates included labor leaders, journalists, and scholars, along with Miller, Ethridge, Bingham, Charles S. Johnson, and other SPC stalwarts.[59]

The conference statement called the NEC report "an essentially true diagnosis of economic conditions in this area." It also agreed with the study's analysis of the "colonial" nature of the region's economy, and went even further in attributing southern poverty to inadequate or misguided national policies. Inattention to agricultural problems, for instance, had strengthened the one-crop, share-cropping, and furnishing systems with all their well-known evils, while the tariff and nationally sanctioned freight rate differentials had kept the South a mere supplier of raw materials to industrial sections. "The harvest of these policies, and of our own shortcomings," the conference asserted, "may be found in the eroded lands of the South; in the dispossessed tenantry; in a people who have too high a percentage of pellagra, malaria, hookworm and other such diseases; in homes... below decent living standards; in inadequate... schools and... institutions of higher learning; in the lowest percentage of home and land ownership in the country; and in the lowest per capita incomes in the country." In short, "the Nation's treatment of the South has been that generally accorded colonial possessions."[60]

To remedy these conditions the conference proposed both federal and state action. Congress should expand FSA rehabilitative work, including farm purchase lending, as well as continue commodity price supports. For industrial workers, the national government should take further steps to assure adequate wage standards and safeguard collective bargaining. Other legislation was necessary to provide federal aid to education and public health, and reform of freight rates was "absolutely essential." The states, for their part, should revise laws on landlord-tenant relationships and create land-planning commissions. Finally, the group vaguely recommended

59 Report of the Atlanta Conference, January 14–15, 1939, in NPC Papers; Graham to Ethridge and Miller, January 11, 1939, in Graham Papers.
60 *A Working Economic Plan for the South* (N.p.: National Policy Committee, 1939), copy in NPC Papers.

state efforts to strengthen civil liberties, but was quite specific in calling for abolition of the poll tax.[61]

Like the SCHW, the Atlanta conference thought in broad terms about what was needed to improve the region, and although it recognized the plight of destitute people, that problem was only one of several concerns. At least one of the members suggested that the group narrow its concentration. James C. Derieux, editor of the *State* of Columbia, South Carolina, thought the primary aim should be to upgrade the working skills of the poor as a prerequisite to other advances. The key to the tenancy problem, for instance, was to correct the "incapacity of so many persons to acquire, own and operate land successfully."[62] This idea was close to the concept of rehabilitation. But Derieux's views were in the minority in a conference concerned mainly with general regional development.

A third organized response to the NEC report was by the Southern Governors' Conference, late in 1939. The state executives' organization was an expansion of the Southeastern Governors' Conference, originally formed to press the case for freight rate reform before the Interstate Commerce Commission. After some initial success in bringing their issue before the ICC, they broadened their interests slightly. On December 14, 1939, in an Atlanta meeting, the governors appointed a committee, headed by Clarence Poe, editor of the *Progressive Farmer* of Raleigh, North Carolina, to devise a ten-year campaign for general economic development of the South.[63]

By December 30 Poe's committee had outlined its major goals and the governors announced their program in the press. Frank Graham, involved in yet another campaign as chairman of its North

61 *Ibid.*
62 Miller to Southern Policy Committee members, May 29, 1939, in NPC Papers.
63 Tindall, *Emergence of the New South,* 601–603; "Report of Committee on Organization and Planning for Ten Year Campaign for 'Balanced Prosperity in the South, 1940–50,'" April 15, 1940 (mimeographed, copy in Graham Papers), 3–13. The committee included the state Extension Service directors of South Carolina and Louisiana, the Tennessee Commissioner of Agriculture, the chairman of the Georgia Public Service Commission, the general manager of the Florida State Chamber of Commerce, chairman H. A. Morgan of the Tennessee Valley Authority and news columnist John Temple Graves.

Carolina subcommittee, wrote to the president and suggested that this latest effort concerned the same conditions which had led to the designation of the South as economic problem number one. At Graham's request, Roosevelt sent a message of congratulations to the governors.[64]

Poe identified two major threats to continued southern economic advancement. He predicted a "crisis in money crops," partly as a result of the closing of foreign markets for staples due to the outbreak of war in Europe. The general answer to this was what Poe had preached for years in the columns for the *Progressive Farmer*: diversified farming, more production for home use, and increased livestock raising. Secondly, he accepted the thesis that freight rate differentials retarded regional industrialization, but thought the governors' recent "epochal triumph" in getting the ICC to consider the matter indicated progress toward its correction. Poe and the committee concluded that, with the beginning of a new decade, the times were propitious for concerted action against these and related problems.[65]

Poe's committee outlined ten goals for the 1940s, all of which centered on the need to "balance" the region's economy. Among these aims were a de-emphasis on staples and increased production of food, feed, soil-enriching crops, and livestock. Farms should be "balanced" with factories, in which "worker prosperity" accompanied "owner prosperity." Other essentials were encouragement of home ownership, and improved marketing of southern products, including elimination of "trade barriers," a clear reference to high freight rates. In general, the committee thought, the South's resources should be made to provide more of the needs of the section's consumers.[66]

64　Southern Governors' Conference press release, December 31, 1939, Graham to Roosevelt, December 30, 1939, and January 4, 1940, Roosevelt to eleven southern governors, January 6, 1940, all in President's Personal File 6410, Franklin D. Roosevelt Library.

65　"A Campaign 'For Balanced Prosperity in the South, 1940–50'" [January, 1940] (printed broadside in Graham Papers).

66　*Ibid.*; "Minutes of Conference, North Carolina State Committee on Organization and Planning Southern Governors' Conference Campaign 'For Balanced Prosperity in the South, 1940–50,'" February 10, 1940 (Typescript in Graham Papers).

These stated goals were little more than platitudes acceptable to a diverse group of governors. As yet they amounted to no specific program and, even if implemented, would not strike at the real destitution of millions of southerners. But they were significant as a sort of recognition by the governors of the needs enumerated in the NEC study. All of the Poe committee's objectives—diversified farming, removal of freight differentials, industrialization, better conservation and management of resources, improved housing and more home ownership, increased local investment, and even a vague reference to the desirability of higher wages—matched the deficiencies mentioned in the report. The governors' goals really constituted a New South statement on regional development, updated for 1940, and reinforced with Poe's emphasis on progressive agriculture.

There were several reasons why these goals were never effectively implemented. The most important was that the governors never saw the ten-year balanced prosperity campaign as anything more than incidental to their freight rate drive. Outlining their plans for regional advancement in January, 1940, they resolved that "concerted effort for economic development along all lines," particularly "increased industrial activity [and] balanced agricultural programs," was necessary to secure the "major benefits of the lower freight rates" they sought. While they considered the transportation problem, they delegated all other planning to Poe's committee.[67]

A second problem was that Poe envisioned a very decentralized campaign. His committee suggested that in each state a governor's committee, utilizing the services of state agencies, colleges, the press, and agricultural and business organizations, survey economic needs and define adequate standards of improvement in such matters as farming methods, crop diversification, community services, health, education, housing, and attraction of industry. Using standard scorecards, the state committees could then grade the advancement of any individuals, communities, school districts, or counties that chose to participate, and award annual "certificates of

67 Press release by Georgia Public Service Commission (for Southern Governors' Conference), January 22, 1940, in Graham Papers.

progress" as a public recognition. Meanwhile, businessmen and chambers of commerce would promote new industries, and farm agencies would encourage diversification. All these efforts depended heavily upon the stimulation of local enthusiasm, and anticipated what Howard Odum described as a "folk movement."[68]

In their conference of April 15–16, 1940, the governors approved Poe's plan, even though some doubted its "tangibility" as a means of increasing prosperity, and turned the campaign over to whatever state committees the executives happened to appoint. The practical results were few. Only five of the committees (Georgia, North Carolina, South Carolina, Alabama, and Tennessee) ever functioned, and those, apparently, only for 1940. None of them mounted more than a campaign for diversified farming with some efforts to encourage local surveys and publication of industrial potential. Perhaps the most concrete achievement was in Tennessee, where 60,000 families were enrolled in a home food production program.[69]

For their part, the governors quickly lost interest in their ten-year campaign. Not only did they remain preoccupied with the freight rate issue, but by the middle of 1940 they developed another economic objective, that of ensuring that the South obtained its share of the new expansion in war industries. Despite Poe's judgment that "the war situation only increases the necessity for going forward with our work," particularly crop diversification, it was clear that the state executives were more intent on other matters.[70]

Finally, at an early stage in the governors' campaign, officials of

---

68 "A Campaign 'For Balanced Prosperity in the South, 1940–50,'" Minutes of Southern Governors' Conference, February 26–27, 1940, Odum to Graham, February 13, 1940, *ibid.*

69 Minutes of Southern Governors' Conference, April 15–16, 1940, "Minutes of North Carolina Committee on Southern Governors' Campaign," February 10, 1940, "Minutes Executive Committee—Georgia's Ten-Year Development Campaign," July 27, 1940, Paul W. Chapman to Poe, April 20, 1940, Poe to five state campaign chairmen, May 24, 1940, Graham to Leon R. Meadows, July 8, 1940, Blake Van Leer to Graham, October 23, 1940, C. C. Flanery to Poe, December 21, 1940, *ibid.*

70 Poe to five state campaign chairmen, May 24, 1940, E. D. Rivers to Graham, June 4, 1940, Minutes of Southern Governors' Conference, September 15–17, 1940, Clyde Hoey to North Carolina committee, undated [October, 1940], *ibid.*

the FSA suggested that the program really overlooked the rural poor. At a Nashville meeting of the Southern Conference on Interstate Problems, where Poe outlined his plan and stressed the need for diversified farming, George S. Mitchell, then assistant administrator of the FSA, read a speech for Will Alexander, who could not attend. Mitchell called for more attention to the "great, ignorant, inert, hopeless mass," of "itinerant farmers." He reminded the group that in some areas 56 percent of the population moved each year, "roam[ing] from one worn out patch to another." Furthermore, due to mechanization and the resulting "pressure of population on the land," they were becoming even less secure. Mitchell noted that "often the annual income for a family of five is about $126" and "you could buy everything the family owns for $25." Warning that unless these destitute people received a better chance the region as a whole could not prosper, he implied that proposals for general economic development could do little for impoverished individuals.[71]

Commenting on this speech to Will Alexander, Clarence Roberts, editor of the *Oklahoma Farmer-Stockman*, summarized the condition of the rural poor as 1940 began, and contradicted the current New South emphasis. He saw the density of the South's country population in relation to its agricultural resources as "in every sense the nation's number one problem." Migration of the impoverished from the farms continued, speeded by mechanization or, in some areas, by unchecked erosion. He concluded that "the nation as a whole must prepare to take care of the surplus population of the South," because the region's "resources . . . simply will not maintain the present population." Furthermore, he wrote: "The real situation is understood by only a few . . . in the field of agriculture who have the facts and are willing to look at them. The general public does not suspect the facts nor their significance. It does not suspect that it has already assumed the burden of support of a part of the South's rural population. . . . They must get ready to support an even larger

71 "The Council of State Governments, Southern Conference on Interstate Problems, Resume and Resolutions," January 25–27, 1940 (Typescript in Graham Papers); "South Plans Own Reconstruction," *Business Week*, February 3, 1940, pp. 24–28.

number in the immediate years ahead." Roberts commended Alexander for stressing these unpleasant conditions to the public, not because he foresaw an "easy, happy solution," but because he hoped that "at least we can soften the blow by an understanding of the facts."[72]

The writers of the NEC report had attempted to promote an understanding of southern conditions and needs. In the process they publicized the region's poverty. The administration made only limited direct use of the study; coming at the end of the New Deal, it did not become the basis for any government program. Some hoped the document would evoke a southern response. As a survey of the region's impoverishment it generated both controversy and wide-ranging discussion of means to achieve general economic advancement. But it produced no concerted attack by southerners on the specific problem of rural poverty.

72   Clarence Roberts to Alexander, January 30, 1940, in Mellett Papers.

CHAPTER X

The New Deal and Southern Poverty

POVERTY WAS DEEPLY ROOTED in the South, and the New Deal's efforts did not eliminate it. President Roosevelt recognized this clearly. On March 3, 1939, in a press conference on board a naval vessel off Charleston, South Carolina, a reporter asked if there had been any change in the South's position as economic problem number one. The president replied, "I cannot say that there is yet. I hope there is going to be." Referring to the current emphasis on regional economic development, he continued that "of course . . . there is no cure-all, like reforming the freight rate problem." He then reiterated his view that "remuneration for work in the South has got to be increased," by which he meant the returns for "all kinds of work," because families with annual incomes of only a few hundred dollars lacked buying power. He went on to say that the impoverishment of great masses of the southern population held back other progress; for instance, it gave "very little incentive for the manufacturer to set up factories in the South." Furthermore, "anything that is done to improve this economic problem No. 1 ultimately comes back to a question of a greater purchasing power on the part of the average Southern family." Raising the incomes of the poor was a key to most of the region's other problems, in the president's opinion. This would help primarily the South, but also the nation, he concluded.[1]

By the late 1960s, after the unfolding of changes begun in the years of the New Deal and the Second World War, and after nearly three decades of economic growth, the South had achieved a general prosperity which made the National Emergency Council's report of 1938 an outdated document. But even after a heavy migration of the poor from the region, and also to its cities, a residual rural poverty persisted. For example, on February 18, 1969, Senator Ernest F. Hollings of South Carolina testified before the Senate's Select Committee on Nutrition and Human Needs about his recent inspection of his state's Sea Island district. "Let me categorically state there is hunger in South Carolina," he declared. "There is substantial hunger. I have seen it with my own eyes. 'Starving'—that is too dreadful a term. But the result is the same."[2]

Hollings continued that he had observed destitution among both races in the coastal area as well as in city slums. He confirmed the existence of severe malnutrition which retarded children physically and mentally. He also described squalid housing, primitive sanitation which resulted in a high incidence of intestinal parasites, and such dietary diseases as pellagra which were supposedly unknown in America in the 1960s. Hollings found still other consequences of poverty—illiteracy, lack of skills, illness—which rendered most of the destitute people he saw unable to work.[3]

Moreover, many of the poor were ignored by state and federal governments alike, and consequently received no public assistance. Hollings admitted that as governor of South Carolina he had minimized discussions of poverty lest publicity about it hinder efforts to attract industry. At the federal level, he charged that because of bureaucratic failures large numbers of those in greatest need knew nothing of the Agriculture Department's food stamp program, and

1 Roosevelt Press Conferences, XIII, 167–68, in Franklin D. Roosevelt Library, Hyde Park, N.Y.
2 *Nutrition and Human Needs, Part 4—South Carolina, Hearings* before the Select Committee on Nutrition and Human Needs, Senate, 90th Cong., 2nd. Sess., and 91st Cong., 1st Sess., 1166.
3 *Ibid.*, 1162–69.

even had they known could not have made even the minimal payments required for participation. Furthermore, he estimated that in "real, extreme poverty areas" perhaps two-thirds of the poor received no welfare aid, often because of technical eligibility requirements. Hearing this, an incredulous colleague asked, "How do they live?" and Hollings replied, "They don't. They barely exist." The obvious needs, according to Hollings, were food, health care, housing, sanitation, and education. But he warned that local people would resent outsiders drawing attention to these conditions.[4]

Hollings' remarks were strikingly like those of many observers in the 1930s. One would not find them out of place, for example, in a Federal Emergency Relief Administration field report of more than forty years ago. They illustrate that for some Americans, at least, little has changed since the New Deal era.

During the early New Deal period the administration's recognition of the depth of chronic need in the South grew slowly. There were about four important reasons for its increased awareness before mid-1935. The decade's outpouring of scholarly and journalistic writing on southern social and economic conditions had begun. By early 1934 the FERA discovered that rural poverty complicated its relief efforts and pragmatically developed a rehabilitation program to deal with it. The Agricultural Adjustment Administration's cotton program, on the other hand, aroused a storm of unfavorable publicity against its tenancy policies, prompted the rise of the Southern Tenant Farmers' Union and other radical critics, and led to dissension and crisis in the agency by February, 1935. Finally, the initiative and patient prodding of Will Alexander and other southern liberals in behalf of the Bankhead bill helped make the New Deal cognizant of southern poverty.

What explains the New Deal's apparent slowness to recognize poverty as a persistent condition requiring extraordinary government efforts to overcome? Despite the fact that destitution was widespread and chronic, and in retrospect obvious, it was not perceived in quite the same manner as in contemporary times.

4 *Ibid.*, 1165–66, 1170.

Americans in the 1960s and 1970s have viewed poverty from the perspective of general prosperity. Partly because the New Deal enacted lasting benefits for landowning farmers, unionized workers, businessmen, and other groups, economic sufficiency has become normal for most. Poverty, while prevalent in isolated or economically stagnant areas such as Appalachia, in the rotting cores of great cities, and among racial minorities, no longer seems pervasive. Accordingly, it has received a revealing designation—"hard core poverty"—which suggests that it affects a residuum of the population which does not respond to overall prosperity. Such people, it follows, need special assistance to attain an acceptable standard of living.

In contrast, for millions in the 1930s economic sufficiency was not a usual condition. This was particularly true in the South. Much of the region's poverty was overlooked precisely because it was a long-standing situation. Tenant farmers, sharecroppers, and laborers never had enjoyed adequate living standards and were not expected to. Moreover, southern agriculture as a whole had known recurrent hard times well before the 1930s. Under these generally unprosperous conditions many simply failed to see the chronically impoverished as a special case. Thus in the early New Deal only the most perceptive government observers—frequently within the FERA—understood that widespread destitution was a problem distinct from the depression.

In the New Deal era thinking about practical ways to improve economic conditions in the South tended to run in three patterns. Some saw parity prices as the region's principal need. Others, more cognizant of chronic poverty, advanced plans for the rehabilitation of the poor. Still others envisioned a general economic development of the South, which would create an overall prosperity. But none of these approaches proved fully adequate.

Price parity programs did not significantly benefit the poor. The concept of parity, after more than a decade of development, became the basic commitment of New Deal farm policy, with which nothing else was allowed to interfere. The administration created the AAA to raise the prices of staple crops by controlling production. But merely increasing prices would do little to improve the abilities and self-direction of the poor, lessen their dependence on landlords, free them from an exploitive credit system, improve the conditions of tenancy, or help them escape it. These fundamental problems of destitute people were beyond the scope of the parity idea. Therefore the view of many planters and AAA officials that parity was the region's principal economic need—that prosperity was largely a matter of twelve-cent cotton—simply ignored the poverty of millions of southerners.

Not only was the concept of parity inadequate to answer the problem of poverty, but the practices of the AAA cotton program favored landlords at the expense of tenants. The cotton contract assigned the lion's share of the benefits to the landowner and allowed him to distribute his dependents' shares to them. Moreover, the very fact that planters were supposed to divide government payments with sharecroppers, but had no such obligation to wage workers, provided a strong incentive to discharge tenants and hire day laborers. Thus, one of the AAA's most serious effects was the impetus it gave to the decline of cotton tenancy, already underway in many parts of the South. Contract terms supposedly designed to prevent this displacement of poor people were, of course, so vague as to be unenforceable.

In the decisive AAA "purge" of February, 1935, Jerome Frank and others tried to broaden the agency's efforts under the contract to protect tenants from displacement, but the cotton section's limited views prevailed. The resolution of this crisis illustrated the AAA's prolandlordism. But even more importantly, it showed the agency's resistance to even the implication by legal section liberals that its concerns should extend beyond the objective of price parity. Although it subsequently accepted some procedural reforms in the contract, neither the first AAA nor its successors ever took forceful steps to halt tenant displacement.

A second New Deal approach to poverty was rural rehabilitation, which meant arranging for poor farm families to occupy land and assisting them with a combination of credit and intensive supervision. The idea had several sources, but it first emerged as a government policy in 1934 when the FERA adopted it in an attempt to get large numbers of destitute country folk off relief rolls in the South. Thus the FERA became the first New Deal agency to start a program aimed specifically at rural need. The relief administration's efforts were hastily devised and not systematically implemented, but later became an important component of the Resettlement Administration.

In some important respects the rehabilitative process had the potential to meet the needs of the rural poor. Since they had always received credit and supervision from one source—their landlords— the same combination under government auspices fit their experience. Substituting for the landlord in two vital matters, the government could exercise supervision to upgrade clients' farming methods and living standards and encourage their self-direction. Likewise, it could extend credit to help propertyless croppers and laborers acquire the workstock, implements, and equipment necessary to raise their status to that of share tenants.

Even as early as 1934, FERA officials perceived that the loan-guidance combination could also be used to assist rehabilitants to purchase small farms. By late 1934 this idea was current in other circles; Will Alexander, Edwin Embree, Charles S. Johnson, and Frank Tannenbaum developed it into the Bankhead tenancy bill, which became the main legislative expression of the rehabilitative concept.

The formation of the Resettlement Administration in the spring of 1935 made rehabilitation the New Deal's major poverty policy. Tugwell and Roosevelt conceived the new agency, but Will Alexander helped determine its scope. By agreeing to become Tugwell's assistant, Alexander probably clinched the undersecretary's tentative decision to take over FERA's rural rehabilitation, the program which became the largest single activity of the RA and the Farm Security Administration. Alexander was also important as a bridge between the RA and the Bankhead proposal. By the middle of 1935 Tugwell and Alexander contemplated a comprehensive rehabilitative plan, reaching all levels of the poor through one agency, and capped by long-term farm purchase loans for the most capable tenants.

For this reason it was unfortunate that Congress did not enact the Bankhead legislation in 1935; this failure was the great lost opportunity of the Second Hundred Days. At least as passed by the Senate, the measure was broad, flexible, and even loosely drawn. It authorized a very large bond issue to finance loans to the landless, and most importantly, would have allowed government initiative in buying and reselling farms to clients, rather than merely extending credit as did the 1937 version. Furthermore, there is evidence that by the summer of 1935 Tugwell had Roosevelt's tentative approval for addition of the proposed program to that of the RA, completing his and Alexander's grand design and establishing in 1935 an agency essentially like the Farm Security Administration of 1937.

The opportunity was lost in 1935 and 1936 because of Marvin Jones's reluctance to push the bill in the House, the urgency of other matters in Congress (first during the Second Hundred Days of 1935 and then when the AAA had to be replaced in early 1936), lack of public endorsement by Roosevelt, and the president's insistence on drastic reductions in its funding. Failure to establish the Bankhead program and link it to the RA before 1937 (when Congress passed much more restricted legislation) delayed and probably weakened the New Deal's comprehensive application of rehabilitative measures.

The Bankhead bill was passed only after the persistent efforts of its advocates and over strong opposition in Congress. Many of the opponents were influential southerners, including many of those on the House Agriculture Committee, who were supposedly well informed on rural matters but who actually had little comprehension of the plight of their poorest constituents. On the other hand, Henry Wallace and other Department of Agriculture officials supported the measure, chiefly for two reasons: they approved its promotion of small farm ownership, and they saw it as a way to alleviate rural poverty without calling into question the price parity policies to which the New Deal was committed.

Especially in 1936 and 1937, radical critics, many of whom were associated with the Socialist party or the Southern Tenant Farmers' Union, attacked the bill. They correctly pointed out that its selective aid would benefit only a few of the poor. However, the measure's supporters had never claimed that credit for purchase of farms was a panacea for rural poverty. Tugwell and Alexander saw the bill as only one part of a comprehensive program of supervision and credit which could also reach poor people not qualified for small owner-ship.

But radical critics also questioned the concept of small owner-ship. They argued that small farms would be uneconomical in an increasingly mechanized cotton belt and charged that the Bankhead bill would merely establish "peasant proprietors." They proposed as an alternative collective farming of large acreages, which they ex-pected to allow the poor to escape tenancy while still preserving the efficiencies of large-scale production.

Supporters of the legislation countered that individual ownership of land need not preclude other cooperation. Indeed, they con-templated joint possession by clients of machinery and breeding stock, as well as cooperative marketing and purchasing, as means of overcoming the economic disadvantages of family-sized farms. Moreover, Alexander and other supporters of the bill were practical men who recognized the profound public and congressional attach-ment to the ideal of home ownership, and the equally deep aversion to suggestions of collectivism. They were convinced that the Bank-head measure was the maximum proposal Congress would enact. Their long struggle to secure its passage confirms their judgment.

The rehabilitation idea was the basis for both the RA and the FSA. The program of these agencies was the most effective New Deal effort in behalf of impoverished southerners. Reaching more than a half-million cases in the region, its functions ranged from extending subsistence grants to the most destitute and dependent to assisting the ablest tenants (after 1937) to buy farms. Yet even these broad efforts were inadequate to reach the bulk of the South's pov-erty. Undoubtedly, an FSA with more funds and congressional back-ing could have benefited more of the destitute. But as mechanization transformed southern agriculture after the late 1930s, and as the FSA's political enemies succeeded in phasing it out in the 1940s, it became clear that most of the rural poor could not become permanently established as small farmers. Thus the rehabilitative approach to poverty failed in its chief objective, although it may have left intangible benefits with many clients in the form of upgraded abilities and new habits of self-direction.

With the return of relative prosperity after 1936, a third view of the South's needs became current. Many southerners turned their attention, in accordance with the New South spirit, to the general economic development of the region. In the summer of 1938 the New Deal became an important contributor to this theme with its National Emergency Council report. This document was not only a cogent review of the South's general underdevelopment, it also pointed out the low living conditions of millions of the section's rural people. But the very breadth of its analysis, summarizing fifteen major economic topics, encouraged southerners to consider the wider question of why the region was impoverished, compared to the rest of the nation, and to that extent diverted attention from the plight of the most destitute individuals.

The document prompted a variety of reactions from southerners, ranging from indignant denunciation of its findings to recommendations by diverse groups and individuals as to how the region and the nation should solve the problems it delineated. But none of these responses focused specifically on the needs of the rural poor. Instead, most of them proposed the remedies of general economic development, especially industrialization and diversification of agriculture. It would be difficult to deny that these objectives were essential for the economic advancement of the South. But at the same time, they were not calculated to uplift the most destitute, ignorant, unskilled, and dependent country folk. Increasingly superfluous as laborers in a changing agriculture, many of them were equally unsuited for new industrial employment.

The New Deal, absorbed with the problems of general depression, never found a completely effective policy for the South's rural poor. Its rehabilitation efforts did the most good, but even these were not sufficiently comprehensive. The consequences of these failures of the New Deal era still trouble the United States and resist solution. Poverty-stricken people still eke out an existence in backwater rural areas, where their plight is occasionally called to public attention by such observers as Senator Hollings. They subsist in chronically depressed sections such as Appalachia, and continue to migrate into the blighted central districts of the great cities. These contemporary problems underscore Roosevelt's judgment that the impoverishment of millions of southerners was "the Nation's problem, not merely the South's." Often forgotten by an affluent country, the poor are the unfinished business of the New Deal.

Bibliographical Notes

THESE NOTES are confined to those sources that have been most essential to this study, with particular attention to primary materials. Numerous books, published documents, and articles provided useful background information, but these have been mostly omitted, as have some of the more infrequently cited materials. Since the documentation in the text has been made as full as possible, the reader should consult the footnotes as well as this essay as a guide to the sources.

Manuscript Collections

Most of the sources for this book were drawn from manuscript collections. The largest single depository of New Deal materials is the Franklin D. Roosevelt Library in Hyde Park, New York. It contains the massive collection of Roosevelt Papers, which is divided into three major file groups. These are the Official File, consisting of the president's papers and correspondence concerning government functions; the President's Personal File, which contains his personal letters, but also much official material; and the President's Secretary's File, collected for reference purposes by his personal secretary. Each division is voluminous, but well organized and indexed. Material pertaining to southern poverty is widely scattered through more than eighty numbered files consulted within the major divisions. This research concentrated on those files, particularly in the Official File and the President's Personal File, concerning southern agricultural and relief matters, and presidential correspondence with government officials, congressmen, prominent southerners, and others interested in the region. In addition to the main file groups, two other divisions of the Roosevelt Papers were consulted. These were the Roosevelt Speech File and the transcripts of presidential press conferences. The latter are most conveniently available as a microfilm publication. The Roosevelt Library also contains the papers of other New Deal figures. Of these collections, the Harry Hopkins Papers were especially valuable for relief administration field reports and surveys. An important item in the Rexford G. Tugwell Papers is Tugwell's typescript diary, covering the New Deal years and open to research through 1935. The papers of Aubrey Williams and Lowell Mellett are also useful.

A second major concentration of manuscripts consulted for this study is located in the National Archives in Washington, D.C. Four record groups, all of massive proportions, were utilized. Record Group 16, "Records of the Office of the Secretary of Agriculture," contains general correspondence of Secretary Henry A. Wallace and other department officials, as well as the files of the Agricultural Adjustment Administration's legal division. Records of the Resettlement Administration and Farm Security Administration are included with those of their successor agency in Record Group 96, "Records of the Farmers Home Administration." Files of the Agricultural Adjustment Administration were consulted in Record Group 145, "Records of the Agricultural Stabilization and Conservation Service." The records of all federal relief agencies compose Record Group 69, "Records of the Work Projects Administration." The most valuable parts of this group were the Federal Emergency Relief Administration's state files, the FERA Old Subject File, and the Works Progress Administration Library. The National Archives also maintains regional depositories. At the Federal Records Center in Suitland, Maryland, material pertaining to the National Emergency Council was sampled in Record Group 44, "Records of the Office of Government Reports."

A small but important collection of Agriculture Department records, memoranda, studies by department economists, and similar data is preserved in the Agricultural History Office, Economic Research Service, U.S. Department of Agriculture. Some important Farm Security Administration documents not found in the archives are included in this material. The Henry A. Wallace Papers at the University of Iowa contain little from the 1933–1940 period, but an isolated fragment of Wallace's typescript diary, covering January–March, 1935, gives insight into the dismissal of the AAA legal staff in the controversy over tenancy policy.

The University of North Carolina Library's Southern Historical Collection is another important depository of primary materials utilized in this work. The most systematically examined large collections were the Jonathan Daniels Papers, the Frank Porter Graham Papers, and the files of the Southern Tenant Farmers' Union. The first two contain a great variety of correspondence, with scattered letters bearing upon poverty conditions. The STFU Papers include much routine union business, but also its leadership's correspondence, a good source for critical views of New Deal policy. Some valuable STFU material is also found in the small collection of William Amberson Papers.

The Frank Tannenbaum Papers, in Columbia University's Butler Library, contain correspondence, chiefly between Tannenbaum and Will Alexander in 1934–1935, which is essential for understanding the origins of New Deal tenancy legislation. Located in the same library is the useful Columbia Oral History Collection, which consists of typescript memoir-interviews of numerous twentieth-century figures. Of most importance to this study were "The Reminiscences of Will W. Alexander" (1952), and "The Reminiscences of Harry Leland Mitchell" (1957).

Two collections are important for southern liberal opinion and efforts to influence the New Deal. The National Policy Committee (NPC) Papers, located in the manuscripts division of the Library of Congress, contain the papers of the Southern Policy Committee, which are valuable for the organization's pamphlet publications and press releases, as well as the correspondence of its leaders between 1935 and 1938. Also useful were the papers of Herman Clarence Nixon, consisting of letters and press clippings, in the possession of the Nixon family in Nashville.

Several other collections were useful in this study. The Trevor Arnette Library at Atlanta University contains the Commission on Interracial Cooperation (CIC) Papers, which include the largest extant body of Will Alexander's correspondence, a considerable amount of which is from the 1930s. The Southern Conference for Human Welfare (SCHW) Papers, also at Atlanta, are most valuable for an important subdivision, the papers of Clark Foreman. Fisk University in Nashville has two large, well organized collections concerning general social and economic conditions of the South in the 1930s, with scattered material specifically on poverty. These are the Julius Rosenwald Fund Files and the Charles S. Johnson Papers. The latter contains both personal letters and unpublished scholarly writings. The Socialist Party of America Papers at Duke University were consulted and yielded information on the Southern Tenant Farmers' Union and left-wing criticism of the New Deal. Finally, copies of reports on the Farm Security

Administration's Non-Commercial Farm Project were obtained from the Department of Rural Sociology Survey Records, in the Department of Manuscripts and University Archives of Cornell University.

Government Documents

Published government documents are a rich source of information on southern rural conditions, the operation of New Deal agencies, and the evolution of legislation in Congress. Among congressional documents consulted in this research, the following were most directly useful:

Agricultural Emergency Act to Increase Farm Purchasing Power, Hearings before the Committee on Agriculture and Forestry, Senate, 73rd Cong., 1st Sess., 1933.

Farm Security Administration, Hearings before the Select Committee of the House Committee on Agriculture, to Investigate the Activities of the Farm Security Administration, House of Representatives, 78th Cong., 1st and 2nd Sessions, 1943 and 1944.

Farm Tenancy, Hearings before the Committee on Agriculture, House of Representatives, 74th Cong., 1st Sess., 1935. Published as an appendix to *Farm Tenancy,* Hearings before the Committee on Agriculture, House of Representatives, 75th Cong., 1st Sess., 1937.

Farm Tenancy, Hearings before the Committee on Agriculture, House of Representatives, 75th Cong., 1st Sess., 1937.

Interstate Migration, Hearings before the Select Committee to Investigate the Interstate Migration of Destitute Citizens, House of Representatives, 76th Cong., 3rd Sess., 1940.

Nutrition and Human Needs, Part 4—South Carolina, Hearings before the Select Committee on Nutrition and Human Needs, Senate, 90th Cong., 2nd Sess., and 91st Cong., 1st Sess., 1969.

Relieve the Existing National Economic Emergency by Increasing Agricultural Purchasing Power, House Report 6, to accompany H. R. 3835, Committee on Agriculture, House of Representatives, 73rd Cong., 1st Sess., 1933.

To Create the Farm Tenant Homes Corporation, Hearings before a Subcommittee of the Committee on Agriculture and Forestry, Senate, 74th Cong., 1st Sess., 1935.

U.S. *Congressional Record,* LXXIX.

The following documents published by New Deal administrative agencies were of particular value:

U.S. Department of Agriculture. Farm Security Administration. *Report of the Administrator of the Farm Security Administration,* 1939. Washington: Government Printing Office, 1939.

———. *Report of the Administrator of the Farm Security Administration, 1941.* Washington: Government Printing Office, 1941.

U.S. Department of Agriculture. Farm Security Administration and Bureau of Agricultural Economics. *Analysis of 70,000 Rural Rehabilitation Families,* by E. L. Kirkpatrick. Social Research Report No. 9. Washington: Government Printing Office, 1938.

U.S. Federal Emergency Relief Administration. *Monthly Reports,* May 22, 1933 to December 31, 1934. Washington: Government Printing Office, 1933 and 1934.

———. Rural Rehabilitation Division. *Objectives and Suggested Procedure for Rural Rehabilitation.* Washington: Federal Emergency Relief Administration, mimeographed, June 27, 1934.

U.S. War Food Administration. *The Annual Report of the Farm Security Administration, 1942–3.* Washington: War Food Administration, 1943.

Two government documents published to promote New Deal policies or viewpoints deserve special mention. The U.S. National Resources Committee's *Farm Tenancy: Report of the President's Committee* (Washington: Government Printing Office, 1937) advocated a coordinated rural poverty program under a Farm Security Administration, and the U.S. National Emergency Council's *Report on Economic Conditions of the South* (Washington: Government Printing Office, 1938), the New Deal's most famous survey of the region's problems, stimulated a wide variety of responses. Finally, the views of a state commission appear in Arkansas Farm Tenancy Commission, *Findings and Recommendations* (Hot Springs, Arkansas, November 24, 1936).

Federal agencies also sponsored valuable work by individual scholars. The Works Progress Administration's Research Monograph Series (26 vols.; Washington: Government Printing Office, 1935–1943) includes several fine studies which provide detailed information on social and economic conditions in the rural South. The two most important volumes for this research were Thomas Jackson Woofter, Jr., *Landlord and Tenant on the Cotton Plantation* (Monograph V, 1936), and Berta Asch and A. R. Mangus, *Farm-*

ers on Relief and Rehabilitation (Monograph VIII, 1937). Olaf F. Larson's lengthy work, *Ten Years of Rural Rehabilitation in the United States* (mimeographed and distributed by the Bureau of Agricultural Economics, 1947), examines the rural rehabilitation program of the Resettlement Administration and the Farm Security Administration in exhaustive detail and includes valuable statistical tables in an appendix. Three published Bureau of Agricultural Economics studies cover the FSA's most intensive antipoverty effort, the Non-Commercial Farm Project. These are Conrad Taeuber and Rachel Rowe, *Five Hundred Families Rehabilitate Themselves* (Washington: Bureau of Agricultural Economics and Farm Security Administration, 1941), Rachel Rowe Swiger and Conrad Taeuber, *Ill Fed, Ill Clothed, Ill Housed—Five Hundred Families in Need of Help* (Washington: Bureau of Agricultural Economics and Farm Security Administration, 1942), and Rachel Rowe Swiger and Olaf F. Larson, *Climbing Toward Security* (Washington: Bureau of Agricultural Economics, 1944). Harold Hoffsomer, *Landlord-Tenant Relations and Relief in Alabama* (Washington: Federal Emergency Relief Administration, Research Bulletin Series II, No. 9, November 14, 1935) examines the tendency of relief to break down the sharecropping system. Thomas Jackson Woofter, Jr., *Rural Planning for More Workers* (Washington: Farm Security Administration, mimeographed, 1940), stressed the need to maintain the rural population on the land at a time when no national economic growth was foreseen.

Books and Other Secondary Sources

Among general histories William E. Leuchtenburg, *Franklin D. Roosevelt and the New Deal* (New York: Harper and Row, 1963) is the outstanding one-volume synthesis of the New Deal era. Easily the preeminent work on the South in the twentieth century is George B. Tindall, *The Emergence of the New South, 1913–1945* (Baton Rouge: Louisiana State University Press, 1967), Vol. X of Wendell Holmes Stephenson and E. Merton Coulter (eds.), *A History of the South*. About half of Tindall's work deals with the 1930s.

This study has benefited from several interpretive works. An important general influence was one of the most cogent of all books on the South, C. Vann Woodward's *The Burden of Southern History* (Rev. ed.; Baton Rouge: Louisiana State University Press, 1968), which points out that chronic poverty has always been one of the region's distinguishing historical experiences. A recent perceptive interpretation, Paul M. Gaston, *The New South Creed* (New York: Alfred A. Knopf, 1970), examines the post–Civil War industrial spirit. Depression-era agrarian critics of American industrialism exerted some influence on government policy; for the classic statement of their views consult John Crowe Ransom *et. al.*, *I'll Take My Stand: The South and the Agrarian Tradition* (New York: Harper and Brothers, 1930).

Of the many social and economic studies of the South published in the 1920s and 1930s, four have been particularly useful. Howard W. Odum, *Southern Regions of the United States* (Chapel Hill: University of North Carolina Press, 1936), contains a mass of data on the southern economy and culture and was the foundation for many later regional studies. The best survey of cotton belt living conditions on the eve of the Great Depression is Rupert B. Vance, *Human Factors in Cotton Culture: A Study in the Social Geography of the American South* (Chapel Hill: University of North Carolina Press, 1929). For two sociological analyses of the economic dependence of tenants and sharecroppers see Arthur F. Raper, *Preface to Peasantry: A Tale of Two Black Belt Counties* (Chapel Hill: University of North Carolina Press, 1936), and Charles S. Johnson, *Shadow of the Plantation* (Chicago: University of Chicago Press, 1934). A general survey of southern backwardness in the 1920s, Frank Tannenbaum's *Darker Phases of the South* (New York: G. P. Putnam's Sons, 1924) is of interest because of its author's later role in developing New Deal tenancy legislation.

The standard work on the concept of agricultural price parity and the origins of New Deal farm policy is Gilbert C. Fite, *George N. Peek and the Fight for Farm Parity* (Norman: University of Oklahoma Press, 1954). Also valuable are Theodore Saloutos, *Farmer Movements in the South, 1865–1933* (Berkeley: University of California Press, 1960), and Van L. Perkins, *Crisis in Agriculture: The Agricultural Adjustment Administration and the New Deal, 1933* (Berkeley: University of California Press, 1969). For a contemporaneous study of the Agricultural Adjustment Administration see Edwin G. Nourse, Joseph S. Davis, and John D. Black, *Three Years of the Agricultural Adjustment Administration* (Washington: Brookings Institution, 1937). Three historians have examined the AAA's impact on sharecroppers. David E. Conrad, *Forgotten Farmers: The Story of Sharecroppers in the New Deal* (Urbana: University of Illinois Press, 1965), is an excellent account of the workings of the AAA cotton program and of the agency's "purge" of 1935. Donald H. Grubbs, *Cry from the Cotton: The Southern Tenant Farmers' Union and the New Deal* (Chapel Hill: University of North Carolina Press, 1971), is a thorough history of the STFU. Grubbs's "The Southern Tenant Farmers' Union and the New Deal" (Ph.D. dissertation, University of Florida, 1963) also has a great wealth of detail on the union. Louis Cantor's *A Prologue to the Protest Movement:*

The Missouri Sharecropper Roadside Demonstrations of 1939 (Durham, N.C.: Duke University Press, 1969) is a good brief account of continuing tenancy problems in one locality under the agricultural policies of the late New Deal.

Despite the fact that it was written to arouse congressional and public opinion, Charles S. Johnson, Edwin R. Embree, and Will W. Alexander, *The Collapse of Cotton Tenancy: A Summary of Field Studies and Statistical Surveys, 1933–1935* (Chapel Hill: University of North Carolina Press, 1935), is the New Deal era's most balanced and scholarly work on tenancy. Socialist criticism of the tenancy system and of the Agricultural Adjustment Act appears in Norman Thomas, *The Plight of the Sharecropper* (New York: The League for Industrial Democracy, 1934). An appendix to the latter work, William R. Amberson, "The Social and Economic Consequences of the Cotton Acreage Reduction Program, Report of Survey made by the Memphis Chapter L.I.D. and the Tyronza Socialist Party under direction of William R. Amberson," contains the results of STFU investigations.

The best secondary sources on the Resettlement Administration and the Farm Security Administration are the exhaustively researched study by political scientist Sidney Baldwin, *Poverty and Politics: The Rise and Decline of the Farm Security Administration* (Chapel Hill: University of North Carolina Press, 1968), and James G. Maddox, "The Farm Security Administration" (Ph.D. dissertation, Harvard University, 1950), by the former head of FSA's rural rehabilitation division. Olaf F. Larson's *Ten Years of Rural Rehabilitation in the United States*, cited above, is also essential. The FSA's most politically popular activity is critically analyzed in Edward C. Banfield, "Ten Years of the Farm Tenant Purchase Program," *Journal of Farm Economics*, XXXI (1949). The FSA's first administrator, who was also a pioneer in the improvement of race relations, is the subject of a sympathetic biography by Wilma Dykeman and James Stokely, *Seeds of Southern Change: The Life of Will Alexander* (Chicago: University of Chicago Press, 1962).

Several monographs on special topics of the New Deal period have bearing on poverty conditions or government policy. Government attempts to create cooperative communities in the 1930s are covered in Paul K. Conkin, *Tomorrow a New World: The New Deal Community Program* (Ithaca, New York: Cornell University Press, 1959), but more recent and specific for the South is Donald Holley's fine study, *Uncle Sam's Farmers: The New Deal Communities in the Lower Mississippi Valley* (Urbana: University of Illinois Press, 1975). Thomas A. Krueger, *And Promises to Keep: The Southern Conference for Human Welfare* (Nashville: Vanderbilt University Press, 1967), carefully examines a southern liberal and radical "popular front" movement. For the American Farm Bureau Federation and its opposition to the Farm Security Administration, see Grant McConnell, *The Decline of Agrarian Democracy* (Berkeley: University of California Press, 1953). James H. Street, *The New Revolution in the Cotton Economy: Mechanization and Its Consequences* (Chapel Hill: University of North Carolina Press, 1957), is valuable for background on a fundamental trend in southern agriculture which was beginning to be felt in the 1930s. Also valuable for general background is Pete Daniel, *The Shadow of Slavery: Peonage in the South, 1901–1969* (Urbana: University of Illinois Press, 1972). Little has been written on the state-level operation of New Deal agencies, but one state has been thoroughly covered by Michael Stephen Holmes, "The New Deal in Georgia: An Administrative History" (Ph.D. dissertation, University of Wisconsin-Madison, 1969).

Among articles which deserve special mention are Edward Banfield's "Ten Years of the Farm Tenant Purchase Program," cited above, George B. Tindall, "The 'Colonial Economy' and the Growth Psychology: The South in the 1930's," *South Atlantic Quarterly*, LXIV (1965), on the clash between New Deal programs and southern industrialism, and James G. Maddox, "Suggestions for a National Program of Rural Rehabilitation and Relief," *Journal of Farm Economics*, XXI (1939), which stresses the need for minimum living standards for all rural people.

Finally, for contemporaneous journalistic insight into the late New Deal period, see the classic travel account of a southern newspaperman, Jonathan Daniels' *A Southerner Discovers the South* (New York: MacMillan, 1938).

Pamphlets and Proceedings

Pamphlet publications, now often found only in manuscript collections, are good sources for the ideas and activities of pressure groups and citizens' organizations. Among publications useful in this study were the Southern Policy Committee's *Southern Policy* (N.p.: Southern Policy Committee, 1935), and *A Working Economic Plan for the South: Recommendations Adopted at Atlanta, January 15, 1939* (Washington: National Policy Committee, 1939). Several of the pamphlets in the SPC series, *Southern Policy Papers* (Numbers 1–10; Chapel Hill: University of North Carolina Press, 1936–1937), provide valuable background. The *Report of Proceedings of the Southern Conference for Human Welfare* (N.p.: Southern Conference for Human Welfare, 1938) is essential for understanding the SCHW. Arthur F.

Raper, *Machines in the Cotton Fields* (Atlanta: Southern Regional Council, 1946), a perceptive short work on technological and social change, was researched mostly during the 1930s.

Author's Interviews

The following persons granted the author personal interviews: Gladys Baker (Washington, October 31, 1969), Clifford and Virginia Durr (Wetumpka, Alabama, August 8, 1972), Brooks Hays (Washington, June 19, 1970), Robert W. Hudgens (Chapel Hill, North Carolina, July 8 and 9, 1970), James G. Maddox (Raleigh, North Carolina, July 10, 1970), Arthur Raper (Oakton, Virginia, December 27, 1969), Gay B. Shepperson (Richmond, Virginia, June 29, 1970), and Robert L. Vansant (Lawrenceville, Georgia, July 16, 1970).

Index